REPORT WRITERS' HANDBOOK

CHARLES E. VAN HAGAN

Head, Publishing Division,
Technical Information Department
Naval Weapons Center

Dover Publications, Inc., New York

Published in Canada by General Publishing Company, Ltd., 30 Lesmill Road, Don Mills, Toronto, Ontario.
Published in the United Kingdom by Constable and Company, Ltd., 10 Orange Street, London WC 2.

This Dover edition, first published in 1969, is an unabridged republication of the work first published in 1961 by Prentice-Hall, Inc.

Standard Book Number: 486-22495-3
Library of Congress Catalog Card Number: 74-96718

Manufactured in the United States of America
Dover Publications, Inc.
180 Varick Street
New York, N.Y. 10014

Preface

This handbook has been prepared as an aid for the men and women who, although they are not professional writers, nevertheless must write an occasional report as part of their work. Practicing scientists, engineers, economists, psychologists, and administrators are the people I have had in mind.

I have tried to give practical solutions to specific problems that may confront the report writer. The handbook deals with workable solutions to actual problems rather than with theoretical solutions to imaginary questions. I have not attempted to include all possible methods of handling each feature of a report, because there are often many satisfactory ways. Instead, I have given certain techniques, styles, and methods that I know are in good usage today, so that a report writer may follow them confidently, knowing that his work will be acceptable.

From time to time I have set special "Notes" apart from the rest of the text. These are points that I have found particularly troublesome for report writers, regardless of their subject matter, the type of their report, or their experience. I hope that the users of this handbook give serious consideration to these notes.

I have tried to cover the major features of report writing. There are some minor points that I have not included, and there are many types of writing closely related to report writing that I have not attempted to cover. This is not a textbook, nor is it a philosophical dissertation; it is a handbook.

I wish to acknowledge the help that I have received in the preparation of this handbook. I am particularly indebted to H. L. Chadbourne, of the U.S. Navy Electronics Laboratory, and T. J. Mathews, of the U.S. Naval Radiological Defense Laboratory, who reviewed the manuscript and offered many valuable suggestions for improvement. J. M. Lesha and W. E. Speedy, of the U.S. Naval Ordnance Test Station, reviewed the chapter on reproduction processes. F. L. Richards, of the Naval Ordnance Test Station, did an outstanding job in preparing the photographs that I have used for illustrations, and I fully appreciate his generous assistance. There have been many on the staff of the Publishing Division here at NOTS who have helped in various ways, according to their talents. I wish to make special mention of the following: W. D. Dickinson, who supplied some of the line drawings; Lonie Cox, Dorothy Morris, and Bernice Patterson, who gave their time and skill in typing the final manuscript; Florence Dinsmore and Dee Gates, who copyedited and proofread the final manuscript; and G. K. Stover, who helped in the preparation of some of the tables.

Finally, I wish to give credit—and much credit is due—to those whose help has extended over many years as the principles recorded in this handbook have been shaped and reshaped until I became content with them. Outstanding among the many are my father, L. F. Van Hagan, Professor Emeritus, University of Wisconsin; D. G. Coleman, of the U.S. Forest Products Laboratory; A. E. Tyler, now with the Jet Propulsion Laboratories; D. T. McAllister, of the Naval Ordnance Test Station; and particularly my wife, Lorraine Van Hagan. The careful guidance and thoughtful advice of these people—although frequently they have disagreed with me—have helped me to settle upon the suggestions presented in this handbook.

C. E. VAN HAGAN
China Lake, California

Contents

1

Introduction

This is the era of the technical report. Since the early years of World War II, the dissemination of technical information through the medium of reports has burgeoned at a constantly increasing rate, until today, practicing scientists, engineers, economists, psychologists, and other professional men and women have come to accept the simple fact that they must write reports year in and year out if they are to be successful.

Although the reasons for this development are many, no attempt will be made to discuss them here. Instead, it is assumed that—regardless of the reason—you are a person in professional life who is faced with the immediate task of writing a report. On the basis of this assumption, this handbook is designed to answer your specific questions, either large or small, about the reports that are part of your daily work.

This is a handbook. It is not intended to be read from the beginning to the end. Rather, it is designed so that you can find solutions to the individual problems that are giving you trouble. If your problem areas are broad, use the table of contents as the key to the pages you want. The index at the back will guide you to the answers to detailed questions.

The formal, long-form technical report serves as the model for the discussions in this handbook, for such a report may include any or all of the various parts that are commonly used. With this as a guide, each part is discussed, with consideration of its purpose, construction, and relation to the other parts. Shorter, less formal variations may not include the full gamut of parts, and—as will be shown later—should not do so unless they serve a definite purpose. It will be easy for you to skip sections that you do not need, depending upon the type and purpose of the report with which you are concerned.

Suggestions on format are integrated with the discussions on the preparation of the manuscript of each part because no report is complete until all necessary copies are off the press, distributed, and in the hands of the intended readers. As a writer, you must be concerned with format, and your reports will be most successful if you write to a predetermined format. Throughout this handbook, wherever variations in format may influence the words you write, the data you record, or the illustrations you use, comments on acceptable format are included.

Since it is not practicable to discuss all possible variations, this handbook offers basic methods, techniques, and styles that are in good standing in major organizations—both governmental and private. You can use these as exact patterns to be followed in detail or as guides upon which to build your own variations. Because report writing is more an art than a science, few "rules" can be set down, and you will undoubtedly wish to adapt the suggestions given here to your own needs.

Although it is customary to speak of "writing" a report, "building" one is probably a more appropriate term, for the modern report is made up of tables and illustrations as well as text, all so interwoven that each is essential to maximum communication. Nothing that does not serve a purpose is included in a report; nothing can be deleted without injuring it. An accomplished writer guides the reader from text to tables to illustrations and back to text as he tells his "story." Each device must be as carefully considered and prepared as the others. In acceptance of this fact, this handbook deals with tables and illustrations in considerable detail.

This handbook is intended to be used by working scientists, engineers, and men and women in other technical fields. The principles and suggestions discussed, however, are not limited solely to this group. They are equally useful to men and women in any field who are engaged in preparing reports, for the principles are the same whether you are writing an administrative report, a report to a city council on the results of a survey, a report to the board of directors of a bank, or any other report that is designed to present useful information in such a way that it will accomplish a specific purpose when read by a predetermined group. Much of the information will also be of interest to authors of professional papers, which are closely allied to reports and are constructed on the same principles.

In addition, this handbook is planned for collateral groups of line administrators who must pass on the adequacy of the end products. It will be useful as well to the production staffs who may support the report writers, including editors, illustrators, and typists, and to the administrators and committees charged with the task of establishing reporting programs. If the information in this handbook is also helpful to students and others interested in reports in a general way, this will be an extra benefit, but its primary purpose is to help the man on the job who must write a report in order to eat.

2

Planning a Report

2-1. FACTORS TO CONSIDER

2-1.1. Purpose of Report

As the first step in planning a report, decide why you are going to write it. To do this, you need to determine two things:

1. Whom do you expect to read it?
2. What use do you expect to be made of it?

These two questions are inseparable; you cannot answer one without considering the other. The combined answers affect everything about your report: the order in which you present your material, the words that you use, the length of your sentences and your paragraphs, the number and complexity of your tables, the type and detail of your illustrations, the material that you include in your appendixes, even the paper on which your report is printed and the manner in which it is bound.

2-1.1.1 POSSIBLE READERS

Report readers can be divided into the following classes:

Technical colleagues. These are the men who work daily in the same field that you do. They have detailed knowledge of your field

4

and are looking for additional information that you can supply. They know the background, and they speak your language.

Specialists in related technical fields. Such men and women have only a general knowledge of your field. They do not keep up with its step-by-step advances. You may assume that they are intelligent and trained to grasp ideas quickly by reading.

Line management. These are the men in your own organization immediately above you in the chain of command. They are the most intimately familiar with your work and also the most critical. They are the men who will have to accept your report before it is passed on to the final readers.

Administrators. These readers have an immediate need for certain types of information. They possess an ability to absorb ideas quickly, but they have little time to spend on any one subject. They have a general background of information on your subject, and they want "the big picture." They are not interested in and cannot comprehend technical details. They want facts and sound advice.

Laymen. Every reader who does not fall into one of the four preceding groups can be considered a layman. In addition to the so-called "general public," all men not familiar with your field are laymen, regardless of their proficiency in some other field. Thus, a nuclear physicist is a layman in the field of paper chemistry, and an expert in automation is a layman in the field of metallurgy.

Ideally, a report should be written for only one group of readers. To do otherwise inevitably introduces certain compromises in your presentation. Because of the extreme pressure on all who write technical reports, however, you may frequently be forced to adapt a single report to serve two types of readers. If you find yourself in this situation, select the most important group as your primary audience and build your report to suit their needs. Then adjust or add as best you can to take care of the needs of your secondary audience.

2-1.1.2 POSSIBLE USES

The uses to which your report may be put fall into the following categories:

1. *Inform for immediate use.* Experimental data, test results, surveys, or studies may be put to use the day your report is off the press if you are working in one of today's fast-moving fields of science.

2. *Serve as a basis for action.* Administrative decisions are often based on reports. Typical decisions of this type are those to increase or decrease funds or personnel, to procure new materials and equipment or to cancel existing orders, to revise procedures, to reschedule work, and to make or modify future plans.

3. *Establish claim to a discovery.* When you are working in a new field of research, particularly one in which the competition is keen, the best way to establish that you have made a discovery may be to publish an account of your work.

4. *Stimulate interest.* You may prepare some reports for distribution to a wide audience to stimulate general interest in the work you are doing. Often, work accomplished for a highly specialized purpose has broad application.

5. *Record for future use.* Your report may find many uses in the future if it is properly recorded and retained in libraries. It may, for example, provide useful information for reopening the work described, for engaging in related work, for tracing the history of a project or organization, for impressing a future employer, or for negotiating a lawsuit (as, a patent suit).

2-1.1.3. COMBINATIONS OF READERS AND USES

To determine the purpose of your report, select a group of readers and combine this with a primary use. For example, you may wish to record all possible information on your project to be used at a future date by technical colleagues; you may want to report to line management so that they can adjust the work schedules; or you may wish to prepare a report for administrators so that they can take immediate action by introducing a new process.

Your report may have to serve a dual purpose. For example, you may be primarily interested in obtaining additional support (money, people, procedures) from your management, and at the same time you may wish to inform your colleagues of your latest achievements. Occasionally, you may prepare a report on a survey for a group of administrators who specifically assigned a project to you, but you may word it in such a way that it can be understood by the general public.

Whatever the combination may be, you will need to have the purpose of your report clearly in mind before you do any other planning.

☐ NOTE

Be sure that anyone in a position to reject your report agrees with you regarding its purpose. This means that you and your line management must be in accord on your selection of readers and the intended use of your report. In large organizations—government or private—there is almost always someone above the report writer who must be satisfied with the end product before the author can consider his job finished. If your supervisor thinks that you are writing your report for a different purpose than you do, you are in for trouble.

If there is no one between you and your client, be sure that both you and he know exactly why you are writing your report. Any lack of agreement here will lead to dissatisfaction and wasted effort. ☐

2-1.2. Kind of Report

Once you have decided upon the purpose of your report, consider the kind of report that will best accomplish this purpose. Decide, for example, whether you need the authority of a formal report or the speed of an informal report. Or, perhaps, a letter report may serve to get preliminary data or recommendations into the hands of a few readers in need of immediate information; a more detailed report may follow if you desire.

Formal reports, which may be of any length, normally carry the full authority of the releasing organization. They serve as vehicles to carry official findings, opinions, and recommendations, and the information that they contain may be used as a basis for action by those who receive them.

Long-form formal reports are written, reviewed, edited, illustrated, and produced to the highest practicable standards. It is expected that the information they contain will be of use for a number of years. They include most of the formal parts (see Section 2-2); under any circumstances, they are clearly divided into preliminary matter, report proper, and supplementary matter.

The official status of short-form formal reports (see Section 6-1) is equal to that of long-form reports, although they include a minimum of preliminary and supplementary matter. The writing and editing are as carefully done as for the long-form reports. Such matters as typography, illustrations, and book design, however, require less regard for the niceties of style. The review process may also be reduced, depending upon local policy.

Informal reports normally do not carry the official weight of the releasing organization; they are primarily the responsibility of the individual author. These reports should carry a statement indicating the extent to which the contents may be used as a basis for action. Usually, they include preliminary information and are sent to a limited number of readers as enclosures to letters. Occasionally, they may be quite lengthy and detailed, but the information that they contain is preliminary or incomplete.

Informal reports do, however, serve as excellent vehicles for transmitting information quickly. It is quite possible, for instance, to prepare a few copies on a typewriter, add diazo or photoprints for illustrations, and distribute the report in not much more time than it takes to prepare a long letter. There is always the danger, however, that informal reports will be used to send out information before it has been verified, and this may result in embarrassment not only to the author but also to his organization if later findings contradict those presented informally.

☐ NOTE

Do not make informal reports look like formal reports typographically, or they will mislead the readers into thinking that they have final information in their hands. The nature of a report should be revealed on its title page and cover. ☐

2-1.3. Relation to Other Reports

In deciding upon a plan, determine whether or not your report has any direct relation to any others already issued. It may, for example, be one of a series dealing with a general subject, one part of a large report that you are issuing piecemeal in order to make your information available as soon as possible, a supplement to an earlier report in which you present additional information, or a revision issued because the information in an earlier report has changed to such an extent that you want to withdraw the original report and substitute a later version of the same material. If your report falls into any of these categories, consider how the treatment of your subject will be affected, and adjust your plan accordingly.

2-1.3.1 SERIES

Some major subjects involve work performed over a number of years, often by many different workers, and occasionally, in different organizations. In such a situation, the information is released in a series of reports. Usually the subjects are determined at the beginning of the project and for convenience and control are assigned numbers, either arbitrarily or in some predetermined order that will eventually result in a logical presentation of the subject when the individual reports are brought together into a final book.

Select an over-all title, to appear on every report in the series, that describes the project as a whole. Then choose a subtitle for each individual report. In the foreword of each report of the series, include a listing of the reports released, those in process, and those planned for the future.

It is not necessary for reports in a series to be released in numerical order if, for example, the work on Subproject 5 is completed before that on Subproject 3. As long as the subjects are listed in each report, the reader will know where a particular report fits into the general pattern.

In the opening sections of reports in a series, make reference to the other work being performed on the major project. Usually a short section headed "Background" or "Related Work" is used to let the reader know how the work recounted in one report fits into the other work on the project. Summarize briefly the procedures or equipment discussed in detail in one of the other reports in order to save the reader time, and draw freely on the data and results presented in earlier reports in the series if they influence your work. In the sections in which you discuss your findings, relate them to work already done as well as suggest how they may affect work not yet reported.

In general, consider that you are preparing one chapter in a book of many chapters and assume that you can lean on what comes before your report and expect that your report will influence those that will follow.

2-1.3.2. PARTS

Usually, when a project is completed, it is reported in a single publication. There are times, however, when certain portions of your work are completed long before the entire project. You then must decide whether to hold the early information until the entire project is finished, or to release it a part at a time as it becomes available. In many fields, it is detrimental to withhold new information, and it should be disseminated even though the entire project may still be several years from completion. If you are working on such a project, issue your report in segments, which are normally identified by "Part" numbers.

As with reports in a series, use a major title for the report as a whole, and part titles for the individual parts. Usually, the parts are issued in numerical sequence, because the work is controlled at one point and progresses from one phase to the next.

In the foreword, the opening section, or both, make clear to your reader your plan for releasing your information in parts, and identify the parts already released.

□ NOTE

If you state in one report that other parts will be released in the future, be sure to follow through with such parts. If you do not, you will find that readers will be writing to you for years wanting to know when you expect to issue the additional parts. □

The first part is likely to be the longest and to fit most nearly the pattern of a formal, long-form report. In this part, present your basic description of methods, procedures, and equipment. Also give the background information needed for the entire series.

Each succeeding part can depend upon the earlier parts for this basic information. In any part, refer freely to the earlier parts, so that the reader will know when he needs to look back. Frequently, for example, Part 1 of a report will include the mathematical derivations leading up to a certain hypothesis; Part 2 will present the experimental procedures and results followed to prove the hypothesis; and Part 3 will discuss the project as a whole and relate it to other work being done in the field.

2-1.3.3. SUPPLEMENTS

When you have new information on a subject that has already been reported upon, issue it in the form of a supplement to the original report. This situation may arise, for instance, when you reopen a project that had been temporarily closed for lack of funds. It also happens when new developments in your field make an earlier area of research once more of interest. Rather than write an entirely new report, it is more practical to publish a supplement.

The main title and the series number should be identical with the original report. In addition, use a subtitle indicating the extent of the new material that you have to offer; for example,

INFLUENCE OF LIGHT ON FERROMAGNETISM

Supplement 1. Effect of Mechanical Vibration

Technical Report 546

Supplement 1

Outline the reason for reopening the work in the foreword, and give sufficient bibliographic information so that the reader can obtain a copy of the original report.

In the opening section of the supplement, describe the entire program as briefly as possible and then go into detail about the new work that is to be described in the supplement. If you have used the same equipment and followed the same procedures that were discussed in the first report, there is no need to describe them again. Simply report the new features of your work in necessary detail. Follow this same style throughout the report, making as much use as possible of the information already presented. In the discussion of the results, be sure to relate the new work to the old.

2-1.3.4. REVISIONS

In many fields of research and development, the work of one year makes that of previous years obsolete, so the reports that have been issued may need to be replaced with the latest information. This is particularly true if you are developing some sort of hardware: aircraft components, electronic devices, or weapons, for example.

In this situation, the changes are usually substantial and are scattered throughout your report. However, if you make any changes in content—aside from typographical corrections—you should issue a revision. To do otherwise will result in your readers not knowing whether they have the latest (corrected) version of the report or not.

Use exactly the same title for the revision as that which appeared on the original report, followed by "Revision 1" or "First Revision" to distinguish the new report from the old one. The revision should also be indicated in the serial number (for example, "Technical Report 546, Revision 1"). The publication date that appears on the title page should reflect the new edition.

□ NOTE

Never issue two publications with identical titles. To do so will lead to confusion because a reader will never be sure that he has the right version. Make sure that the title and the serial number clearly show the revision number. □

You must prepare a completely new publication for a revision. Although the manuscript may be prepared by marking changes in the old report, the entire report will have to be republished. Except for a statement in the foreword or preface explaining the reasons for issuing a new edition, there is no need to refer to the earlier version. Since your intent is to retire the earlier report and have the readers use only the latest revision, your report should contain all of the required parts from title page to distribution list.

2-1.4. Secondary Factors

In addition to the factors already mentioned, there are a few secondary factors that need to be considered before you have all of the basic information necessary to determine the plan of your report. Although, theoretically, these secondary factors should not be allowed to influence the preparation of your report, in actual practice they do directly affect your plan.

2-1.4.1. MONEY

The amount of money available for the writing, reviewing, and production of a report has a strong influence upon the plan. If, for instance, there are ample funds, you can pay for quality art work if it will help to tell your story. If you are lacking certain photographs, you can send a photographer to get them and pay artists to retouch them in order to get a particular effect. You can afford to have your report set in hard type, which means that you have a great variety of type faces to work with and can, accordingly, go into as much detail in mathematics, chemistry, and similar fields as you wish. Or you can pay for professional book design to make reading easy and enhance the appearance of the publication.

When your money is limited, however, you usually must make do with whatever materials you have at hand. If your illustrations are inadequate, you must go into more detail in your text. You will probably have to be content with typewriter typography, and you will need to keep the number of copies of your report to a minimum. There are many other ways in which the amount of money available affects your plan, so in the early stages of your work determine how much money you are going to have and adjust your plan accordingly.

2-1.4.2. TIME

To prepare a report in any form takes a certain amount of time; the better job takes more time. Conversely, the less time available, the simpler the report must be.

If you have an indefinite amount of time, you can make your report as inclusive and as detailed as you wish. You can wait to have the illustrations worked up in just the style that you need. You can spend time working out tables until they present your information in the best possible way. And you can afford the time necessary for top quality typography and book design. All of these elements make for a more effective vehicle for communication. However, they do take an appreciable amount of time after you have finished writing your manuscript. It also takes time to have your work carefully reviewed by several competent reviewers, and this must enter into your planning.

There are situations, however, that require you to write and produce a report as quickly as possible. The matter of timeliness appears to be more critical in reports than in any other form of publication. As your time scale is shortened, you must adjust your plan accordingly. It is impractical to plan an elaborate treatment of a long text if there is not sufficient time to produce it.

□ NOTE

If your time is limited, get an accurate estimate from your production staff as to how long it will take to produce the report you have in mind before you begin to write it. You may defeat your best efforts if you attempt to prepare a report that cannot be produced in the time available. Confine your manuscript to limits agreed upon. If you exceed these limits, you cannot expect your report to be produced in the time allotted. □

The production of a report is like the building of anything else; there is a certain minimum amount of time that must be allowed for. Do not overlook this fact.

2-1.4.3. PROCESSING SUPPORT

The processing support that is available to a report writer can vary from none at all to a full-scale publishing group complete with editors, photographers, artists, book designers, and typographers; the amount usually depends upon the policy of your organization. The extent of this support has a direct effect upon the plan of your report and should always be considered in the early stages.

Lacking support, you must plan your report to include only those elements that you can produce yourself. If you are a competent draftsman, for example, and have plenty of time, you can use detailed engineering drawings in your report; but if you lack sufficient experience or time, you must use very simple figures and write your text in more detail. You will have to make use of whatever photographs are at hand and, again, depend upon your text to bring out a particular point instead of retouching illustrations. In addition processing a report yourself takes a great deal of time, so it is wise to limit it to a size that can be produced in the time available.

As you have more and more support available—editors, artists, compositors, proofreaders, etc.—you can confine yourself to preparing your manuscript, leaving other phases of the work to people who are trained and experienced in handling them. This gives you more time to concentrate on your professional specialty.

As you begin your planning, it is wise to determine exactly what support you can expect and then develop your plan to make the best use of this support. In general, every report should be edited; the final copy should be proofread; and the illustrations should be prepared by professionals.

2-2. ORDER OF PARTS

Reports are traditionally divided into a number of distinct parts, such as the opening section, the discussion, and the conclusions. There is no need to try for a smooth flow from one part to the next as is often done in narrative writing. In report writing, you make it clear to the reader when you shift from one part to another by inserting a descriptive heading, and then you proceed with your exposition in as direct a manner as possible.

The number of parts in a report depends upon its length and complexity. A formal, long-form report includes many standard parts, each distinct from the others. In an informal, short-form report you can omit many of the parts and combine others. As you begin to develop your plan, however, make your first outline by listing the major parts in the most effective manner.

2-2.1. Parts of a Report

The parts will be considered here in three groups: the front matter, the report proper, and the supplementary matter. It is quite possible that you will not want to use the stylized headings listed here, particularly if you are writing for a nontechnical audience; but the following parts should be considered regardless of what you may call them.

2-2.1.1. FRONT MATTER

The front matter, which is normally on pages numbered with lower case roman numerals (i, ii, iii, iv, etc.), includes the following parts:

Title Page	Acknowledgment
Letter of Transmittal	Abstract
Foreword	Table of Contents
Preface	(Glossary)

The parts of the front matter are usually short—only one or two pages. In a formal, long-form report, however, they should be treated as major sections, and each should start on a new page. The title page (see Section 3-2) should always be a right-hand page. Unless you are preparing an elaborate report and using a half-title page (see Section 3-2.3) to be backed up with a frontispiece, the title page is considered to be page i, but the number does not actually appear on the page.

□ NOTE

If your report is to be printed on both sides of each leaf, give odd numbers to all right-hand pages and even numbers to all left-hand pages. A blank left-hand page is assumed to carry a number, even though one does not appear. If your report is to be printed on one side of the leaf only, number each page consecutively. □

Because right-hand pages are more quickly seen by a reader thumbing through a report than left-hand pages, start your more important parts on right-hand pages; for example, the title page, foreword, preface, and table of contents should normally begin on a right-hand page.

2-2.1.2. REPORT PROPER

The report proper may contain a great variety of parts, and it is impossible to say that you must have certain parts without knowing the purpose of your report and the type of material that is to be reported. Typical major parts, from which you can select those that apply in your situation, are as follows:

Introduction	Procedure	Discussion
Background	Derivations	Summary
Materials	Results	Conclusions
Equipment	Evaluation	Recommendations

You probably will never use all of these parts in one report, and you undoubtedly will use others from time to time.

2-2.1.3. SUPPLEMENTARY MATTER

The miscellaneous information that would be useful to some of the readers of your report, but is not essential to the basic exposition, is classed as supplementary matter. It is useful to place this material at the end of the report so that it is out of the way of the primary group of readers. (Although the list of nomenclature is classed as supplementary matter here, there are some circumstances in which it more naturally fits immediately after the opening section; for example, if you plan to include a mathematical derivation in which your nomenclature is not apt to be familiar to the bulk of your readers.)

Supplementary matter is usually grouped at the end of the report in the following order:

Appendixes	List of References	Abstract Cards
Nomenclature	Bibliography	Distribution List
Glossary	**Index**	

Readers are in the habit of turning to the back of a report for these items, and to place them anywhere else only results in confusion. The distribution list may be located on the inside (or even the outside) of the back cover. Abstract cards are often printed on a heavy card stock and bound as the last sheet before the back cover. Indexes are rare in reports, but if you have one, it should be the last basic part of the report (just preceding the abstract cards or distribution list, if any). The list of references or the bibliography should immediately precede the index.

2-2.2. Relation of Similar Parts

Some of the parts listed in the preceding section are similar in content but serve a slightly different purpose in a report. Although each of these parts is discussed in detail later in this handbook, it is useful to point out the similarities and the differences here so that you may build your plan with the proper parts to achieve your purpose.

2-2.2.1. FOREWORD AND PREFACE

Both the foreword and the preface are considered front matter, and they should be separate from the report proper. Usually they are written after the rest of the report has been completed. The principal difference between them is that a preface is written by the author, whereas a foreword is written by someone other than the author, usually someone in the administrative chain of command above him. Each of these parts contains direct comments to the reader about the report.

In the preface, you may explain why you wrote the report in the way that you did, for whom you wrote it, how you expect the information to be used, and how you plan to tie the report in with others that you have produced or intend to produce. Acknowledgments may be made part of a preface.

In the foreword, your supervisor may comment upon the quality or background of the work, your success or skill in your profession, and the reason the work was performed, in addition to stating such facts as the period during which the work was done and the method of funding the work.

A majority of report readers do not read either the foreword or the preface. Therefore, do not put something in either of these parts that is essential to the understanding of the report unless you repeat it in the opening section.

2-2.2.2. FOREWORD AND OPENING SECTION

The foreword and the opening section may be considered complementary parts. Each may contain information that is needed in the over-all picture that the report presents. Certain essential items that could appear in either part include (1) the dates during which the work was performed, (2) task assignment identification, project numbers, or similar funding information, (3) relation to other reports, and (4) a statement as to whether or not the work is to be continued.

If you present these items in the foreword, it is usually not necessary to repeat them in the opening section. Since they should be recorded somewhere, however, any of these items that are not in the foreword should be included in the opening section.

In some organizations, local policy is to publish reports without a separate foreword or preface. If such is the policy where you work, put all of this information into your opening section. Since much of this information is of interest to only a few readers, however, it is advisable to use a foreword if possible and to include in the opening section only such information as the typical reader needs to understand the content of the report.

2-2.2.3. ABSTRACT AND SUMMARY

Although the words *abstract* and *summary* are often considered to be synonymous, they have slightly different meanings in report writing. The abstract has certain physical limitations and should be kept quite short (not more than 200 words), since it is used on library catalog cards. Because the summary on the other hand does not have this limitation, it can be two or three pages long if necessary. Both these parts are abridgments of the report; but an abstract is usually confined to stating the problem and giving the more important results, findings, or recommendations, whereas the more extensive summary includes information on the manner in which the work was done, the equipment or processes that were used, and a brief discussion of the results.

An abstract is handled as part of the preliminary matter; a summary, as part of the report proper. A summary may be located at the end of the report as the closing section, or it may be placed either at the very beginning of the report proper or just after the opening section, depending upon the audience and the purpose of the report.

A summary may include an illustration if you think it is desirable as an aid in covering your subject as briefly as possible. It is sometimes particularly helpful to show in a figure results of tests and experiments that would be difficult to describe in words. It is also practical to use a table in a summary if in this way you can summarize the results of many tests in a small space. On the other hand, neither illustrations nor tables are appropriate in an abstract.

You may have both an abstract and a summary in the same report. When you do, you may be concerned because you seem to be saying the same thing again and again as you move from one part to another. Remember, however, that the summary is part of the report proper and the abstract must be considered to be separate from the main report. It is quite acceptable to cover the same points in both parts.

2-2.2.4. CONCLUSIONS AND RECOMMENDATIONS

In the normal sequence of parts, the conclusions and recommendations are located at the end in the closing section. Your report may include either one or both of these parts, depending upon its content and purpose. Also, depending upon the purpose, you may place one or the other of these parts at the beginning or immediately after the opening section, where it may be easily found and read by those people who are not likely to read the entire report.

These parts must be based logically upon the information set forth and discussed in the report. They must not introduce anything new. If, for example, you recommend that a certain action be taken, the justification and support for this recommendation must have been covered in previous sections of the report. Or, if you conclude that a certain finding is true, an interested reader must be able to find the reasons for your conclusion clearly presented in an earlier section.

The difference between the contents of these parts is indicated by the terms *conclusions* and *recommendations*. Conclusions are "reasoned judgments" that have been reached after careful consideration of the results of your study, survey, or experiments; that is, because of what you have found out through your work, you believe that certain things are true. In many projects, all of your work will have been done in order to arrive at your conclusions. They should be logical, clearly supported, and simply stated. Conclusions do not call for any action; recommendations do.

Some engineering or scientific projects are performed solely to provide advice for your customer in deciding upon a course of action. For example, you may "conclude" that it is more economical to use diesel locomotives to haul freight over a section of railroad than to use electric locomotives, and you therefore "recommend" that the railroad company discontinue the electric locomotives and replace them with diesels immediately.

When you include both conclusions and recommendations in one report, it is best to separate them into two parts with the conclusions preceding the recommendations.

2-2.2.5. REPORT PROPER AND APPENDIXES

Use appendixes as supplements to the report proper. The type of information contained in an appendix is exactly the same as that which is contained in the report proper, except that it is more detailed. It is advisable to keep the report proper as brief as is practicable, because your readers can then follow your presentation more easily. While great masses of detailed test results, for example, may be necessary to determine or confirm your conclusions, they tend only to confuse the presentation when they are given in the normal evolution of your report. If you believe that it is necessary to have bulky supporting information immediately available to the readers, it is best to remove it from the report proper and place it in an appendix. In this way, your story is unencumbered and, consequently, may be more readily understood.

In some situations, you will wish to include illustrations to prove what your tests have revealed. If you have only a few such illustrations, include them in the report proper; but if you have many of them, place them in an appendix and show only typical examples in the report proper. The decision as to whether material serves your needs best in the report proper or in an appendix depends upon the quantity of repetitive items and your own judgment as to how many of these items will hold the reader's interest before he begins to skip over them.

□ NOTE

Do not include so many repetitive pieces of information in the report proper that the reader loses interest. If he begins to skip over your text, he may inadvertently skip some points that are essential to his understanding of your thesis. Place bulky detail in an appendix. □

In addition to bulky information, you should place in appendixes information that is of interest to only a small portion of your readers. Particularly when you are using one report for two or more groups of readers, you will find that some material, essential to the uninitiated, is well known by most of your readers. Or there may be information that is important to your technical readers but of no interest at all to your administrative readers; an appendix is the best place for this.

Typical kinds of information that should be placed in appendixes are specifications (detailed), lists of drawing numbers, detailed mathematical derivations, historical background, repetitive test results, and tables of data.

2-2.2.6. Results and Discussion

In a report on a series of experiments or tests, a survey, or a study, always present the results of your work, at least in summary form. These should be simple statements of facts offered in such a way that the reader can know exactly what you found out. Having presented these facts, it is customary to discuss them in a section in which you interpret your results as they may be affected by the extent of your work and the accuracy of your methods and equipment, and to point out what they can logically mean.

At the time you write your report you are the expert on the information that you are presenting, and your readers rightly expect you to explain your results to them. Also, the discussion section gives you an opportunity to guide the thinking of your readers into the desired channels. You can make sure that they do not overlook any points that may be important to the theme of your work. The explanations and interpretations of the results should be gathered into the part entitled "Discussion," while the recording of the actual findings is contained in the part headed "Results."

2-2.2.7. DISCUSSION AND CONCLUSIONS

Although the difference between the content of the sections on discussion and conclusions appears to be evident from the headings that are usually given to them, many authors apparently become confused in separating their material.

In the section entitled "Discussion" give your interpretations, explanations, and arguments, as pointed out in Section 2-2.2.6, but do not carry this discussion over into the final section on conclusions, which should present the final statements to which all the rest of the report was leading.

Keep these two sections distinct. The conclusions should be as straightforward and brief as possible. Many readers have time to read only the opening and closing sections. They do not want the conclusions hidden or confused by qualifying opinions and discussions. If they question any of your conclusions or are curious to know what they are based upon, they can look back into the report to the discussion section.

2-2.2.8. TABLE OF CONTENTS AND INDEX

Both the table of contents and the index serve as devices by which a reader can locate particular portions of a report. However, they have some basic differences. The table of contents, which is at the beginning of a report, keys a reader to the primary sections of the report in the order in which they appear and, in many reports, locates specific figures and tables. It also furnishes the reader with a skeleton of the report so that he can see how you have presented your information.

The index is situated at the end of a report. It provides no clue to the organization of a report; instead, it tells the reader the specific pages on which a particular subject is mentioned. It gives no indication as to whether the item is discussed in detail on a given page or simply mentioned in passing. An index is much more detailed than a table of contents, but it does not key the reader to either illustrations or tables.

Except in short-form reports, you will always include a table of contents, but you will have a need for an index only if your report is long and complicated and if you mention the various items in several places so that the reader will have to skip about through the report to get the full story about a single item.

2-2.2.9. REFERENCE LIST AND BIBLIOGRAPHY

A reference list and a bibliography both supply information necessary for a reader to locate particular publications that you think might interest him. The difference is that a reference list includes only the names of those publications that you refer to in your report, whereas a bibliography includes the titles of publications that you think will be of interest to your readers whether or not you referred to them in your text.

Entries in a reference list are placed in the order in which they are mentioned in your text—not in any sort of alphabetical order. Entries in a bibliography, however, are arranged in alphabetical order— either all by authors or all by titles. They may be further broken down into groups by subject matter, but within these groups they are listed alphabetically, regardless of their order in the text.

Occasionally—but rarely—you will find it useful to include both a reference list and a bibliography in one report. Usually, report writers depend upon the reference list alone.

In deciding upon the parts that you want to include in your report, you should understand the slightly different functions performed by the parts that have been discussed in this section and select those that fit the report that you are planning. The selection of major parts should be made early in your planning; the smaller sections can then be grouped around them. Selection of a wrong part can throw your entire plan awry and may cost you considerable time in reworking your material.

2-2.3. Combinations of Parts to Achieve Various Purposes

When you know the different parts of a report that you can use (Section 2-2.1) and are aware of the relationship of similar parts (Section 2-2.2), you are ready to select the parts that you want to use and determine the most desirable combination and arrangement to accomplish the purpose of your report.

□ NOTE

As a report writer, you are at liberty to determine the most effective combination of parts. Do not blindly follow a skeleton outline chosen by some other writer in a different situation. Remember that there is no single combination that will serve all purposes. □

Up to this point in your planning you should keep an open mind about your method of presentation, but now it is time to sort out the parts that you will use and arrange them in the proper order. The following examples demonstrate ways of moving the parts around to obtain different results. They may be used as guides, but any combination that will be effective in accomplishing your purpose is completely acceptable.

1. *Report of Basic Research for Specialists in the Same*
   Field to Put to Immediate Use

Front Matter	Report Proper	Supplementary Matter
Title page	Introduction	Appendixes
Foreword	Background	Nomenclature
Abstract	Materials	References
Contents	Equipment	Abstract cards
	Procedures	Distribution list
	Results	
	Discussion	
	Conclusions	

2. *Report of Current Status of Project to Obtain Additional Funds From Line Management*

Front Matter	Report Proper	Supplementary Matter
Title page	Recommendations	References
Foreword	Introduction	Abstract cards
Abstract	Background	Distribution list
Contents	Status	
	Conclusions	

3. *Report of Progress to Line Administrators*

Front Matter	Report Proper	Supplementary Matter
Title page	Summary	References
Foreword	Introduction	Abstract cards
Contents	Materials	
	Equipment	
	Procedures	
	Results	
	Discussion	

4. *One of a Series of Reports Describing a Step in a Continuing Project*

Front Matter	Report Proper	Supplementary Matter
Title page	Introduction	Appendixes
Foreword	New Procedures	References
Contents	Results	Abstract cards
	Discussion	Distribution list
	Summary	

5. *Terminal Report on a Research Project*

Front Matter	*Report Proper*	*Supplementary Matter*
Title page	Summary	Appendixes
Foreword	Introduction	Glossary
Preface	Background	Bibliography
Abstract	Materials	Index
Contents	Equipment	Abstract cards
	Procedures	Distribution list
	Results	
	Evaluation	
	Conclusions	
	Recommendations	

6. *Short-Form Report on a Survey*

Front Matter	*Report Proper*	*Supplementary Matter*
Title page	Summary	Abstract cards
Abstract	Recommendations	Distribution list
	Introduction	
	Background	
	Methods	
	Results	
	Discussion	

2-3. DEVELOPMENT OF THE OUTLINE

2-3.1. Preliminary Title

As you begin to develop an outline for your report, it is helpful to write down a tentative title. Do not assume that the first group of words that occurs to you will necessarily be the final title of your report. Almost without exception you will revise it as you work on the manuscript, adjusting it from time to time so that it will identify your work more exactly. The title should be related to the purpose of your report, and a tentative title will serve to help you keep this purpose in mind as you write the first draft of the manuscript. Put your title on a card and keep it in front of you whenever you work on your report. If your manuscript begins to stray away from the title, either bring it back into line or adjust the title.

2-3.2. Preliminary Outline

A successful report must first be outlined. The amount of detail depends upon the length of the report and how experienced you are. A short report—say four pages—requires an outline of only the major sections; and, if you are an old hand at the business of writing reports, you can carry the outline in your head without ever putting it down on paper. Opposed to this is the long report, which must have a written outline regardless of how experienced you are. If you are inexperienced, you will do best if you outline a major report in great detail, developing the outline to fourth- and fifth-order headings.

☐ NOTE

A carefully developed outline will greatly speed up your writing. It will eliminate repetition and ensure adequate coverage of all essential points in the most effective sequence. ☐

To develop your preliminary outline, first determine the major parts that will be required (see Section 2-2.1 for possible parts that you may need). Then consider various combinations of these major parts (as suggested in Section 2-2.3) until you arrive at the most effective arrangement. Next, expand this basic outline into a detailed outline by adding under each major heading the second-, third-, and fourth-order headings that are needed to present all the information.

During this stage you should keep the order of your details flexible. The tendency is to freeze an outline too early in the planning stage. Among the many methods that are used, one of the most successful is the "card method." Put each minor heading on a 3- by 5-inch card coded with the number of the major part in which you plan to use it. As you consider the material that you have to present, keep adding new cards and filing them under the major headings. It is useful to use a color code in this process; for example, put all major headings on blue cards, second-order headings on white cards, third-order headings on green cards, etc. This will help you to keep them sorted. When it appears that you have most of the subjects grouped under major headings, sort the cards in each group into a tentative sequence. Lay out all the cards for your report on a large table. Then remove or add cards to eliminate duplications and fill in gaps. This procedure makes adjusting your outline as simple as shuffling cards, and you can revise it indefinitely until you finally arrive at the most satisfactory arrangement.

2-3.3. Final Outline

When your card outline is settled, copy it into standard outline form, with major (first-order) headings aligned on the left, second-order headings indented, third-order headings double-indented, etc. You now have determined the order and value of the different subjects that you will present.

There are three methods that can be used to report your material: text, tables, and illustrations. The final outline should indicate how you plan to use each of these.

□ NOTE

The ability of your primary audience to understand your subject matter and to make use of detailed information determines the number and kind of tables and illustrations that you will need or be able to use. Consider the needs of these readers carefully as you develop your final outline.   □

The ideal situation is one in which you can add illustrations at will when you need them to present your material. Practically, however, either because of time, money, or other circumstances beyond your control, you often are forced to make do with the illustrations that are available. If this is the case, enter them in the outline where they will accomplish the most good, and then plan to expand the text to make up for any deficiencies in illustrations.

When the text, tables, and illustrations have been charted, there remains the matter of balance to be planned. Again, this is influenced by the primary and secondary groups of readers, and the purpose of the report. Balance cannot be determined exactly in advance, but you must make a rough estimate of the percentage of the total report that

TITLE. The Weather at NOTS, 1946-1958

Subject	%	Tables	Figures
Foreword	...	...	...
Abstract	...	...	...
Introduction	5	...	...
Surface climatology	35	1. Summary of surface measurements 2. Ave. monthly surf. pressures 1946-58 3. Max & ave. daily temperature ranges	1. Ave. monthly surface pressures 2. Max & ave. daily temperature ranges 3. Max & ave. temperature observed at Field X 4. Days with temperatures of 100°F or more
Upper-air data	40	4. Annual mean temperature by months	5. Relative humidity and spread 6. Monthly ave. tropopause heights over NOTS 1955-57 7. Monthly ave. potential temperatures of tropopause over NOTS 1955-57
Misc. phenomena	15	...	...
Summary	5	...	...
References	...	...	...

Figure 2-1. Typical report outline listing major sections. The approximate proportions are indicated as percentages, and the tentative tables and illustrations are assigned to the appropriate sections.

will be devoted to each major section, or you will run the risk of overemphasizing a minor point or underemphasizing a major point. There is a normal tendency to overwrite in the early portions of your work and then to cut down as you approach the end of the manuscript. The nearer you get to the end, the more you want to get the whole thing over with and the more you tend to skimp on your writing. By planning the balance as you develop your outline and holding reasonably close to these proportions as you write, you will avoid this error. A typical outline is shown in Fig. 2-1.

When your outline is settled into the form illustrated in Fig. 2-1, check it out with your line supervisor, project leader, section head, or person to whom you report. Since your supervisor will usually have to pass upon the adequacy of your manuscript, it is most satisfactory to incorporate his suggestions before you begin to write. This will save you the time that might otherwise be required to rewrite or reorganize your report.

When the final outline has been established to your satisfaction and approved by your supervisor, you are ready to begin writing the first draft of your report.

3

Front Matter

3-1. COVERS

3-1.1. Content

For routine reports, you need to consider only the front cover (Fig. 3-1a). This should contain enough information so that a reader may know exactly what report he has in his hand without opening it.

☐ NOTE

In planning the cover of a report, remember that many copies will be recorded, stored, and retrieved by librarians who daily handle hundreds of other reports. Place sufficient information on the front cover so that a librarian will not need to open it to be sure that it is the one requested. This will save a great deal of time for everyone who handles the report. ☐

Normally, you should include the following items on the outside of the front cover:

Title	Series number
Part, Revision, or Supplement title	Copy number (if classified)
Name of your organization	Classification (if classified)

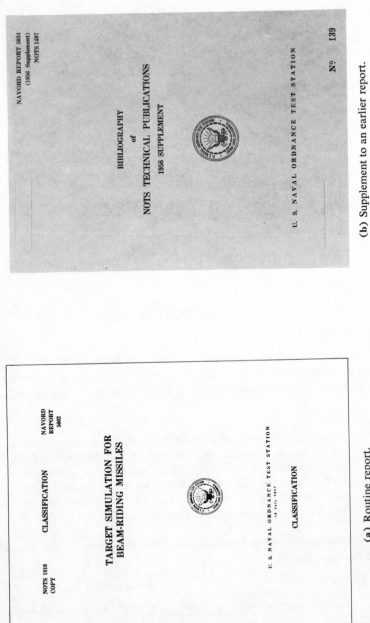

Figure 3-1. Typical covers.

(b) Supplement to an earlier report.

(a) Routine report.

NAVORD REPORT
5562, Part 1

TEMPERATURE TABLES | Part 1.
One-Layer Plate,
One-Space Variable,
Linear

U. S. NAVAL ORDNANCE TEST STATION

NOTS 1756

(d) Special cover designed with various type faces only.

NAVORD REPORT

NOTS TP 2322   NAVORD REPORT 6590

SOLVING DIFFERENTIAL EQUATIONS
BY FOURIER SERIES

By

H. J. Fletcher and C. J. Thorne

Research Department

Copy № 149

(e) Window cover, with a die-cut window that permits the title, names of the authors, and serial numbers to show through from the title page; a second window is cut out over the copy number.

Figure 3-1 (*cont'd*)

(f) Cover for a technical brochure.

(e) Special cover that combines a photograph and artwork.

Figure 3-1 (*cont'd*)

NAVORD REPORT 5396

U. S. NAVAL ORDNANCE TEST STATION
F. L. Ashworth, Capt., USN   Wm. B. McLean, Ph.D.
    Commander   *Technical Director*
China Lake, California

Rocket Quarterly

BULLETIN OF ACTIVITIES IN THE
ROCKET PROGRAM

CONTENTS

VOL. 4, NO. 3 AND 4   JUNE AND SEPTEMBER 1956

NOTS 1649

(h) Self-cover, with title page information and table of contents.

T3061-2

APSWP   TP   T3061-2
NAVORD SWOP T3061-2

TECHNICAL MANUAL

OPERATION AND MAINTENANCE INSTRUCTIONS

COMPONENT TESTER T-3061

U. S. NAVAL ORDNANCE TEST STATION
CHINA LAKE, CALIFORNIA

Published under the authority of the Secretary of the Navy and the Chief, Armed
Forces Weapons Project.

(g) Cover for a technical manual.

Except in rare circumstances, the title on the cover should appear exactly as it does on the title page (Section 3-2). As one of your last steps, cross check the wording, spelling, and punctuation of the title between the cover and the title page. Occasionally, when you have a very long title, it is acceptable to use a short version on the cover. If you use a shortened version, be sure that you do not introduce any new words that are not included in the full title given on the title page.

The name of your organization (the publisher) may be given in its complete form, or you may use a seal, trademark, or other device that incorporates some form of the organization name. In any event, the cover of your report should inform the reader of the name of the organization that releases it.

Since most reports are assigned series numbers (Section 3-2.1.8), this number should appear on the outside—either on the front cover or on the spine. Reports from an organization are frequently filed in libraries by series number, and placing this number on the outside speeds up the handling process.

If your report contains classified information, it may be controlled by copy number as well as series number. (If it contains Secret information, it must be controlled in this way.) As with the series number, the copy number located on the outside of the front cover simplifies handling the report.

When you issue a report in separate parts, release a supplement to a report already published, or revise a report, show the title of the new edition on the cover (see Fig. 3-1b). These are usually further identified by a part, supplement, or revision number, which should be placed on the cover.

When you are preparing a nonroutine report, consider the front cover, the back cover, and the spine. (The spine is the left side of a book when you are looking at the front cover—the portion that covers the bound edges of the pages.) Most reports are bound by side-stitching (Section 7-4) or by punching and inserting fasteners; the spine may or may not be covered with binding tape. With bindings of these sorts there is no way to put words on the spine. On unusually thick reports or those bound with cloth covers or in leatherette binders, however, it is possible to include some information on the spine.

3-1.2. Window Covers

A device often used by organizations not equipped to print special covers is the "window" cover. This is a cover in which a "window" has been die-cut in such a location and of such a size that the report title, the series number, and, possibly, the names of the authors show through the cover from the title page. It is helpful to order them with the name of the organization preprinted. Window covers are also used for assembly-line production of reports when, for speed or economy, it is not desirable to prepare special covers for each report (see Fig. 3-1c).

Window covers can be purchased or made in a wide variety of forms. Some of the more elaborate ones have transparent acetate covering over the window to protect the title page. Others have openings cut with dies of special shapes, but these take time and cost more money.

A serious disadvantage of windows is that they weaken the covers, which are apt to tear during use. If your reports are likely to be stored in crowded file drawers, window covers will shorten their lives.

3-1.3. Format Variations

3-1.3.1. STANDARD FORMAT

A satisfactory format to use as a standard for routine formal reports is shown in Fig. 3-1a. This calls for the title in bold letters at or slightly above the optical center of the cover. If the organization's name is spelled out, it can be placed near the bottom of the cover. The series number (and copy number) can be located in the lower center or in the upper right corner, where it is easy to find. When a seal is used, place it at the center horizontally and slightly below the center vertically. Optional items can be added as you wish, but try to avoid a cluttered cover.

3-1.3.2. DECORATED COVERS

Individual appeal can be given to covers if you are supported by typographers or artists, and if your report is to be reproduced by photo-offset or letterpress methods or bound with cloth covers as a book. The advantages of decorated covers are that they call attention to your report if it must compete with similar reports for readers, and that they are likely to impress nontechnical audiences and get them into a receptive mood to absorb the information that your report contains. Ordinarily, formal technical reports planned to be read by your colleagues or other specialists do not need the extra drawing power of a decorated cover.

Although it is possible to cement photoprints onto report covers that you prepare yourself, it is not advisable unless you plan to produce a limited issue—say, 5 or 10 copies. Photoprints are expensive, and cementing them to covers is time consuming. Occasionally, however, you may want to use them. When you do, be sure that the photograph illustrates the title as a whole, rather than only a portion of the report. Also, use only top-quality prints, so that they do not detract from the appearance of the report.

Unusual and pleasing covers can be worked out by the use of various type faces, without the assistance of special art work (see Fig. 3-1d). Work with your layout expert; explain the effect that you want and then take his advice.

☐ NOTE

Avoid overcrowding your cover. Select type faces that emphasize the title; be sure that the type faces are compatible. Report covers should be conservative rather than garish. Serious work deserves dignified treatment. ☐

When you have the help of an artist or a book designer, you can prepare interesting and unusual covers that will make your reports stand out from others that might appear on your reader's desk. An example of such a cover is shown in Fig. 3-1e. As the author of the report, you are responsible for setting the tone of these covers. Because you know the type of audience that you expect to read the report, you are in a position to tell the artist what kind of cover to prepare. You should also tell the artist the precise wording that must appear on the cover.

3-1.3.3. BROCHURE COVERS

The covers of technical brochures are almost always decorated in one way or another (see Fig. 3-1f). These publications are often directed at different audiences than the usual formal technical reports and must compete for readers with each other and with many other types of reading matter.

The first purpose of these covers is to induce the reader to pick up the brochure. You cannot afford to waste the back cover of a brochure; it should be designed with enough appeal so that the publication will be noticed even if it lies face down on a desk.

The second purpose of a brochure cover is to attract the reader to the extent that he will open it to see what is inside. Paper stock, color of stock, and color of ink must all be considered. The reader's eye must be drawn quickly to the title, which must be stimulating enough to arouse his interest. Keep the design simple.

3-1.3.4. HANDBOOK COVERS

Covers for handbooks and manuals (see Fig. 3-1g) are normally quite different from covers for technical brochures. You can assume that the reader is vitally concerned with the contents of your handbook and will read it regardless of what kind of cover it has; he is, in effect, a captive audience. Your one concern, then, is to put enough information on the cover so that the reader knows that he has the right publication in his hand. Be sure that the title stands out clearly from everything else on the cover so that it can be read at once. If there is room on the spine, the title should also appear there. It is frequently helpful to print the title vertically along the right edge of the back (near the binding) so that, if the handbook is kept in a bookcase or filed in a filing cabinet, the title can be read without pulling the handbook all the way out.

3-1.3.5. SELF-COVERS

There may be times when you will wish to produce simple reports, bound by saddle-stitching (see Section 7-4.4), without using special covers. This is acceptable if you do not expect the report to get hard use. In such a situation you can use a self-cover (see Fig. 3-1h), printing the cover on the same stock as the text. No special back cover is designed, and the text may continue on the inside and even the outside of the last sheet of paper (which in a saddle-stitched report is the same sheet of paper as the front cover). Put the title page information and the table of contents on the outside front cover if you wish, or use the front cover as the title page and follow it with the table of contents on the reverse side. The latter method allows you to begin the opening section on the first right-hand page (numbered page 3), and your reader may begin the report without working his way through several pages of preliminary matter. If you do not plan to use a table of contents, you may condense the title page information at the top of the front cover and begin the text below it (in which case, the cover is actually page 1 and a continuation of the text is page 2). This method is economical and simple, and makes for easy reading.

3-1.4. Use of Inside of Covers

If you use individually printed covers on formal reports, you can reduce the cluttered effect of the outside front cover by moving some of the information to the inside of the cover (but check your security regulations first). For example, if the report is classified, the espionage statement can be placed on the inside, as well as other information such as the names of the president, the senior scientist, the director, or the department head. Information regarding the number of copies printed, dates of various printings, and similar publisher's information may also logically be located on the inside of the front cover.

In less formal reports, the table of contents, the abstract, or the foreword may be printed on the inside of the front cover so that the opening section can begin on the first right-hand page.

On the inside of the back cover, you may want to place such items as a distribution list (when one is required) or a list of references. If additional copies of the report are available upon request, it is useful to state the method of obtaining them on the back cover.

3-2. TITLE PAGE

3-2.1. Content

The title page of a report is definitive with regard to the wording and spelling of the title, the names of the authors, and the date of publication. It is imperative, therefore, that you make certain that all entries on your title pages are exactly as you want them.

3-2.1.1. TITLE

The title of a report is the label with which you describe its contents so that the publication can be identified and so that potential readers will have some idea of whether or not they might be interested in reading it. Make the title of each report distinctive as well as descriptive.

The title will also serve to catalog your report according to its subject in library card files, bibliographies, and other listings. Although you may send your report to your principal readers, with the reasonable certainty that they will know the subject matter because your covering letter prepares them for it, most research and development reports are also filed in libraries for the use of people who are interested in the same or related fields of work. You must give your report a title that is suitable for indexing and cross-indexing. Poor titles not only mislead readers but also cause documents to be misfiled by librarians, who depend chiefly on titles. If a document is misfiled, many potential readers are lost.

Titles of technical reports are traditionally long—as opposed, for example, to titles of novels. A two- or three-line title occurs so frequently that it rarely causes any comment. The following title is typical:

PRELIMINARY INVESTIGATION OF THE RELATIVE EFFECTS
OF VARIOUS CURING FACTORS ON THE COMPRESSIVE
STRENGTH OF AN ASBESTOS-FILLED MOLDED
PHENOLIC RESIN

Although such a title is unwieldy, the author probably thought that it was necessary to identify his work to this precise degree in order to avoid possible confusion with other publications. A better solution would have been to make use of a subtitle, as follows:

COMPRESSIVE STRENGTH OF ASBESTOS-FILLED
MOLDED PHENOLIC RESIN

Preliminary Investigation of the Relative
Effects of Various Curing Factors

The technique of using a title and a subtitle permits the title to be as specific as possible with secondary identification of the subject matter accomplished by the subtitle. Also, subtitles give the reader the scope of report coverage (in this instance, a preliminary investigation) and the angle of attack—theoretical, practical, mathematical, etc. In deciding upon a title, you must compromise between the desire to qualify your report completely and the need to keep the title within reasonable bounds.

A short title is good, because it can be remembered and used with ease; the longer your title becomes, the more difficult it is to use. Therefore, make every effort to use as few words as possible in your title, without obscuring the meaning. Eliminate such phrases as "A Report on . . ." and similar unnecessary phrases or words, and resist the temptation to overqualify it. Make your titles specific, unique, concise, and unclassified wherever possible; avoid unnatural word inversion.

In selecting a title, it is best to be serious. Some authors try to be "cute" with their titles, presumably on the theory that they can trick potential readers into requesting copies. Although clever titles have a definite place in brochures prepared for a general audience with little original interest in the contents, the majority of readers of technical reports are inclined to place more confidence in a report that is identified by a serious title.

Write your title in telegraph style rather than in sentences. Do not begin with an unnecessary article. Phrase the title in such a way that a minimum of punctuation is needed, but be sure to punctuate it correctly.

The final title should be determined after the manuscript has been completed. Cross-check it with the information that is actually contained in the report—frequently this is quite different from what you thought you were going to write when you first started out on the manuscript. Remember that the report will be designated by this title forever, and it ought to be something that you can live with.

3-2.1.2. Part Titles

When a report is issued in parts released at various times, the parts are distinguished by giving each an identifying part title. The title of the report as a whole appears on the title page of each part; below it is placed the specific part title, usually numbered (Part 1, Part 2, etc.), and phrased to make clear to the reader exactly what portion of the work is described in each part. Supplements to reports already published (see Section 2-1.3.3) are similarly identified by number and descriptive supplement title.

□ NOTE

When a report is issued in parts, the title of the report as a whole cannot be changed in any way from one part to another. The order of the words, the spelling, and the punctuation must be repeated exactly in each part. Since to change it in any way results in a new report, be sure that the main title is one that you will be willing to use throughout the series. □

3-2.1.3. AUTHOR'S NAME

It is customary for the name of the author or authors to appear on the title page of a report. (There are, however, some organizations, both government and private, that have a policy of not naming authors on reports on the theory that the report is the product of the organization and not the individual. This is a defensible policy, but such organizations are in the minority.) Here, as in the signature on a check, the wishes of the author as to spelling and style are sacred. If you wish to use your middle name instead of your first name, do so. Though you may be called "Ed" around the laboratory, your name can appear on your title pages as "E. Thorndyke Smith" if that is the way you want it. Remember, however, that it is wise to follow the same form and spelling through the years. Unless there is good reason, do not vacillate from one form to another.

3-2.1.4. MULTIPLE AUTHORS

It is common to name several authors of a technical report, although usually only one person does the actual writing. There are various policies in this matter, but the following is one of the more workable: the first name listed (senior author) is that of the man who had the most to do with the project; the names of the men who worked with the senior author follow in the order of their contribution to the work; finally, the name of the senior author's supervisor is given. Any one of these men may be the one who writes the report. A professional writer may even be used, but his name does not appear on the title page at all.

If you have done all the work on a project, and have written the report as well, you may be resentful if your supervisor insists that his name be included. Remember, however, that your report will be more widely accepted if it carries the name of a man with a reputation in the field than if it travels only over the name of a new and unknown worker. It is also true that your report must be reasonably good or he would not want his name on it.

3-2.1.5. PUBLICATION DATE

Every title page should include a publication date. Because of the rapid advances that are being made in almost all fields of science and engineering, readers are particularly interested in the date of a technical report. It is important for them to know whether or not they are spending time on a report that may contain obsolete information.

Policy varies with regard to the date that is shown on the title page. Two are considered acceptable: the date on which the material is approved for publication (if the author is supported by an editing and publishing group), or the date on which the report is released (if a limited number of copies are prepared by the author's immediate staff).

Occasionally you will issue a report on work done some years before. In this situation, the date on the title page should be related to the report—not to the work reported. The date on which the project was completed should be given in either the foreword (see Section 3-4) or the opening section (see Section 4-1.1).

3-2.1.6. PUBLISHER

The name of the organization responsible for publishing the report should always appear on the title page. This is the name of the company, partnership, corporation, or government activity for which you work. The only exception to this rule occurs when you issue the report on your own responsibility and not as the product of an organization.

Give the full name of the publisher; do not use any abbreviation on the title page. Be sure to use the official spelling, capitalization, and punctuation. Again, the title page is definitive.

3-2.1.7. PLACE OF PUBLICATION

Show on the title page the name of the town or city and the state in which your organization is located. Do not abbreviate. If the report is to have a foreign distribution, add the statement "Printed in the United States of America." If the city is well known (for example, Chicago, Philadelphia, or San Francisco), you need not include the state. If, however, the city is not known to readers throughout the world, or if there is more than one city or town with the same name (for example, Madison, Hollywood, or Glendale), give the name of the state.

3-2.1.8. SERIES NUMBER

Most organizations that publish more than a few reports each year control the processing by assigning a series number to each report. This number should appear on the title page. Many libraries file reports from an organization by number and use the numbers to retrieve them when a user requests certain reports.

☐ NOTE

Never assign the same number to more than one report. To do so will lead to confusion throughout the life of the reports. If a number is assigned to a report that is subsequently withheld from distribution, cancel the number. ☐

3-2.1.9. CUSTOMER'S NAME

When a report has been prepared as the end product of a study, survey, or other project requested and paid for by an organization, the name of this "customer" should appear on the title page, preceded by some such statement as "Prepared for . . ." or "Submitted at the request of . . ." Use the official spelling of the customer's name. Avoid abbreviations.

3-2.1.10. MISCELLANEOUS ITEMS

Additional items of information may be included on a title page, according to the policy of your organization. These differ from one organization to another, but they should be consistent within a single organization.

A few such items are as follows: name and title of the technical director or senior scientist (in research laboratories); name and rank of the commanding officer (in military activities); name of the organizational unit for which you work (branch, division, etc.).

In a report concerned with classified matter, see the applicable security regulations for the placement of the classification and the phrasing of notices that may be required.

If a copyright notice is used, it conventionally appears on the back of the title page.

□ NOTE

Avoid the use of facsimile signatures on the title page. This is a carry-over from correspondence, when responsibility for the contents of a letter is assumed when a man actually signs the ribbon copy. Reports, on the other hand, are released in quantities of a dozen to thousands, and reproduction of a signature is an unnecessary requirement. It has long been accepted that a man's name set in type on a title page or at the end of a foreword acts instead of a signature to indicate authority of release and responsibility for content. □

3-2.2. Format

In designing a title page, try to indicate relative importance of the items by typography and placement. Title pages of technical reports are frequently overly crowded, and to lay one out in a pleasing manner requires ingenuity.

3-2.2.1. TRADITIONAL STYLE

Usually, the items are centered horizontally on the page and placed so that they are in the shape of an hourglass (see Fig. 3-2a). The title is located slightly above the center of the page, arranged in an inverted pyramid. The name of your organization appears near either the top or bottom of the page—ordinarily near the bottom. Because they are short, the series number and date can be placed near the center of the page, or they may be used to balance each other on opposite sides of the page.

The title is normally the most important item on the page and should stand out. In typewriter typography, it should be in capital letters and underscored. This permits you to set part or supplement titles in capitals and lower-case letters underscored, indicating to the reader that they are of less relative importance than the main title.

If your report is to be produced in typewriter typography, it is advisable to use the traditional style. You do not have enough typographical flexibility to attempt much variety.

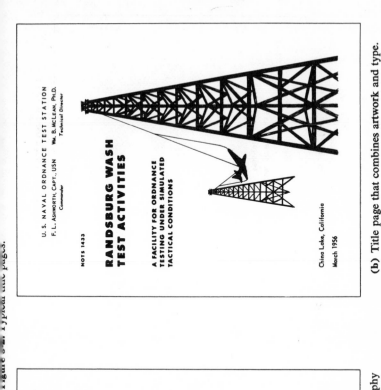

(b) Title page that combines artwork and type.

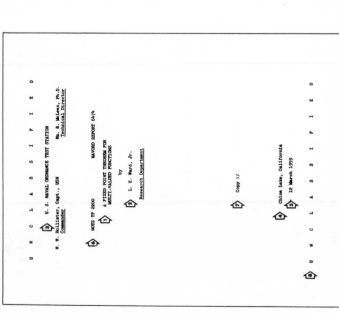

(a) Traditional title page in typewriter typography showing acceptable location of (1) title, (2) author, (3) name of releasing organization, (4) place of publication, (5) date of publication, (6) serial numbers, (7) copy number, and (8) classification, if any.

Figure 3-2 (*cont'd*)

WISCONSIN HIGHWAYS
1835-1960

(d) Half-title page used with (c).

WISCONSIN HIGHWAYS

1835 ~ 1960

COMPILED AND EDITED
BY THE
HIGHWAY PLANNING SURVEY

STATE HIGHWAY COMMISSION OF WISCONSIN
MADISON, WISCONSIN
1 9 6 0

(e) Typical title page planned for hard-type typography.

Figure 3-2 (*cont'd*)

OP 2786

ROCKET CATAPULT MARK 1 MOD 0

(AIRCRAFT EJECTION SEAT)

DESCRIPTION, OPERATION, AND MAINTENANCE

U. S. NAVAL ORDNANCE TEST STATION

CHINA LAKE, CALIFORNIA

23 NOVEMBER 1959

(f) Title page for a technical manual.

Technical Bulletin No. 479 January 1940

UNITED STATES DEPARTMENT OF AGRICULTURE

WASHINGTON, D. C.

STRENGTH AND RELATED PROPERTIES OF
WOODS GROWN IN THE UNITED STATES

By L. J. Markwardt and T. R. C. Wilson, *senior engineers, Forest Products
Laboratory,[1] Division of Research, Forest Service*

(e) Title page including table of contents and acknowledgment.

3-2.2.2. VARIATIONS

If you have the support of artists or typographers and your report is to be reproduced by photo-offset or letterpress methods, the variations of title page design are almost limitless. With your designer you may work out the most effective combination of type faces and the most stimulating placement on the page.

☐ NOTE

Guard against using lettering styles or type faces in such a way that they fight each other. As with colors, certain styles clash with other styles. The selection of type or lettering styles is a matter of education and good taste. ☐

When your report is to be reproduced by the photo-offset or letterpress process, you have the advantage of being able to combine artwork and type on the same page. You may find it an advantage to use an organizational seal, any of various art devices, or even a photograph as a background (see Fig. 3-2b).

3-2.3. Half-Title Pages

A half-title page is a page that carries only part of the information required on a full title page. It should be used only in the more formal and elaborate reports. If you have planned your report to be read by a nontechnical audience and you wish to impress the readers with the extent of your work and therefore the importance that should be attached to the contents, you may elect to use a half-title page backed up with a frontispiece. Such a page immediately precedes the full title page. Although the half-title page usually carries only the title of the report, occasionally it may also include the name of your organization across the bottom.

☐ NOTE

Although a half-title page is a standard part of a book, it is rarely used in a technical report. Following the principle that nothing is included in a report that does not contribute directly to the communication of useful information, a half-title page is an unnecessary nicety. ☐

When you are preparing an unusually long report separated into chapters or distinct parts, you may want to emphasize the break between chapters by using chapter half-title pages. Such pages carry only the chapter or part number and the title of the unit. These pages are always right-hand pages and are not generally backed up. They are included in the pagination of the report, but the page number is not printed on the front or back (if not backed up).

A half-title page can be used to introduce an appendix when you wish to begin the appendix proper on a left-hand page. This is particularly useful when your appendix consists of tables spread across two facing pages.

3-3. LETTER OF TRANSMITTAL

3-3.1. Content

The letter of transmittal (or letter of promulgation) presents your report to the customer. It accomplishes much the same purpose as a foreword (see Section 3-4), and if you use one, you do not need the other.

Write this letter directly to your intended reader; for example, if a specific individual requested you to do some work for him and financed the project, address the letter of transmittal to him by name, or to his company to his attention.

Open the letter with a brief description of the project upon which you are reporting. If it is appropriate, give the date upon which the work was begun. Then describe in a paragraph the report, its contents, and your suggestions for its use. If it is related to any other publication—either superseding or complementing it—discuss the relationship.

If your task was to reach certain conclusions or to make specific recommendations, they should be presented in this letter. Your customer will read it first, and in brief form it should justify his expenditure.

If you want your project to be continued—for example, if you have carried it to the point originally requested but believe that additional work will give considerably more information—state this fact in the letter of transmittal.

A letter transmitting classified information should include instructions regarding the handling of the document.

In private industry, the letter of transmittal is usually signed by one of the officers of the company responsible for the report. In the government, it may be signed by the head of the activity responsible for the work. Thus, for example, it might be signed by the Technical Director of the U. S. Forest Products Laboratory or by the Chief, Bureau of Naval Weapons. In any case, the man whose name appears on the letter of transmittal is the individual who is ultimately responsible for the content of the report.

If your report is to be distributed to others than the management of the organization that financed your project, it is best not to include a letter of transmittal as an integral part of your report. Instead, use a foreword or preface in the report, and submit the report as an enclosure to a separate letter of transmittal to your primary customer.

3-3.2. Format

Prepare a letter of transmittal in standard business correspondence style, and reproduce it under the official letterhead of your organization. The signature is usually handwritten, but a facsimile may be used if you have photo-offset or letterpress reproduction methods available and plan to reproduce a considerable number of copies of the report (see Fig. 3-3). The paragraphs may be numbered or not as you prefer; unless, however, you expect the paragraphs to be discussed separately, there is no need to number them.

3-4. FOREWORD

3-4.1. Content

It is advisable to include a foreword in most formal, long-form reports. Ideally, it is prepared by someone other than the author; for example, by your line supervisor. The content should be in the nature of information supplied by a person looking at the report over the author's shoulder. To establish individual authority for the release of the report as well as for the accuracy of the statements made in it, the name of the releaser is frequently printed below the foreword in the position of a signature.

JACKSON and CLYBOURNE, ENGINEERS

842 Rutledge Street   Chicago, Illinois

May 21, 1960

Clark County Power Commission
Monroe, Iowa

Attention: Mr. C. W. Thorkleson, Manager

Gentlemen:

In fulfillment of our agreement of April 10, 1959, we submit this report on the engineering and economic feasibility of the proposed expansion of the existing generating facilities of your present hydroelectric plant.

In this report, we have presented our findings and comments concerning the design features of the proposed construction, and we have included what we consider to be a conservative estimate of the probable financial operation of your system during the period of debt financing.

On the basis of this information and an independent verification of your construction cost estimate, it is our conclusion that the proposed design is sound and that the system financial operation will be able to support the proposed debt without distress. There are features of the design that indicate possibility of a real advancement in power station economy; these will doubtless be watched with interest by the entire electric utility industry.

Respectfully submitted,

JACKSON and CLYBOURNE, ENGINEERS

Walter I. Jackson

Walter I. Jackson
President

WIJ:rac

Figure 3-3. Typical letter of transmittal.

☐ NOTE

Limit the number of names that are given after the foreword. There is often a strong desire to list the managers of all administrative units concerned with a project. Actually, only the name of the man who assumes full responsibility for releasing the material is needed. If this authority has been specifically delegated by someone in a higher position, that man's name may also appear, although it is not necessary.　☐

In a foreword give information about the financing of the project, the authority for performing the work, and the dates during which the work was performed. The last information is particularly useful if the work was done some time before the report was written.

If the report has been reviewed for technical accuracy, give the names of the reviewers in the foreword. It is always wise to have your report reviewed by one or two others in your field in order to cross-check your work and help you avoid oversights; when you do so, it is a courtesy to the reviewers and a benefit to the readers to list their names.

The relation of your report to others produced by your organization may be discussed in the foreword. If, for example, your report is one of a series, you should mention this fact and supply sufficient bibliographic information about the others in the series for the reader to obtain copies if he needs them.

The foreword may also contain comments upon the project on which you are reporting so that the reader knows whether the work is continuing or completed, whether the information is preliminary or final, or whether the report covers a portion of the work or the entire project.

It is appropriate for the man who writes the foreword to comment upon the work of the author of the report if, for example, he believes that the report is unusual in any way. The foreword should not, however, include the sort of comment that belongs in an acknowledgment.

The foreword should be coordinated with the opening section. Between them, they should include all of the information needed to set the stage for the body of the report and the conclusions. If, for example, there is a statement about the funding in the foreword, there need not be one in the opening section. Or if the dates of the beginning and end of your project are stated in the foreword, it is probably not necessary to discuss them again in the report.

☐ NOTE

Experience indicates that many readers ignore the foreword of a report in their impatience to get into the subject matter, a habit which must be considered in your planning. For this reason, information may appear in the opening section as well as in the foreword. ☐

In less formal reports intended for limited distribution, you may wish to omit a foreword. If so, the information commonly contained in the foreword should be placed in the opening section.

If you have done the work and prepared the report on your own responsibility, you will not have a supervisor available to write the foreword. In this situation, use a preface instead (see Section 3-5).

3-4.2. Style

In the usual report, the foreword should be quite formal and should consist of straight text, without tables, illustrations, or footnotes. Do not use personal pronouns, and, of course, do not try to be humorous.

An exception to the rule of formality occurs in technical brochures, where the foreword should follow the style of the text. You may replace the heading "Foreword" with a more appealing and less formidable heading. You may use personal pronouns, and may include an illustration or cartoon if one is in the spirit of the brochure.

3-4.3. Format

Since the foreword is an important part, it should begin on a right-hand page in a formal, long-form report, usually on the first right-hand page after the title page. In less formal reports, it may appear on the inside of the front cover or on the reverse side of the title page.

The heading is a first-order heading, set in the same typography as the other major headings of your report. In typewriter typography, it is usually typed in all capital letters, underscored, and centered on the page. If the text of the foreword is relatively short, it can be set in narrow measure and located at the optical center of the page. Otherwise, it should be set in the same type style as the text of your report. Place the name of the man who releases the report and his title immediately below the text and preferably against the right margin (see Fig. 3-4).

3-5. PREFACE

3-5.1. Purpose

A preface is a preliminary part in which the author may offer introductory comment upon the report itself as well as upon the project being reported. The principal difference between a preface and a foreword (see Section 3-4) is that the author writes a preface, whereas someone else writes a foreword.

Although it is fairly standard for an author of a book, particularly a textbook, to make use of a preface, a preface is rarely used in a technical report. Normally the stage is set for the author by his supervisor in the foreword. Nevertheless, under unusual circumstances, you may wish to make some remarks that would be out of place in the opening section, which is the section in which you usually establish contact with your reader.

As an example of such a situation, you may be issuing a series of reports that you intend eventually to publish as a book and you may have planned to release them over a period of years. If this is so, you should explain your plan to your readers, tell them what you have accomplished so far, and indicate how you expect to put the pieces together. You may also have such factors as an equation numbering system worked out for the book as a whole that would not make sense to someone reading only one report of the series; they would require discussion in the preface.

If you are issuing a report on your own responsibility and do not have a foreword, use a preface to present the information generally included in a foreword (see Section 3-4).

Write a preface in the first person singular. Place your name at the end, followed by the city and state where you work and date you write it. You may be reasonably informal in this section, even if the report itself follows the impersonal style of the formal, long-form report.

Studies on the Influence of Light on Ferromagnetism. II

FOREWORD

This report describes the results obtained in a second series of experiments studying the effect of light on ferromagnetism. These experiments were carried out at the U.S. Naval Ordnance Test Station during 1958 as a part of a program to evaluate new possibilities of radiation detection for use in missile studies and were financed by exploratory and foundational research funds.

Results of the first series of experiments were reported in NAVORD Report 5840, "Influence of Light on Ferromagnetism," by Julian L. Thompson, published at this Station.

This report, released at the working level for information purposes only, was reviewed for technical adequacy by A. E. McKay.

F. M. ASHBROOK, Head
Instrument Development Division

iii

Figure 3-4. Typical foreword in typewriter typography. The man whose name appears at the end of a foreword is the man who has authorized the publication of the report in its present form. A facsimile signature is unnecessary.

3-5.2. Format

The format for a preface is similar to that for a foreword. Start with a first-order heading—usually the word "Preface"—set in the style of other first-order headings in the report. In typewriter typography this is usually in capital letters, underscored, and centered horizontally on the page. If it is short, the text can be set in narrow measure, but most prefaces run more than half a page and are, therefore, set full measure. The preface of a long-form report is located on the first right-hand page after the title page. If your report also includes a foreword, it should immediately precede the preface.

Footnotes, subheadings, illustrations, and tables are out of place in a preface. If you refer to other publications, give the necessary bibliographic information in the running text.

3-6. ACKNOWLEDGMENT

3-6.1. Content

If anyone, other than the men and women named on the title page, has made a substantial contribution to the work that you are reporting, acknowledge their help in a special section. You may name individuals, organizational units, or even companies, depending upon the type of assistance that was given.

Although the statement of acknowledgment has been known to run to two full printed pages on major undertakings, limit your list to those who made unusual contributions. Following this principle, you would name a man who helped you develop the basic plan of your project, but you would not name your secretary, although she may have done an excellent job of typing your manuscript. Or you would acknowledge the help of a colleague who worked out a system of quality control that enabled you to complete your project much sooner than you had expected, but you would not list your office manager because he kept the supplies moving in on schedule. There is no need to name the members of your staff who did only what they were paid to do as a part of their jobs.

3-6.2. Style

An acknowledgment should be made simply and with dignity. Resist any tendency to be overenthusiastic in your praise of those who have helped you. A statement of a man's name (correctly spelled) and the contribution that he made is sufficient. Instead of:

> The author wishes to acknowledge the great amount of work done by Mr. Kenneth R. Jacobs in deriving an unusually unique method for measuring small quantities of powder and without whose devoted help this project could never have been completed.

say

> The contribution of K. R. Jacobs to the test program is gratefully acknowledged.

Do not use adjectives needlessly in your acknowledgment; they tend to detract from the sincerity of your thanks. However, be sure that you do acknowledge real help that you have received, for the time that a colleague gives to your work must be taken from his own. You will never lower your own stature by admitting that others have helped you in your work.

□ NOTE

Make your acknowledgment brief and sincere. Name those who have given you unusual help, but do not overburden the list with the names of those who only did their jobs. □

3-6.3. Format

In formal, long-form reports the acknowledgment is usually placed on a page of its own and included in the preliminary matter. It fits logically on the back of (or immediately after) the foreword or preface. It carries a first-order heading (normally centered and set in capital letters in typewriter typography). If it is short, it can be set in narrow measure, and it should be located as a unit at the optical center of the page.

If the format of your report calls for the title and the name of the author to appear at the top of the first page of the opening section, you may include a short acknowledgment as a footnote to the name of the senior author. In this style, it is helpful to use an asterisk or some other symbol separate from your basic system of indicating footnotes, because the acknowledgment is not a part of your regular series of notes. Place the footnote of acknowledgment at the bottom of the page (without any heading), but above any other footnotes that might appear on that page.

A typical example of an acknowledgment for a formal, long-form report is shown in Fig. 3-5. The style of acknowledgment in a footnote is included in Fig. 6-1.

3-7. ABSTRACT

3-7.1. Purpose

3-7.1.1. WITH THE REPORT

Many organizations have a fixed policy that an abstract must be included in every report released. This is a sound policy that should be followed except in unusual circumstances. Bound into a report, an abstract is treated as part of the preliminary matter. It is intended to present the major points in the report so that by reading it the user may determine the gist of the material and decide whether to read the report from beginning to end, to read only the opening and closing sections, or to file it, unread, to be consulted when he needs it.

The abstract is probably the "most-read" part of any report. Combined with the information on the title page and in the table of contents, it should give a reader a complete thumbnail sketch of the information contained in the report.

3-7.1.2. APART FROM THE REPORT

Abstracts are often separated from reports for use in abstract journals, bibliographies, library file cards, and special subject files of individual users. Here they are intended to convey information in capsule form for the many readers who need only a brief account to keep up with the field in general. They also serve to make readers aware that certain information exists and is available.

Listed in bibliographies, abstracts act as a key to the literature on a given subject so that a man making a search for information may know which reports to request for detailed study. A list of titles alone is not nearly so helpful as a list of titles and abstracts because many titles are misleading, vague, or incomplete.

3-7.2. Content

An abstract is a brief summary of the significant information presented in a report. In the main, it is constructed by bringing together

Yawing Motion of Tangent-Finned Rockets
_____

ACKNOWLEDGMENT

The contributions of Grace Rowlison in the reduction
of the telemetered records, G. W. Younkin for the preparation of Appendix B, and Martin Seaholm for the design of
the telemeters is sincerely acknowledged. The Ballistic
Division Shop did much of the fine machine work necessary
for the test vehicle, and the Liquid Propellant Division
supplied many tangent fins for this work. The help of
these people and others who made contributions is acknowledged with appreciation.

ii

Figure 3-5. Typical acknowledgment in typewriter typography.
Acknowledgments in formal reports should be brief and conservative. It is not necessary to sign them.

the meat of the opening and closing sections. It should contain a comment concerning the reason for the work, anything unusual about the methods used, and a clear recapitulation of the principal findings, results, conclusions, and recommendations. Do not give historical background, descriptions of routine procedures, or discussions of the results. Try to limit the abstract to the facts, being sure to include anything that is new and significant.

Avoid writing an abstract that only describes the type of work that was done in the project and the scope of the information without presenting any concrete results. Faced with such an abstract, the only way that a potential reader can determine whether or not the information will be useful to him is to call for a copy of the report and read portions of it. Often, this is a needless waste of time and effort.

Do not use illustrations in an abstract. Remember that it will be reproduced in a variety of places, many of which may not have facilities for reproducing illustrations. Also, libraries file abstracts on 3- by 5-inch cards, and there is not space for illustrations on these cards.

References to other works are out of place in an abstract. If you refer to a publication listed with the other references at the end of your report, it will be useless when the abstract is separated from the report. Footnotes, subheadings, and tables should also be avoided.

Avoid using abbreviations or symbols that are explained only in the body of your report. Because the abstract must stand alone, they should be explained or written in full in the abstract.

□ NOTE

Prepare your abstract after you have finished writing your report —not before. An abstract should never contain anything that does not appear in the report itself. Authors who write an abstract first and then prepare their report often find that, in the writing, reviewing, or revising processes, important items are added or deleted that make the abstract incorrect. As a general principle, you cannot abstract something that does not exist.   □

An abstract for the ordinary report should be not more than 200 words in length. A short abstract can be read quickly and best serves the purposes outlined above; a two-page "abstract" may never be read at all by a busy reader. In addition, abstracts are placed on file cards in libraries and in various individual files; if they are longer than 200 words, they require two or more cards, which causes confusion.

3-7.3. Format

In a formal, long-form report, the abstract should appear on a page alone. Because it is an important part, it should preferably be on a right-hand page (although it may back up the foreword). For the heading, use the word "Abstract" treated typographically as a first-order heading. In typewriter typography, it is normally typed in capital letters, underscored, and centered. If the body of the abstract is short, type it in narrow measure and place it at the optical center of the page (see Fig. 3-6).

In short-form reports, the abstract may be located just before the opening section; it may be on the left-hand page facing the opening section, or it may appear immediately below the title and author's name and just above the beginning text on page 1. If several type faces are available, set the abstract in boldface type in a smaller face than the body of the report.

3-8. TABLE OF CONTENTS

3-8.1. Purpose

A table of contents indicates to your reader your method of organizing your material and, in addition, tells him on what page he will find a particular section. A careful reader will examine the table of contents before he begins to read your report. If he plans to read it in its entirety, the table of contents will let him know what to expect as he passes from section to section. It also gives him an indication of the extent of your subject coverage.

When your report is used as a reference work by some colleague working in the same field—as many research and development reports are—the table of contents directs him to the specific information that he wants, and it is not necessary for him to leaf through the entire report in order to find a single item. A well-planned table of contents can save the users a considerable amount of time.

In a short-form report, a table of contents is not needed. It only adds to the bulk of the report without accomplishing any real purpose. In all formal, long-form reports, however, tables of contents are necessary.

NAVORD REPORT 6415

ABSTRACT

From experiments performed at the Naval Ordnance
Test Station, it was concluded that the effect of light
on ferromagnetism is largely due to the red and near-
infrared portions of the spectrum. Thermal changes of
permeability are shown to be applicable to the detection
of steady illumination. Domain boundaries in the ferro-
magnetic films are shown to move under the influence of
mechanical vibration, and by analogy, light is believed
to produce the same effect.

v

Figure 3-6. Typical abstract for formal report in typewriter
typography. Abstracts should be short and with no unnecessary
statements. Abstracts that give positive information are preferable
to those that only indicate the type of material that can be found
in the report.

3-8.2. Content

3-8.2.1 SECTION HEADINGS

Basically, a table of contents is made by listing the section headings in the order in which they appear in the report (see Fig. 3-7). In an average report (20 to 60 pages), the list usually is composed of the first- and second-order headings. Listing only the first-order headings does not supply enough information; if you show third- and fourth-order headings (see Section 4-1.3), you are apt to confuse the general picture of the report with too much detail.

Prepare your table of contents by listing the section headings exactly as they appear in the report. Be sure to keep the sequence the same, as well as the wording, spelling, and punctuation. Although a table of contents is in outline form, it is not exactly the same as the outline that you use to write your report. The outline usually is more detailed than a table of contents; the wording of the subjects is often not so precise as your final section headings; and a consistent format is not so important in an outline as in a table of contents.

☐ NOTE

Prepare the table of contents after you have completed your report—not before. When the table is made up before you have finished writing, there is a strong chance that you will add or delete a section or rearrange the order of some sections, which will make the table of contents incorrect. One of the last steps in writing a report is to cross-check the entries in the table of contents with the actual section headings, including the page numbers. ☐

Begin the primary listing in your table of contents with the foreword and other preliminary material (exclusive of the table of contents itself), list the headings in the report proper, and end with the supplementary material, including the appendixes, list of references, and index (if any).

3-8.2.2 FIGURE LEGENDS AND TABLE TITLES

Figures and tables may or may not be listed in a table of contents. They are actually integral pieces of the various sections described in the primary listing, and a reader will come upon them at

TECHNICAL REPORT 1234

CONTENTS

Figure 3-7. Typical table of contents in typewriter typography. In this example, the text, figures, and tables are listed together. Another acceptable style is to list these items on three consecutive pages, headed "Contents", "Illustrations" and "Tables" respectively.

the right time as he reads the report. There will be situations, however, in which the figures or tables are also important by themselves, and users of the report may wish to refer to a particular figure or table without making any further use of the text that supports it. If this is the case, list all of the figures together, with the word "Figures" in the location and typography of a first-order heading, and the figure legends in the typography of second-order headings (see Fig. 3-7). Following the figures, you may wish to list the tables in a similar fashion.

With figures, it is acceptable to give only the basic legend in the table of contents and not show any additional notes or comments that may appear in the legends beneath the figures. Similarly, you may list only the primary titles of tables and not include any subtitles if they are unusually long or not required in order to direct the reader to the proper table. Be sure to cross-check all legends and titles shown in the table of contents with those that actually appear in the report.

If you identify your figures by numbers only as in a mathematics report, you should not attempt to list them in the table of contents. It is of no use to tell a reader that "Figure 6" is on page 19 if you do not tell him what "Figure 6" shows. Similarly, if you do not plan to number your pages (as in some brochures), there is no purpose in listing the figures or tables because you have no device to lead the reader to them.

3-8.3. Format Variations

Figure 3-7 shows a typical table of contents in typewriter typography. It includes first- and second-order section headings, regular preliminary and supplementary matter, figure legends, and table titles.

Some organizations prefer to divide a table of contents into three units: one for the section headings, one for the legends, and one for the table titles. While this policy is quite acceptable, it is becoming outmoded. It is a holdover from the days when figures were used, not as integral parts of a discussion, but as devices to decorate reports. Now the trend is to make everything in a report serve a useful purpose.

Some authors use a table of contents as a variation of a summary of their report. In this style, they include a brief abstract of the contents of each section immediately after the listing of the section heading. For certain types of publications—for example, textbooks—such a table of contents may be very useful to the readers.

In short reports, you will probably list only the first-order headings. This is good form for reports of 10 to 20 pages, where the subject matter is not sufficiently involved to require more detail.

4

Report Proper

4-1. TEXT

4-1.1. Opening Section

4-1.1.1 PURPOSE

The opening section of a report serves to bring you, the author, and the reader onto common ground so that the process of communication will be as easy—and at the same time as thorough—as possible. You must make clear to him exactly what you are writing about, why he should read your report, and what he can expect to find in the pages that follow. If you begin to give the details of your report to your reader without first conditioning him, he will not be receptive. The opening section serves somewhat the same purpose as the introductory comments given by a good master of ceremonies before a speaker takes over.

□ NOTE

Every report—regardless of its length—should have an opening section. You should always make contact (even though briefly) with your reader before you begin the report proper. □

4-1.1.2. Content

As you design your opening section, consider discussing the following items:

a. Purpose of report	f. Limits of work reported
b. Authority for work	g. Method of work
c. Historical background	h. Statement of findings
d. Review of theory	i. Method of presentation
e. Specifications	

It is seldom necessary to include all of these items, but consider each and use those that are applicable. Items (a), (f), (h), and (i) will almost always be used—usually in that order. Occasionally, however, you may want to follow (a) with (h) so that you can give the reader at a glance both the reason for doing the work and a brief statement of what you learned.

In some organizations, the authority for the work (item b) is given in the foreword (see Section 3-4) or in the letter of transmittal (see Section 3-3); in others, it appears in the opening section. The location depends upon local policy. It should, however, be included in one or the other of these sections. Because a considerable amount of time and money may have been spent in performing the work that you are reporting, it is wise to state early who authorized the expenditure.

The need for a summary of background information (item c) or for a review of the theory (item d) on which the work was based depends upon the type of report and the audience. For example, if you·are preparing a routine test report for a limited audience completely familiar with your program, a review of the historical background would be superfluous; but when you are preparing a long-form report to be read by a general audience, such a review will be essential to their understanding of the information that you have to offer. In addition, such summaries are traditional in the fields of chemistry and mathematics. In these sections, credit the research men who have preceded you and clearly indicate the work that they have done before you begin to discuss your own work. Go as far back as necessary, but do not attempt to cover the entire field each time you move one step forward. The real problem arises when your report must serve more than one audience. It is well in such circumstances to label your review sections with an appropriate heading so that those familiar with the background can skip it and go on to the report proper.

A brief statement of pertinent specifications (item e) is often useful in setting the stage for an engineering report. If, for example, your task has been to design a water system with a specific capacity that can be installed for a fixed amount of money, record this in the opening section. If the specifications are long and detailed, however, include in the opening section only the major or unusual features and place the complete specifications in an appendix, for you do not want to make the opening section so tiresome that your reader loses interest before he gets into the main body of the report.

Your readers will always want to know the limits of the information (item f) that you plan to give them. In the opening section, state in a few words what you will cover and—if there is any doubt—what you will not cover. The following statement is typical:

> This survey covers the off-street commercial parking facilities in the City of Milwaukee in the area between the Milwaukee River and Lake Michigan and bounded by Wisconsin Avenue on the south and North Street on the north. It does not include public parking lots and garages nor individual private garages.

Make a particular point of establishing the limits if there is anything unusual about them. A discussion of limits is unnecessary only if your audience is small and the matter to be discussed is clearly indicated in the title. For example, a report entitled "Slide Rule for Computing the Density of Atmospheric Air at Ground Level" probably would not require further comment concerning its limits in the opening section, whereas a statement would be needed in a report entitled "Hot Gas Blow-Down Experiments With Counter-Thrusting Nozzles."

When you are reporting on research work or a survey, your readers will usually want to know how you went about it (item g). If you followed standard procedures, a simple statement to this effect will be sufficient. Readers familiar with these techniques can then scan your later sections on methods and procedures and move to the more interesting sections on results, while newcomers to the subject can read your sections in order. Anything unusual about your methods should certainly be pointed out in the opening section.

A statement of your findings, results, conclusions, or recommendations (item h) is useful in this section. Be as brief as you can, but cover the major points. A more elaborate summary will be made in the closing section.

☐ NOTE

There will be many readers who will not get past your opening section. Because of the press of work or individual reading habits, they will scan the first page or two and then put the report aside to "read later when there is more time." If the points you wish to make are important, place them where they cannot be missed— they will bear repeating at the end without loss of effectiveness. ☐

A statement of results is easily made if, for example, you have been asked to report on the ability of a particular metal to withstand a certain compressive force and you can say simply that it did. It is more difficult if your findings are complicated and need to be qualified, but a short statement of your findings in the opening section will benefit the great majority of your reports.

At the end of the opening section, outline the manner in which you intend to present the information in your report (item i). This portion also should be brief—not a repetition of the table of contents. The reader would like to know, however, if you plan to emphasize certain features of the work or to omit other areas. Tell him if you are discussing the items in the standard order, or if you are introducing any unusual sections. This forecast of the information to come will help the reader to understand the report.

4-1.1.3. LENGTH AND BALANCE

The length of an opening section is primarily determined by the knowledge of the people whom you expect to read your report. The greater their knowledge of your field of endeavor in general and your phase of work in particular, the less you need to explain to them in order to get onto common ground. Conversely, the more general your audience, the more detailed your opening remarks must be.

It is important not to let your report get out of balance by holding a reader too long in the opening section. Most report readers quickly become impatient; they are anxious to get on with the business at hand—if, indeed, they intend to read the entire report. It is advisable, therefore, to keep your opening section short; a good rule of thumb is to limit it to no more than 10 percent of the total number of pages, exclusive of any appendixes.

To stay within this limit and still include a sizable section on background information, you may find it useful to use a heading such as "Introduction" for your basic remarks, followed by another heading of equal importance—for example, "Review of Previous Studies" —to introduce the background material. Although the two sections combined make up the complete opening section, the reader is innocuously led to believe that he has finished with the preliminary remarks and gotten into the "meat of the thing" much earlier than is actually the case.

4-1.1.4 USE OF ILLUSTRATIONS

Be sparing in your use of illustrations in the opening section. Holding to the theory that every illustration in a technical report must serve a purpose, you will find that few of your opening remarks require the support of an illustration. Certainly, detailed pictures of test apparatus or results will be withheld for the proper sections in the body of the report. General illustrations, however, may definitely assist you in orienting the reader, and figures that set the theme are appropriate in your opening section. Typical of such figures would be an aerial view of the downtown section of a city to illustrate a report on a proposed plan for a new civic center, a photograph of a prototype of a new rocket in a report summarizing the research and development work that brought it to the production stage, or an artist's conception of a new type of extrusion press being introduced by your report. The point to keep in mind is that your illustrations should complement your verbal introduction; otherwise they should be eliminated.

4-1.1.5. STYLE AND LANGUAGE

More than any other section, the opening section of your report must be written with care and thought, for you can lose a potential reader in the first few paragraphs if your style does not appeal to him. Consider your readers and write in the style that is best suited to them. If you expect your report to be read by more than one group of readers, write first for your most important audience.

Try to be direct rather than devious, but avoid the style of a newspaper reporter. Since you are striving for sincerity coupled with understandability, avoid exaggeration and flamboyancy. For example, instead of:

> The ultimate in wood preservatives has at last been developed. One treatment with Composition X will render all types of wood invulnerable to termite attack for a hundred years.

use

> This report describes Composition X and its use in preserving certain deciduous woods against termite attack. This promising new preservative appears to be a distinct improvement over current commercial preservatives. A series of accelerated tests performed at the American Laboratories indicates that Composition X will retard the attack of termites in oak, ash, maple, and walnut for more than 20 years.

Since you want to capture your reader's attention quickly, open your report with something that seems certain to interest him. After the first paragraph, you can back off and cover the other information suggested in the foregoing section, returning to a summary of the main points of your report near the end of the opening section.

Avoid the use of abbreviations and jargon that would not be understood by the majority of your readers, at least until you have explained these terms. For example, instead of:

> At a meeting of representatives of NOTS, NOLC, and NRL, it was decided to replace the Mark 42 with the Mark 44.

use

> At a meeting of representatives of the Naval Ordnance Test Station (NOTS), the Naval Ordnance Laboratory Corona (NOLC), and the Naval Research Laboratory (NRL), it was decided to replace the Torpedo Mark 42 Mod 6 with the Torpedo Mark 44 Mod 1.

Once you have defined your abbreviations and even jargon to your readers, you are free to use the shortened forms if you feel that they will make for easier reading.

4-1.1.6 SLANTING

On the premise that every technical report is written for a specific purpose and intended for a predetermined audience, it is reasonable to expect that the author will slant his writing as best he can to achieve his purpose. There is nothing unethical about this practice because the purpose of the report is stated at the outset. Slanting is simply a matter of stating the facts in such a way that they will create a desired impression on the reader.

If your report is an over-all summary of all the work done on your project, to be put in the archives for possible use by colleagues at some later date, you can forget about the problem of slanting. If, however, you are on the verge of a major breakthrough in your work and are reporting to your management in the hope of obtaining additional funds to keep you going for another year, it is only good sense first to point out the advantages of carrying on the work before you mention the disadvantages, as you are ethically bound to do. In such a situation, your opening section should reflect your enthusiasm and call attention to the importance of the progress that you have made. Your recommendations should appear early in the section and should be backed up with a summary of your work that supports them. Later, as you discuss the results of all of your tests, you can report the reverses that you have had.

On the other hand, if you are convinced that your project has been only a dreary repetition of blind alleys and that further work would be fruitless, in the opening section point out the reverses that support your recommendation to discontinue the project.

This is "slanting." It is an acceptable practice even in the field of technical reports, but it should be done with care and with skill.

4-1.1.7 USE OF HEADINGS

In reports written in normal narrative style, it is usually not necessary to break up the opening section with second- and third-order headings. If a historical review is included (see Section 4-1.1.2), introduce it with a first-order heading; otherwise the use of headings should be governed by the principles described in Section 4-1.3.

There are, however, certain types of form reports (Fig. 4-1) that are prepared on sheets that contain preprinted headings. Their opening sections may contain such headings as "Purpose," "Date," "Fund Source," and "Test Number." After each heading there is a space that is to be used to supply the information. Such a device is useful for

U. S. NAVAL ORDNANCE TEST STATION
Engineering Evaluation Branch
Room 130   Michelson Laboratory

TEST DATA MEMORANDUM

DATE 2 September 1959

JOB ORDER NO. 160498

TDM NO. 60-59

REQUESTOR W. E. Kummings,
Code 5512

TEST (Give type of test, item tested, applicable dwg. no. Be clear but concise.):

To check the Upper Pressure Valve Rod Assembly on the J48 engines,
Part 207285.

OBJECT (State precisely the object of the test; that is, raise the question that the report answers.):

To check by metallographic means the Magnaflux inspection indication found
on the clevis-end of the rod during the Magnaflux inspection of a number of
these rods for failure of the threaded ends.

APPARATUS & PROCEDURE (Mention all major apparatus. Identify specimen. Give
enough detail so that test could be duplicated by junior personnel.):

A Section of the rod containing the Magnaflux indication was removed and
a longitudinal section was cut, mounted, polished, and etched for metallurgical
examination. Reference - Metallurgical Investigation No. 1014, Micro-specimens
231 and 232.

RESULTS (Give results only.):

No crack was found in the parent material.

DISCUSSION (Discuss only results obtained in this test. Avoid generalities based on results from
only a few tests.):

It was obvious that the Magnaflux indication was caused by the holding
tool used during the swaging operation which enlarges the end of the tube to
permit insertion of the clevis. The holding tool slightly depresses the tube
and during the swaging operation the cadmium plate was sufficiently folded
over to create the appearance of a crack.

CONCLUSION (Answer the question raised in the "Object." Do not introduce new ideas.):

The Magnaflux indication found did not indicate a cracked part.

Witnessed by

Report by

Date

Approved by

Figure 4-1. Typical form report. The headings, which will serve for a series of
similar reports, are preprinted at optimum locations, and brief instructions are
given as to the type of information that is to be included in each section.

gathering information into categories or for pl[...]
that it can be found quickly by the readers. It [...]
pletely restrict the author and prevent him from a[...]
suit his information.

In general, be conservative in the use of hea[...]
section. If your statements are brief, you will lea[...]
report proper before you need headings either to [...]
relieve the monotony of your discussion.

4-1.1.8 FORMAT

The opening section usually begins on a right-hand page, and, except in reports which have self-covers (see Section 3-1.3), it should begin on page 1. (The title page and other preliminary items are numbered with Roman numerals.) If you have used a title page, it is not necessary to repeat the title on the first page of the opening section. Start with the primary heading that you have chosen for your opening section (for example, "Introduction") located approximately one-third of the way down the page from the top (this is called "sinking" the heading). Then proceed in normal text style (one or two columns, as the case may be).

If you are using a self-cover, count it as page 1 (although you do not actually number it), and begin the opening section on page 3. When it is necessary to place your first illustration where it can be seen by the reader as he reads the first few pages, it may be located on the left-hand page facing the first page of the opening section. Usually, however, it should appear at the bottom of page 1 or on page 2.

You may wish to include the abstract on the first page of the opening section in order to save space (see Section 6-1.2.1). In this situation, it is well to place the title of the report near the top of the page followed immediately by the name of the author. Below this you can place the abstract in narrow measure. Next, in normal measure, begin the text of the opening section. There are variations of this format; the abstract is put in a box in the center of the first page of the opening section, for example. Variations are acceptable and may be used to suit your taste. The following pages of the opening section are then arranged in normal format for running text.

sing Section

4-1.2.1. PURPOSE

Most reports are improved by the inclusion of a section at the end that summarizes the main points that have been made in the report proper. The principle here is similar to that followed by good speakers and teachers: they close by restating the main points that they want their listeners to remember. Throughout the body of the report you move carefully from point to point, but as your reader considers one, he may lose track of an earlier argument. The longer the report, the more this is apt to happen. As a final step, then, array the points that you have made where they can be considered together by the reader.

Even though you may have placed a summary or list of recommendations at the beginning of your report, you should include a closing section at the end of it. Doing so enables you to satisfy the needs of several audiences. You place the summary at the beginning of the report for the readers who can spare only a little time and must get your major points quickly. The closing section is for those who will read your report from beginning to end. A third group of readers should also be considered—those who will read your opening section and skip to the end of the report to read what you have to say in the closing section. They are accustomed to reports being constructed in this manner and seldom, if ever, read the body of the report.

Although you should usually try to close your report with a final summary, there are a few reports in which a closing section is not appropriate. Typical of these are bibliographies and some survey reports. If a closing section is obviously inappropriate, omit it, but always use one when it is logical to do so.

□ NOTE

Plan to end your report with a closing section. It is an unusual report that does not need one. Omit it only after you are convinced that it will add nothing.   □

4-1.2.2. TYPES

Depending upon the subject of your report, you will (1) summarize your major findings, (2) draw conclusions from your work, or (3) make recommendations based upon the material that you have presented. Frequently you will divide your closing section into two subsections, one for your conclusions followed by one listing your recommendations. Often the type of closing section is determined by the task that was originally assigned to you. If, for example, you have been asked to make a study of three possible sites for a flood-control dam and to recommend the best one, you obviously will summarize the advantages and disadvantages of each site and close your report with a specific recommendation.

4-1.2.3. CONTENT

In preparing a closing section, remember that every point you make must either have been made in the report proper or (in the case of recommendations) must be based upon the results and arguments that you have presented in the body of the report.

□ NOTE

Do not introduce a new idea in the closing section. Everything that you say must have been said before or be supported by information that you have previously presented. □

Write the closing section after you have completed the body of the report. Although a few authors prefer to write their conclusions first and then build the report toward them, if you do so, there is the possibility that the information in the body of your report will not justify the conclusions. Too often, something is overlooked when this method is used. It is far safer to select the points to be presented in the closing section by reading through the body of the report.

Keep the statements in the closing section as brief as possible. This is not the place for discussion, which is properly located in the body of the report. If it is appropriate, use a short narrative paragraph to introduce the final section and then summarize the points.

Because you are not introducing anything new, you will have no need to refer to any items in your list of references. Similarly, footnotes are rare in this section.

It is always advisable to cross-check the closing section with your remarks in the opening section. If at the beginning of a report you indicate that you are going to prove certain points, they should appear in the closing section. Although you touch upon the same items in both sections, you should present a much more detailed and thorough summary in the closing section than in the opening section.

4-1.2.4. USE OF ILLUSTRATIONS

You seldom have need for illustrations in the closing section of a long-form report. Since you are recapitulating points that you have made before, the illustrations supporting these points will have been shown during the presentation of the results or the discussion of them. If your closing section is a summary, you may wish to repeat a particularly descriptive figure shown earlier in the report—especially if you believe that your more important readers may read only the opening and closing sections. In general, however, illustrations are out of place in the closing section. If you believe that you need one in this section, you have probably failed to complete the body of the report.

4-1.2.5. USE OF TABLES

Tables are rarely used in the closing section of a report. There are exceptions to this rule, of course, depending upon the purpose of the report. For example, if your project was to determine which among a number of alloys would make the best motor casing, you might very well compare the characteristics of each in a summary table and then point out that one of them is the best.

4-1.3. Section Headings

4-1.3.1. PURPOSE

The primary purpose of section headings is to indicate when you have completed the discussion of one subject and are about to move on to a new one. They define the new subject specifically. By their typography and location on the page they show quickly the relation of one section to those that precede and follow it. Section headings make the report more readable by visibly breaking up the blocks of text on the page—a device that noticeably speeds up the reading of the man who is scanning your report for general information.

Section headings are also invaluable to the man who uses your report for reference. The headings, combined with a reasonably complete table of contents, make it a simple matter to find a specific part of the text without losing time in paging back and forth through the report. Therefore, use sufficient headings so that they will guide the user quickly to the information that he wants. In report writing it is better to have too many than too few section headings.

4-1.3.2. STYLE OF PHRASING AND PUNCTUATION

Headings actually are titles and should be worded in the manner of titles. Write them in telegraphic style, with a minimum of articles. Avoid the use of verbs and gerunds. For example:

> Instead of: Many Problems Were Encountered in Developing the Machine
>
> use: Machine Development Problems
>
> Instead of: The Testing of the Samples
>
> use: Test Results
>
> Instead of: The Amount of Fermentable Sugar Was Determined for the Five Bark Samples
>
> use: Fermentable Sugars in Barks

☐　NOTE

Keep your section headings as short as possible without making them ambiguous. Use qualifiers only when they are absolutely essential.　☐

Punctuation of section headings should be kept to a minimum. Headings that stand on a line of their own should not have end periods, whether they are located in the center of the page or flush against the left margin. The only headings that require end periods are those that are run into the following text; for example:

> *Definition of Dielectric Heating.* Dielectric heating, as the name implies, is the process of generating heat in . . .

Avoid the use of parentheses and dashes with numbers or letters to identify section headings. They are old-fashioned and add nothing to the readability; for example:

> Instead of: (c) *Rockets in Use*
>
> or: c.—*Rockets in Use*
>
> use: c. *Rockets in Use*

The only situation that justifies the use of parentheses is when you have at least five orders of headings and are working in typewriter typography.

In section headings of two or more lines try to avoid breaking words at the end of a line and using hyphens; for example:

> Instead of: *Action of Resin Glues Under Ex-*
> *ternal Heat and Electronic Heat*

> use: *Action of Resin Glues Under External*
> *Heat and Electronic Heat*

4-1.3.3. CONTENT

In reports, section headings tell the reader the general subject coverage of the text that follows. This is contrary to the way in which headings are sometimes used by journalists. Newspaper practice often requires that headings be inserted every few inches whether there is a distinct change in subject matter or not. There, a heading is keyed to a statement that appears somewhere in the next paragraph or two, but it may not indicate any real shift in thought. For example, a newspaper heading may read as follows:

HUBBUB FOLLOWS

> Thomas became the first man to high jump seven feet indoors here two weeks ago.
>
> During the hubbub that followed, Olympic champion Charley Dumas tried to clear seven feet and dislodged the bar . . .

In a report, however, a section heading is supposed to indicate the main topic of the material that follows; for example:

ROCKET HEAD

> The rocket head is known as the payload of the rocket because this is the part that will do the damage when the rocket gets to the target . . .

4-1.3.4. FORMAT

In general, the section headings that define the major portions of a report (first-order headings) should be prominently displayed (usually in the center of the page horizontally) and set in large, bold type. Selection of the location and typography of succeeding orders of headings depends upon the number of orders to be used in a report. As the headings are less and less important, they are made to stand out less and less from the rest of the text on the page. They may be moved to a line of their own flush against the left margin, and finally run into the first line of the text. Thus, in typewriter typography three orders of headings could be set up as follows:

<pre>
             FIRST ORDER, CENTERED

SECOND ORDER, FLUSH LEFT

     Third Order, Run-In. Following the third-
order heading, the text is continued on the same
line, immediately after the heading...
</pre>

To handle five orders of headings in typewriter typography, however, the format might be varied as follows:

<pre>
        FIRST ORDER, CENTERED, ALL CAPS

   Second Order, Centered, Caps and Lower Case

THIRD ORDER, FLUSH LEFT, ALL CAPS

Fourth Order, Flush Left, Caps and Lower Case

     Fifth Order, Run-In. Note that here each of
the first four orders of headings stands on a
line of its own. The fifth-order heading is
followed immediately by text on the same line...
</pre>

If your report is short and you plan to use only two orders of headings, you may want to go directly from a centered heading to a run-in heading, disregarding the flush-left heading standing on a line of its own; this is a matter of personal preference.

□ NOTE

Once you have selected a system of headings, follow it with absolute consistency throughout your report. Nothing will confuse a reader more than inconsistency in the typography of your headings. □

If your report is to be composed on cold-type composing machines or in hot type for letterpress or offset reproduction, you have much greater flexibility than if you must work with a typewriter. Here you can discard the underscore used so extensively in typewriter composition and take advantage of the variety of type faces, styles, and sizes, For example, if your text is composed in a serif type face (say, Garamond), you can change to a face without serifs (say, Futura) for your headings. You may increase the point size as you wish to get variation or use boldface or italic in almost limitless combinations.

When your report is to be set in hot type, you need the advice of a professional book designer or, at least, a printer. To give you some idea of the variations possible, however, the following is an example of the headings used for a report that required seven orders of headings set in hot type:

FIRST-ORDER HEADING

SECOND-ORDER HEADING

Third-Order Heading

FOURTH-ORDER HEADING. Followed by text . . .

Fifth-Order Heading. Followed by text . . .

Sixth-Order Heading. Followed by text . . .

Seventh-order heading. Followed by text.

4-1.4. Footnotes

4-1.4.1. RELATION OF FOOTNOTES TO TEXT

A footnote is used to present information that supports but is not essential to your main discussion. On the assumption that not all of your readers will be interested in such additional information, you remove it from the body of the text and place it at the bottom of the page. As an indication to the reader that there is more supplementary material if he cares to read it, you insert a "flag"—such as a superscript number or án asterisk—at the appropriate point in the text, and you put the same flag at the start of the footnote.

☐ NOTE

Since not all readers take the time to read footnotes carefully, do not put anything essential to your argument in a footnote. Only "extra" information should be removed from the text and placed in footnotes. ☐

Authors of technical reports are much less inclined to use footnotes than are authors of technical books, perhaps because the former either say all that needs to be said in the text or simply refer the reader to another publication (given in the list of references or the bibliography) and let him look up the information for himself. Nevertheless, the footnote is a useful device that, if used correctly, will enable you to keep your main text comparatively free of unessential detail and thereby improve the presentation. There are two types of footnotes: the comment type and the bibliographic type.

4-1.4.2 COMMENT-TYPE FOOTNOTES

Comment-type footnotes vary widely in the kinds of information that they contain. In general, they are a continuation of the text, ranging from a single word to several paragraphs. It is quite permissible to include tables or simple figures (usually line drawings) if necessary. The following examples are typical of the content of such footnotes:

Example 1

The distance x from the center-line of pile to the center of gravity of the transformed area is

$$x = \frac{567}{97.0} = 5.84 \text{ in.}$$

This value of x is sufficiently close to the trial value of 6.0 and no correction is needed.* In case there is too large a . . .

---

* With the value of 5.84, a recalculation gives the second value of 5.86 for distance from center-line to center of gravity of transformed section.

Example 2

. . . I believe that social study should begin with careful observation of what may be described as communication: that is, the capacity of an individual to communicate his feelings and ideas to another, the capacity of groups to communicate effectively and intimately with each other. This problem is, beyond all reasonable doubt, the outstanding defect that civilization is facing today.[1] The studies of Pierre Janet, of which I shall have more to say . . .

[1] See Chap. IV, infra, for detailed discussion of the importance of "listening" as the basis of communication.

Example 3

If the terminal point in any vector addition of revenue and benefit quotients falls on the axis *OC,* the condition defined is one wherein road user benefits just balance motor vehicle revenues. In other words, the road user, in this case, derives benefits exactly commensurate with the taxes he pays.* There is no particular advantage to him . . .

* This is not true unless motor vehicle imposts are used exclusively for highway purposes. It is substantially true when the only diversion is a small deduction for collection and administrative expenses.

Example 4

When allowance is made for the lack of perfect matching among the several moisture-content sets, it is possible to derive from the data on each species a value of M_p that is acceptable for all of the strength properties.[8]

[8] Convenience in the use of formulas for moisture-strength adjustment, as is shown later, makes a single value of M_p for all properties of a species desirable.

From these examples you may see that in a footnote the author of a report is speaking directly to the reader, giving him an additional bit of information to aid him in understanding the text. Consider, then, the knowledge and background of your intended readers in deciding whether certain information should appear in the text or be removed from the text and placed in a footnote; again, consider the variety of readers that you anticipate in deciding upon how far you should go with supplementary information in your footnotes.

In addition to the type of material shown in the foregoing examples, you can use footnotes to supply essential facts that would not otherwise be available to your readers. For example, if you want to document information that you received by telephone, you can foot-note it as follows:

> ¹ Supplied to the author by Dr. J. D. Jacobson of Pacific Propulsion Laboratory in a telephone conversation on 14 July 1960.

Or you can refer to correspondence in a footnote, as follows:

> ¹ Stated in a personal letter to the author from R. M. Richards, Head, Physics Department, Strand Corporation, dated 22 June 1960.

Or you can refer to a publication that is in manuscript form at the time that you are writing your report—and therefore not available to a reader—as follows:

> ¹ Described in a report now in preparation by R. F. Blan-chard, Senior Engineer, Navy Electronics Laboratory, San Diego, on the subject of the relation of underwater tides to the transmission of sound.

□ NOTE

In referring to a publication that is not yet actually off the press, give the subject rather than a proposed title. If, as so often happens, the title is changed during the processing stages, your reference will result in confusion for your readers who attempt to obtain a copy. □

4-1.4.3. BIBLIOGRAPHIC FOOTNOTES

When you refer your reader to another publication, you may instruct him to look in the list of references (see Section 5-3) at the end of your report for the bibliographic information he needs to find the publication, or you may supply that information in a footnote located on the same page as your reference to it. The decision as to which method you use is purely arbitrary but is based on the follow-ing principle: if you have only a few (five or six) references scattered throughout your report, use footnotes; if you have more than six references or if you refer to some publications more than once, use a list of references at the end of your report.

In supplying bibliographic information by the use of footnotes, furnish only the information that you have not already given in the text. Thus, if you mention the author's name in the text, do not repeat it in the footnote; for example:

> I shall make no attempt to describe at length that which has been already and fully described. The interested public is well acquainted with *Management and the Worker.* . . . The same public has not yet discovered *The Industrial Worker,*[1] by another colleague, T. North Whitehead.

---

[1] Cambridge, Harvard University Press, 1938, 2 vols.

In this example, since the name of the author and the title of his book were given in the text, they were not repeated in the footnote. Your purpose is to see that your reader has all of the information that he needs in order to find the right publication.

In the use of bibliographic footnotes, it is also possible to make use of abbreviations to relieve you of the need to repeat information. They are as follows:

> *ibid.* (*ibidem*), in the same place
>
> *loc. cit.* (*loco citato*), in the place cited
>
> *op. cit.* (*opere citato*), in the work cited

These are used in the following manner:

Example 1

[1] Edward Jenks, *Law and Politics in the Middle Ages* (London, John Murray, 1913), 2d ed., p. 71.
  [2] *Ibid.,* p. 72.

Example 2

. . . I have elsewhere described the bonus plan [1] and shall not repeat this detail here. . . .

---

[1] Elton Mayo, "Revery and Industrial Fatigue," *loc. cit.*

Example 3

. . . The first two operate to make an industry *effective,* in Chester Barnard's phrase [1], the third to make it *efficient.*

---

[1] *Op. cit.,* p. 56.

4-1.4.4. FOOTNOTE IDENTIFICATION METHODS

In reports of not more than 50 or 60 pages in length, which are not separated into chapters, it is customary to use one series of numbers for all footnotes in a report, beginning with page 1 and continuing through to the end of the report, including appendixes.

☐ NOTE

Do not start a new footnote numbering series for each appendix. To do so will result in duplicate numbers; for example, there will be two or more footnotes numbered "1," which is. likely to lead to confusion. ☐

In large reports that are divided into formal chapters or parts, you may want to identify the footnotes for each chapter. They may be numbered 1—1, 1—2, 1—3 for Chapter 1; 2—1, 2—2, 2—3 for Chapter 2; etc. This procedure is particularly useful during the writing and production stages when you may be adding or deleting footnotes, a process that requires renumbering all footnotes after the new note.

Footnotes for text tables (see Section 4-1.5.4) are included in the same series as all other footnotes to the text. The footnotes to formal tables (see Section 4-2.5), however, are handled in separate series because they are a part of the tables rather than of the text and, as such, may be moved about to a certain extent by the typographer, thus disrupting the proper sequence of numbers.

☐ NOTE

Be sure that your footnotes are numbered consecutively. If, for example, footnote 4 precedes footnote 3, your reader will be confused. If you insert a footnote as an afterthought, renumber all of the notes after it; do not use such numbers as 14a or 22b. ☐

If you have very few footnotes in your report, you may use symbols for reference marks, such as the asterisk and dagger. When you use this method, however, you soon find yourself faced with the need to use such marks as the double and triple daggers, which become more trouble than they are worth. On the other hand, if you attempt to start over with an asterisk, then a dagger, etc., on each new page, your production problems become complicated and you are forced to re-mark your footnotes after the report has been typed or composed in final form. For technical reports, it is far easier to hold to one series of numbers for your reference marks.

4-1.4.5 FORMAT

In hot-type typography, footnotes are set in the same face as the text, but usually two points smaller. In typewriter typography, a short line (about an inch long) at the left margin is used to separate the text and the footnote. The footnote may be indented as a paragraph or it may be placed flush against the left-hand margin. The reference mark should be raised.

Use normal sentence punctuation, ending the footnotes with periods. Start each footnote on a new line· unless the notes are very short, in which case they may be set two or more to a line or in columns.

Begin every footnote on the same page as its reference. If you have a long footnote that must be carried over onto a following page, arrange it so that you break the note in the middle of a pararaph, thereby avoiding starting a new paragraph on the succeeding page and the resultant confusion.

In bibliographic footnotes that start with the author's name, use normal rather than inverted order; for example, "R. C. Whitman," rather than "Whitman, R. C." Since footnotes appear in the order in which they are mentioned in the text, there is no need to place the last name first for alphabetizing as there is in a bibliography.

4-1.5. Displayed Text

4-1.5.1. PURPOSE

Certain points that are particularly important to the theme of your report can be emphasized by displaying them in a format different from that of your running text. By the device of separating such points from the text, you call the reader's attention to them, and he inevitably considers them more carefully than he does other material. For example, in this handbook there are certain important points that should be remembered—even if you do not absorb anything else; to call your attention to these points, they have been set in narrow measure and flagged with the word "NOTE." You will find that, if you scan through these pages, your eye consistently hesitates at these notes. This is one of the purposes of displayed text.

Through the technique of displayed text, it is also possible to explain some concepts better than you can in running narrative. It is often helpful to array information in outline form either when you are leading into a difficult section of your report or when you wish to summarize your findings. In this way, you can show relationships and make comparisons more easily than by any other device. For example, a review of information about nonpressure wood-treating plants can be arranged thus:

> 8 nonpressure plants treating fenceposts and some small poles. The treating liquid is creosote and oil in varying proportions.
> 1 million or more posts treated, or 6 million board feet.
> 34 men employed in the treating process.
> 62,600 man-hours of labor.

Arrayed in this manner, the information is easy to comprehend; if it had been presented in normal running text, it would have been obscure.

Displayed text is also useful when you are presenting material that you expect to be used often by readers who turn to your report for reference. By displaying it, you make this information readily accessible and eliminate the need for searching through the report for a desired passage.

4-1.5.2. PRINCIPLES

Be conservative in your use of displayed text. If you use it too frequently, or if a single display is too long, you lose the benefits of this device. If, for example, every other paragraph is displayed, you lose both emphasis and easy reference. Displayed text that runs for a full page or more gives the reader the impression that you have changed to a new format, and he no longer considers the material to be displayed.

Keep to a consistent style in each block of displayed text. Lack of consistency may confuse the reader; at best, it will irritate him and draw his attention away from the theme of your presentation.

□ NOTE

Do not change style in the middle of a block of displayed text. This principle applies to sentence structure, punctuation, capitalization, abbreviation, and physical arrangement. □

The following examples indicate the difference between consistency and the lack of consistency in displayed text.

Inconsistent	*Consistent*
Following are a few ways by which the output of existing kilns may be increased:	Following are a few ways by which the output of existing kilns may be increased:
1. Dry lumber longer on yard before bringing it into kiln.	1. Dry the lumber longer on the yard before bringing it into the kiln.
2. Laminate thick stock instead of making it of one piece.	2. Laminate thick stock instead of making it of one piece.
3. The Kiln Stickers Should Be Planed to ¾ Inch.	3. Plane the kiln stickers to ¾ inch.
(4) Use forced circulation in the kilns.	4. Use forced circulation in the kilns.

If you begin a list of displayed items in the imperative style, continue this style for all the items; if you use sentence style (subject and verb) in some of your items, use it in all. If none of the items in a list are complete sentences, do not use final periods, for example:

The woods used in this series of tests were as follows:

Softwoods

    Cedar, northern and white
    Fir, balsam and commercial white
    Hemlock, eastern
    Pine, southern yellow

Hardwoods

> Aspen and largetooth aspen
> Basswood
> Cottonwood, black and eastern
> Poplar, yellow

On the other hand, if you have a comment in sentence form requiring a final period in any of your items, use a final period in all items, thus:

> . . . In applying the formula, it is necessary to break down the cost components and apply to each the service-life value that best fits the case. The following breakdown will generally be sufficient:
>
> 1. Roadbed and rights of way.
>
> 2. Roadway surfacing.
>
> 3. Structures. These should be segregated by types in accordance with service life.
>
> 4. Miscellaneous appurtenances.

4-1.5.3. FORMAT

In addition to the suggestions concerning the format of displayed text indicated in the foregoing discussion, some other points should be made. Remember that displayed text is handled by the typographer (or typist) in the same manner as normal running text; that is, it is begun when it is encountered in your manuscript regardless of where it may fall on a page. When the typographer reaches the bottom of a page, he simply breaks the display and continues it on the next page, whether the remainder is a dozen lines or only one. If a display begins on a right-hand page and carries over onto the left-hand page that follows it, you may lose the benefit of the display when the reader cannot see the entire group at once.

Displayed items may be numbered or not, according to your needs. If you refer to the items in your text, or if you wish to convey order of importance, they should be numbered; otherwise, numbers add nothing and are better omitted.

Displayed text does not require a title or heading. Lead directly from the narrative into the display, as indicated in the preceding examples.

The following three types of displayed text are common:

Flush	*Hung*	*Paragraph*
1. Your first item	1. Your first item	1. Your first item.
2. Your second item with run-over lines brought flush left	2. Your second item with run-over lines indented	2. Your second item with run-over lines brought back to the left margin.
3. Your third item	3. Your third item	3. Your third item with run-over lines.

The paragraph style is preferable when your items are long, running consistently to more than one line. "Hanging" the run-over lines is useful when most of your items are short—not more than one line. While the flush style is satisfactory for short items, it is seldom employed. If you use it, be sure that you leave a vertical space between the items so that the reader will not be confused.

4-1.5.4. TEXT TABLES

A useful variation of displayed text is the "text table," in which related information is arrayed in two or more vertical columns, instead of being presented in running text. As with other forms of displayed text, a text table is set exactly where it appears in the manuscript and cannot be moved about by the typographer. This gives you the advantage of being certain that the reader will see the items precisely when you want him to (which may not be true with a formal table); but it has the disadvantage that it may be continued from the bottom of one page to the top of another, depending upon how long it is and where it happens to fall on the page. A text table is excellent for making quick comparisons among a limited number of items; however, it is not a successful method of presenting a large quantity of information. In designing your text tables, the following suggestions should be kept in mind:

1. Restrict the table to not more than four columns. If you try to use more, you will lose the advantage of quick comparison.

2. Do not use a table title or a table number. These are used with formal tables (see Section 4-2.6); they are no more necessary in text tables than they would be in running text.

Example 1

. . . The following slopes are considered necessary to produce joints
as strong in tension along the grain as the solid woods:

Species	Slope
Birch, yellow	1 in 12
Gum, red	1 in 8
Mahogany	1 in 10
Poplar, yellow . . .	1 in 8
Oak, red	1 in 15

Example 2

. . . These tunnels are to be very similar in cross section and capacity
to the Holland tubes. The published estimate of cost originally covered
the following items:

Construction and initial equipment for operation ..	$57,800,000
Engineering, administration, and contingencies	8,700,000
Real estate	17,000,000
Interest during construction and financing	12,500,000
Total estimated cost	$96,000,000

Example 3

. . . The following data give a general idea of the operating conditions
of the retort. The data are a composite of numerous trials and are intended only to show the typical performance of the retort.

Speed of rotation, rpm	3
Temperature, discharge end, $^{\circ}$F	1250
Temperature, feed end, $^{\circ}$F	350
Feed, lb dry wood material per hr	100
Retention time, min	25

Example 4

. . . there was a possibility that some of the consignees in the Chicago
district with wharf facilities might be able to take advantage of the
new rates. Sample rates per net ton are indicative of the proposal.

Origin group	Local rail delivery rates to Chicago	Lake-cargo rates to Chicago
Clinton, Indiana	$1.65	$1.25
Southern Illinois	1.90	1.55
Western Kentucky	2.40	1.90

Figure 4-2. Typical text tables. When entries in the first column are uneven,
align them to the left and use leaders (as shown). If entries of figures are
similar, as in the second and fourth examples, align them on the decimal point.
If they are dissimilar, as in the third example, align them on the right.

3. If you need to footnote an item, include it in the regular series of footnotes to the text and place it at the bottom of the page on which it falls (rather than immediately below the last entry in the table).

4. Use column headings if you need them, but they are not required if the text that introduces the table explains it sufficiently.

5. Follow the examples in Fig. 4-2 for alignment of entries, use of leaders, location of units of measure, capitalization of words in column heads, etc.

4-1.5.5. EQUATIONS

If you have many equations in your report, obtain the assistance of a professional editor or at least enlist the help of a technical typist who is experienced in the composition of such matter. For the many report writers who introduce mathematics only occasionally, the following suggestions will be of help.

First, determine the capability of the staff that will help you produce your report. If you are supported by cold-type compositors, or if your report is to be produced in hot type, you can include complicated equations as often as necessary. The only restriction is that you should try not to use a character or symbol that your compositor does not have. Check with him if you are in doubt about some unusual character. If your report must be composed on a typewriter, however, with all but the simplest characters to be inserted by hand, keep your mathematics to a minimum. Where it is possible, refer your readers to some other publication, or summarize your detailed calculations in your report and let the few readers who want the details write and request them. Then keep the following suggestions in mind:

1. When your report is composed in hot type, all letter symbols (with the exception of chemical symbols and vector symbols) should appear in italic, but all figures in Roman, whether they appear as part of the running text or in displayed text; thus

... to illustrate, if a ball drops on a pavement from a height h_1 and bounces to a height h_2, e is given by the relation $h_2 = e^2 h_1$, or

$$e = \sqrt{\frac{h_2}{h_1}} \qquad (3)$$

In typewriter typography, however, because you do not have the opportunity to use italic type, you must resort to some other device to be sure that the reader recognizes letters as mathematical symbols and does not try to make words out of them. The accepted technique is to underscore letter symbols, which has the significance of italics. You will find it both practical and understandable if you underscore letter symbols in running text, but omit the underscore in equations or formulas displayed separately; thus:

. . .The strain or deformation in the pile at the load R is RL/AE, where L is the length of the pile, A the cross-sectional area, and E the modulus of elasticity of the concrete. The loss of energy in temporarily compressing the pile is therefore:

$$\text{Energy loss} = \frac{R^2 L}{2AE} \qquad (6)$$

2. Do not underscore numerals in typewriter typography. You would write:

Compression in the strut equals W/3 pounds.

3. Do not underscore Greek letters in typewriter typography.

Using 1-deg intervals in the equatorial co-ordinates of the right ascension, α, and the declination, δ, the following expressions were used to determine the ecliptic longitude, λ, and ecliptic latitude, β, and the galactic longitude, l, and the galactic latitude, b:

4. Where it is possible, in typewriter typography, use the solidus
(/) and write fractions on one line instead of built up; thus:

$$(W/3) \times (B/h) \text{ instead of } \frac{W}{3} \times \frac{B}{h}$$

5. When a mathematical expression or equation is too long to fit on
one line and must be broken, break after a plus or a minus sign;
thus:

$$2160 = 699 + 538 + 274 + 434(Z-9) + \frac{25.0(Z-9)^2}{2}$$

but break before an equals sign; thus:

$$P = 0.7 \times 1150 \times 0.64^{2.5} \times 0.5$$
$$= 132 \text{ pounds}$$

6. When you have a series of two or more equations without any
intervening text, they should be aligned on the equals signs and so
located that the longest equation is centered on the measure; thus:

$$R = 1,660,000 \left[-0.15 \pm \sqrt{0.15^2 + \frac{174,000 \times 2}{1,660,000}} \right]$$
$$= 1,660,000 \,(-0.15 \pm 0.48)$$

7. When your explanation requires connecting words between
equations, they should be set flush against the left margin, either on
lines of their own or on the same lines as the following equations;
thus:

Rankin's theory gives the following formula for the
increment of active pressure:

$$u = w \frac{1 - \sin \phi}{1 + \sin \phi} \tag{22}$$

in which

$w =$ weight of soil per cubic foot
$\phi =$ angle of internal friction

8. If, in your text, you refer to specific equations, number them all
consecutively, beginning with the first equation that you encounter in
your report and continuing through the report and all appendixes. It

is most satisfactory if equation numbers are placed flush against the right-hand margin, as shown in the example above. If equation numbers are located against the left-hand margin, they are apt to be confused with the numbering of other displayed items.

9. Although it was once universal practice to use punctuation marks throughout displayed equations on the principle that they were integral parts of the text and should be punctuated as sentences, this style is becoming outmoded. It is recommended that you omit punctuation in displayed equations on the assumption that the line breaks supply adequate visual indication of the relationship of the parts. Thus, whereas the more conservative authors would punctuate a series of equations in the following manner:

> . . . Then the components of the velocity of any particle P are
>
> $$v_x = \bar{v}_x + z'w_y - y'w_z ,$$
> $$v_y = \bar{v}_y + x'w_z - z'w_x ,$$
>
> and
>
> $$v_z = \bar{v}_z + y'w_x - x'w_y .$$

it is recommended that you do not use the end punctuation (in this case, the commas and the period).

4-1.6. Figure Legends

4-1.6.1. PURPOSE

Figure legends serve two purposes: they supplement the text by identifying the illustration and pointing out important features, and they serve to refresh the memory of the user who returns to your report for reference. Depending upon the use that you have made of an illustration, the legend may be as short as a few words or as long as several lines. Figure legends should be written carefully and cross-checked against the text to be sure that between the two you have adequately covered the subject under discussion.

□ NOTE

Except in unusual circumstances, every figure in your report should have a legend and a number. The number makes it possible for you to refer your reader to a figure with certainty; the legend explains the figure. □

It is not necessary that your figure legends be so complete that each figure would stand on its own if removed from the text. The figures and text should be so closely interwoven that neither is complete without the other. For example, your text might read: "The results of the firings of this rocket against armor plate, as shown in Fig. 16, clearly indicate that the rocket will effectively destroy tanks protected by as much as 12 inches of modern armor." The corresponding legend might read: "Fig. 16. Results of Rocket X Impacting on 12-Inch Armor Plate at an Angle of 45 Deg. Note that the rocket completely penetrated the plate (see arrow) and exploded on the far side." Thus, the text plus the figure and its legend are required to tell the full story.

4-1.6.2. CONTENT

The first portion of a figure legend should clearly identify the figure. Write this part in title style with a minimum of words. Thus, the title of a figure might be

> Fig. 3. Example of Highway Relocation To Accommodate Increased Traffic.

rather than

> Fig. 3. The Increased Traffic Between Racine and Kenosha Made Necessary the Relocation Shown in This Picture.

Observe that all words are capitalized in this style except articles, prepositions, and conjunctions of less than four letters. For example, do not capitalize *the,* but capitalize *This.*

You will frequently wish to include more information about the figure; such comments follow the figure title. Normally they are given in sentence style, and are punctuated like sentences, thus:

> Fig. 3. Example of Highway Relocation To Accommodate Increased Traffic. The volume of local traffic increased 200 percent, and that of non-resident traffic increased nearly 350 percent during the last 5 years. Relocation of highways to eliminate dangerous curves, as shown in this figure, has become a necessity rather than a luxury.

On the other hand, it may be necessary only to qualify the information shown in the figure, and this may be done with a minimum of words, thus:

> Fig. 10. Pile Driver Used To Drive Concrete Piles for
> Exposition Building. 5,000-lb. ram; 36-in. drop.

The major exception to the policy of supplying a legend with every figure is the illustration used as part of a mathematics study. There the figure is a direct extension of the text, and a legend could be supplied only by repeating a large block of text. In this situation, the figures are numbered for easy reference, but no legends are given.

4-1.6.3. NUMBERING OF FIGURES

Number your figures consecutively from 1 to 100 or more, beginning with the first figure in the report and continuing to the end, including all appendixes and supplementary matter. Assign numbers to the figures in the order in which they are mentioned in the text. If you think, for example, that Fig. 12 should come between Fig. 4 and Fig. 5, there is something wrong with the organization of your report; either you have numbered your figures incorrectly, or you are not discussing your material in the proper sequence.

□ NOTE

Never use the same figure number for two different figures, and never use identical legends for two figures in the same report. To do either will invariably confuse your readers. □

In long reports divided into chapters or parts you may want to vary the principle stated above and identify your figures according to the chapter in which they appear. If so, number them thus: Fig. 1-1, Fig. 1-2, etc.; Fig. 2-6, Fig. 2-7, etc.; or Fig. 4-10, Fig. 4-11, etc., for the figures in Chapters 1, 2, and 4. As with footnotes and references, the method of numbering by chapters is very helpful in long reports during the writing and processing. If you add or delete a figure, you need change numbers of only the following figures in that chapter instead of on all figures to the end of the report.

Occasionally, in a long and formal report you may wish to use a frontispiece. Generally, these have no place in technical reports, but if you feel that you must have one, note that it is not numbered in the same series as the other figures. It is customary for a frontispiece to have a legend with no number at all. Some authors place the word *Frontispiece* before the legend, although, since it is quite obvious what it is, there is no need to do so.

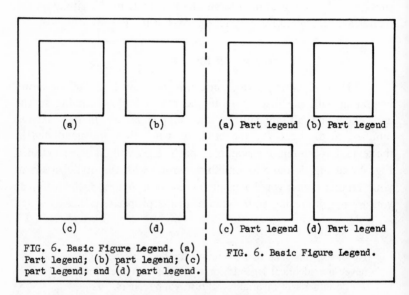

Figure 4-3. Two styles for handling legends for figures with parts. (a) Preferred style when part legends are long. (b) Preferred style when part legends are short.

4-1.6.4. Legends for Figures With Parts

In reports, it is common for figures to have several parts, each part being a variation of the main topic of the figure. If parts are closely related, identify them as a single figure, but in the legend make clear the different features that should be seen by the reader. The part legends should follow the primary legend, thus:

Fig. 6. Construction of Panels for Tests of Dimensional Stability of Synthetic Board Materials Used as Core Stock. (a) Flat-grain panel with one-ply veneer faces; (b) close-packed, edge-grain panel with two faces; and (c) spaced edge-grain panel with three-ply faces.

When this style is followed, the identification letters are placed below each part as shown in Fig. 4-3a. It is also good practice to locate the actual part legend below its corresponding part, giving only the primary figure legend below the entire figure (Fig. 4-3b).

□ NOTE

Legends are usually located below the figures to which they refer. If a figure is turned so that it is read from the side of the report, the legend should be turned with it, so that it is always below the figure as the reader looks at it.   □

4-1.6.5. FORMAT

Consistency is important in the treatment of figure legends. The two most common styles are (1) legends centered below the figures with the second, third, and following lines arranged in inverted pyramids, and (2) legends with the first line starting flush with the left edge of the figure and all run-over lines brought back flush left. If you are working in hot type, have the legends set in a type face different from the face used for the text: for example, 2 points smaller; or if the text is in Garamond roman, have the legends set in italic or in a sans-serif face, such as Futura. If you are working in typewriter typography, be sure to leave sufficient space between your legends and the surrounding text.

Because you are usually concerned with saving space in figure legends, use abbreviations as much as possible. The decision as to whether to use *Fig. 1, FIG. 1,* or *Figure 1* at the start of a legend is a fine point, however, of more interest to editors than to authors. But once you have selected a style, use it consistently throughout your report.

4-1.7. Word Usage

To a considerable degree, your success as a report writer will depend upon the words that you use. If you choose your words well, you can convey a difficult concept simply and accurately, but if you choose poorly, you can confuse the most elementary statement. It is essential that you give careful thought to your words and that you base your selection upon the ability of your intended audience to understand them.

The basic principle is to use words so well suited to your subject matter that the reader thinks only of the information they convey. Like brush strokes in an oil painting, your words should blend into a comprehensive whole to carry your message to your audience. This is not easy.

Your "style" will be determined by the words that you use as much as by the manner in which you put them together. And many strange and wonderful things can happen when you finally begin to write. Some lean toward the "I have a cat. The cat's name is Tom. Tom is a good cat." school. Others find that when they think "cat" they write "feline"; while some, afraid of being trapped into a flat statement on anything, qualify the information by writing, "Based upon the limited data available, all indications point to the strong possibility that I may be in possession of an animal referred to by many as a cat."

4-1.7.1. LENGTH OF WORDS

In choosing your words, try for the "right" word, keeping in mind the primary readers and the purpose of your report. A great deal of unfortunate advice has been supplied to potential authors in regard to the words that they should use if they wish to be understood; much of it has urged writers to use shorter and shorter words, as though all problems of communication would vanish if you could write entirely in words of one syllable. Such a suggestion is as unfounded as the implication—often encountered—that you can measure the success of a sentence by counting the number of words it contains. At the risk of overburdening you with even more advice, it is suggested that you keep in mind that the usual report is intended for an intelligent audience, frequently made up of extremely well-educated men and women who have been trained to learn by reading. Therefore, concentrate upon finding the word that best conveys your meaning and ignore the number of syllables.

4-1.7.2. WORDS IN GOOD USE

Your first consideration in selecting a word is to make certain that it is in good use. It should be a word that means the same in all parts of the country; it should be accepted by present-day authors and publishers as being neither obsolete nor archaic; and it should be in good repute, that is, not slang, a barbarism, or a word that might offend a reader.

It is well, for example, to avoid such words as *whilst, hither,* and *anon.* These words long ago dropped out of good usage; they have no place in report writing.

Slang not only is in bad taste, but it also has the more serious disadvantage of ambiguity. Although you may be tempted to introduce slang into your writing in an effort to make it more "readable," this is a trap. For example, the noun *corn,* which in America means *maize,* in slang may mean a kind of whiskey, or a type of music, or a rather dreary class of joke. If you consider using a word in a way described as slang by your dictionary, discard it and try another.

Under no circumstances should you use a word that would be offensive to some of your readers. Such a word will immediately divert attention from your ideas and will prejudice your readers against you. Occasionally, an author feels that a bit of profanity will make his writing more forceful. Unfortunately, it merely emphasizes his ineptness in the use of the language.

4-1.7.3. JARGON

Prominent among the words that you should not use are those classed as jargon, which is the name given to "the technical or secret vocabulary of a science, art, trade, sect, profession, or other special group"—in short, shop talk. Jargon is particularly insidious because you are apt not to recognize it. Every group, however, develops a form of verbal shorthand that simplifies day-by-day discussion. Most jargon is made up by a very few people and never finds its way into a dictionary.

☐ NOTE

If you are certain that you must use a word not listed in the standard unabridged dictionaries, define it the first time that you use it so that your readers will not be in doubt as to the meaning. Then you are free to use it without further definition throughout your report.   □

4-1.7.4. PERSONAL PRONOUNS

Many authors are undecided whether or not to use the personal pronouns, *I, you, he, we,* etc., in their reports. Policies vary in this matter, depending upon the desires of the local management. If there is not a fixed style, however, it is best to maintain an impersonal style when you write long-form, formal reports. This is the usual practice in the majority of both private firms and government activities, based upon the concept that it adds to the dignity and sincerity of the presentation. In addition, the impersonal style permits an author to speak for his organization as well as for himself, which is not possible if the first person is used. In informal reports, there is no objection to using personal pronouns, and many writers can actually do a better job of writing when they use this style. They often tend to stiffen up when they attempt to write in an impersonal style, and their sentences become stilted and tedious.

4-1.7.5. CONSISTENCY OF MEANING

There are a great many words in the English language that have more than one meaning. Such words as *show, fire, light, activity, cognizance,* and *instrumentation* have various meanings. The choice of meanings is usually easy enough for a reader to make unless you shift from one meaning to another without warning. Such a shift, particularly in one sentence, is likely to make your reader stumble. Although he will quickly recover, he will rightly feel that he has been badly treated and for the moment will be diverted from your line of thought. A second reading of your manuscript will enable you to catch and eliminate such difficulties. Be consistent in the meaning of each word that you use.

4-1.7.6. COINING NEW WORDS

With research moving ahead as rapidly as it is today, you will occasionally find that you must coin a new word to describe some new item or concept—"spaceography," for example. Ideally, when you are in this situation, you should call for the assistance of a professional etymologist so that the word that you devise will be sound and defensible. The number of barbarisms being perpetrated by unskilled inventors of words is appalling. The production of technical reports moves so rapidly that such words no sooner appear in the works of one author than they are picked up and repeated by many others, and before a competent etymologist can devise a truly suitable word it is too late: the barbarism is already permanently accepted as a respectable part of technical language. Such terms as "paintability" and "roadability" are bad enough; "the rocket 'self-destructed' itself" is worse. If it is at all possible, get help from a trained and experienced colleague unless you have made a careful study of word formation and are confident that you can coin an acceptable word.

4-1.7.7. SHORTENED FORMS

Avoid the use of shortened forms of words in formal reports. Like jargon, they may be misread. At best, they give an impression of casualness that is undesirable. For example, use *laboratory,* not *lab; telephone,* not *phone; airplane,* not *plane; potentiometer,* not *pot;* and *propeller,* not *prop.* While shortened forms are quite acceptable in speech, they are out of place in formal writing.

4-1.7.8. TRADE NAMES

Trade names are copyrighted property and must be capitalized in publications that are given general distribution. Many of them, from *Coke* to *Carborundum,* have become so familiar that they are often mistakenly thought to be ordinary English words. In technical report writing, no author is apt to be sued for neglecting to capitalize a trade name, but ethically you must be meticulously careful to give proper credit wherever it is due, and the proper handling of trade names is one of these areas.

4-1.7.9. FOREIGN WORDS

Many technical writers have a habit of using foreign words in their reports even though there are English words that convey exactly the same idea. With some, it is probably a result of their training; while they were learning their profession they studied so many books that included foreign words that they do, in fact, think in those words, and so use them when they write. With many others, it is a form of affectation—they believe that to scatter a few foreign words through-out their writing will prove conclusively that they are very learned men, indeed.

With such words as *a priori* and *a fortiori,* it may be debatable as to whether the English equivalents are equally descriptive, but as a rule, use English rather than any other language. When you drop into Latin, French, or German, there is always a strong chance that your reader will not know the exact meaning of the word or phrase. If he does not, communication has been clouded rather than improved. You will find that a high percentage of your readers do not even know the meaning of such common abbreviations as *i.e., e.g.,* and *viz.* In consideration of these readers, it is just as easy to write *that is, for example,* and *namely,* and you will be certain that you are under-stood. It is wiser to communicate in English than to be obscurely im-pressive in Latin.

4-1.7.10. CONTRACTIONS

Avoid contractions in formal writing. Such terms as *can't, don't,* and *won't* are better written out as *cannot, do not,* and *will not.* There is room for argument on this point; many writers claim that the use of contractions results in a lighter, more easily read style of writing. They make the point that everyone uses contractions in daily speech, and therefore it is natural to use them in report writing. Although the argument certainly has merit, most organizations require their writers to use the formal style.

There is no problem of possible misunderstanding when contrac-tions are used, however, and they are becoming more and more ac-ceptable in informal reports. If you feel strongly about this matter—and there are many who do—use them in your "quickie" reports in which you are rushing information to a limited audience. In these, contractions may even help to create an impression of immediacy in the report. You are apt to find, though, that after you have expressed yourself this way in a few reports, it no longer is such an urgent point after all. Actually, contractions add nothing to a report, and they give a feeling of casualness that may detract from the seriousness of your information. It is better to have your writing a little stiff than to run the risk of offending some of your readers who object to this style.

4-1.7.11. COMMONLY CONFUSED WORDS

There are many "look-alike" words that have given trouble to report writers through the years. These words either are spelled almost the same or are pronounced very much alike; for example, *accept* and *except* or *advise* and *advice*. Although they still cause trouble, they have been so well advertised in recent years that most writers are conscious of them. Nevertheless, words of this type will always be a problem, and in order that you give proper consideration to them, a list of words that are commonly confused follows:

accept (*v*), to take; to agree to.
except (*v*), to leave out; to exclude; to omit; to take
    exception.

advice (*n*), encouragement; counsel; information.
advise (*v*), to give advice; to counsel; to recommend.

affect (*v*), to act upon; to influence; to move emotionally;
    to attack.
effect (*n*), result or product of some cause or agency.
effect (*v*), to bring about; to cause; to achieve; to accom-
    plish.

adapt (*v*), to adjust to a situation; to make suitable; to
    conform.
adopt (*v*), to accept as one's own; to take and use as if
    one's own.

among (*prep*), in the midst of; mingled with.
between (*prep*), in the space which separates two places
    or objects; intermediate in relation to.

assure (*v*), to make certain; to convince; to give assurances
    to.
insure (*v*), to make sure or secure; to guarantee.

complement (*v*), to add to; to supplement; to make com-
    plete.
compliment (*v*), to pay a compliment to; to show regard
    for.

device (*n*), a plan or scheme; a contrivance; a fanciful
    design or pattern.
devise (*v*), to invent; to contrive; to scheme; to construct.

farther (*adj*), at a more distant point in space; at a more
    forward stage.

further (*adj*), more advanced in time or degree; additional; wider or fuller.

foreword (*n*), an introduction; preface.

forward (*adj*), near the front; in an advanced state.

imply (*v*), to intimate something not expressed; to signify; to hint at.

infer (*v*), to deduce or accept on the basis of evidence; to conclude.

inter- (*prefix*), between; together; intermediate.

intra- (*prefix*), within.

later (*adv*), at a subsequent time.

latter (*adj*), the second of two persons or things mentioned.

loose (*adj*), not fastened or confined; unbound; not dense.

lose (*v*), to part with unintentionally; to mislay; to waste.

objective (*adj*), having the nature of an object; that which is thought of or perceived; directed to or pertaining to an object or end.

subjective (*adj*), relating to or conditioned by mental state; proceeding from or taking place within the thinking subject.

practical (*adj*), pertaining to or governed by actual use and experience or action; having reference to useful ends to be attained.

practicable (*adj*), feasible; usable; that can be put into practice.

precede (*v*), to go before; to occur or exist before.

proceed (*v*), to go on or forward; to continue; to renew motion or action after rest.

principal (*adj*), first in rank, character, or importance; chief; outstanding.

principle (*n*), a general truth or law; a law of nature as illustrated in the mechanical powers; a settled rule of action.

purpose (*n*), plan; design; aim; the thing to be attained.

propose (*v*), to offer for consideration; to put forward; to plan; to make an offer.

respectfully (*adv*), with respect or esteem; deferentially.

respectively (*adv*), singly in the order designated; relating to particular persons or things.

site (*n*), position; situation; plot of ground set apart for some specific use.

cite (*v*), to bring forward proof.

stable (*adj*), standing firmly in one place; fixed; having durability or permanence.

staple (*n*), a principal commodity; chief element or main constituent of something.

stationary (*adj*), fixed; remaining in one place.

stationery (*n*), writing materials; paper.

therefore (*adv* & *conj*), for that reason; on that account; accordingly.

therefor (*adv*), in return for this or that.

More detailed definitions of the words given above can be found in an unabridged dictionary, but the meanings listed are sufficient to indicate the differences between the members of each group. There are many pairs of similar words. Since each author has his own "problem pairs," it is suggested that you add to this list additional words that cause you trouble so that you have them close at hand whenever you write.

4-1.7.12 REPEATING WORDS

If a word is repeated too frequently in a sentence, paragraph, or even a section, it may distract the reader from the thought that you are discussing. Words that draw the special attention of the reader should be eliminated. Nearly every writer has certain words that he unconsciously uses again and again. Although he does not notice them, his readers do. If possible, they should be weeded out of your writing.

On the other hand, some words must be repeated many times throughout a report. Many of your terms are precise, and any substitute will change the meaning and may confuse your readers. In report writing, it is quite acceptable to repeat words that identify items, materials, equipment, and methods. To try to get variety into your writing by substituting other words that mean "about the same" is not desirable. If you are discussing a "rocket motor," for example, you will only confuse your readers if you suddenly give it another name, because your readers identify that item with the name you gave it when you first mentioned it, and any variation will lead them to think that you are writing about something else.

As a general rule, then, do not repeat endlessly such common words as *great, important, significant, effective,* and *magnify* (persistent repetition will draw attention to them); but do not attempt to subsitute for fundamental technical terms, such as *strength, procedure,* and *capability.* Particularly, do not substitute for descriptive terminology.

There are some uncommon words that are not technical terms but still should not be repeated too often. For example, you may wish to use the word *concomitant,* which is a perfectly good word meaning "accompanying, conjoined, or attending." However, if you were to use this word several times in a short discussion, your readers would begin to notice it. In this situation, substitution is advisable.

4-1.8. Compound Words

You will help your readers if you use hyphens carefully and consistently throughout your writing. Like other punctuation marks, they should not be used without reason, for they can change your meaning and thereby defeat your attempts to achieve accuracy and clarity. Since the hyphenation of compound words may not have been stressed by those who taught you grammar, some of the principles of hyphenation are presented here with examples to give you something to check against in your writing.

Of the two classes of compound words—permanent and temporary—permanent compounds are the easiest to understand. There are three stages in the natural evolution of permanent compounds: first, the words are written separately with a space between them; next, they are joined by a hyphen; and finally, they are written together as one word. For example,

wave length   wave-length   wavelength

Because the accepted forms have been established and recorded in dictionaries, you will have little difficulty with permanent compounds. Whenever you are in doubt about the use of a hyphen in what you believe is a permanent compound, look it up in an unabridged dictionary and follow the usage given there.

There are exceptions to this principle, however. In many fields the evolution of words is taking place so fast that compound words reach the final one-word stage and are accepted by the writers and publishers in the field although the dictionaries still record them as two-word or hyphenated compounds. When you find that the transition has been accomplished and a one-word form is in use by the leading publishers in the field, use this form even though it does not yet appear in the dictionaries.

Distinguished from the permanent compounds are the words that are joined together in a particular instance for reasons of syntax. These temporary compounds are always written with a hyphen, which serves as a punctuation mark to aid the reader in rapid understanding of the text. Some of the underlying principles of compounding are presented in the following pages to guide you in the preparation of your manuscripts.

4-1.8.1. BASIC RULES

The following basic rules serve as a foundation upon which you can make specific decisions in determining whether a compound should be written as two words separated by a space, two words joined by a hyphen, or one word.

1. In general, do not hyphenate noun compounds (*bombsight*).
2. Write short, familiar compounds as one word (*horsepower*).
3. Hyphenate adjectival compounds (*heat-treated steel*).
4. Do not hyphenate adverb-adjective combinations (*recently delivered*).
5. Hyphenate two-word unit modifiers (*four-wheel drive*).
6. Do not hyphenate unit modifiers involving capitalized words (*New York City*).
7. Combine a prefix and a verb into one word *(overestimate).*
8. Make exceptions to these rules for emphasis or clarity (*technical and non-technical*).

These suggestions will be amplified in the following pages, and specific examples will be given with which you can compare the combinations that you want to use. Although no attempt is made to cover all possible situations, the major problem areas will be discussed and patterns will be demonstrated.

4-1.8.2. COMPOUND NOUNS

It is customary to write compound nouns either as two words separated by a space or as one word; for example:

air blast	center line	horsepower
air flow	crosswind	feedback
graph paper	backbone	downwash
butt weld	bandwidth	bombsight

As exceptions to this general rule, there are some multiple-word compounds that the dictionaries record as hyphenated; for example:

by-product	cross-feed	right-of-way
foot-pound	cave-in	stern-wheeler

When you join a single, descriptive capital letter to a noun to form a compound word, use a hyphen; for example:

I-beam	Y-axis	X-ray
U-bolt	O-ring	A-frame

4-1.8.3. ADJECTIVE AND NOUN

Frequently, compounds comprised of an adjective and a noun have become so familiar in the language that they have acquired a single meaning. Write these as one word; for example:

afterbody	highway	goodwill
anyone	headway	greenhouse

If, however, the compound is preceded by an adjective that modifies the first part of the compound, separate the parts. A hyphen is frequently introduced to indicate the correct interpretation; for example:

aircraft, *but* lighter-than-air craft

ironworker, *but* structural-iron worker

taxpayer, *but* income-tax payer

4-1.8.4. PREFIXES AND SUFFIXES

When you make a compound by adding a prefix or a suffix to a noun or adjective, write it as one word; for example:

antisubmarine	hydrostatic	clockwise
bylaw	infrared	lifelike
bipropellant	interview	faceless
cooperate	nonlinear	fireproof
counterclockwise	rework	carload
decentralize	semiautomatic	broadside
gyroplane	supercooling	spoonful

4-1.8.5. PREFIXES *Ex* AND *Self*

Use a hyphen when you make a compound word by joining either the prefix *ex* or the prefix *self* to a noun. This usage is generally accepted even though compounds made by combining other prefixes with nouns usually do not require hyphens. The following examples are typical:

ex-soldier	self-defense
ex-prize fighter	self-sacrifice
ex-president	self-control

4-1.8.6. VERB AND PREPOSITION

When you combine a verb and a preposition to form a compound verb, write it as two words without a hyphen. If you use the same two words as a noun, however, either write it as a single word or use a hyphen; for example:

As a verb	*As a noun*
pull off	pulloff
pull out	pullout
set up	setup
take off	takeoff
go between	go-between

When you combine a verb and a preposition to form a compound adjective, join them with a hyphen; for example:

As an adjective

the blow-off point

the cut-off date

the break-in period

the pull-on lever

the lead-in wire

4-1.8.7. UNIT MODIFIERS

Frequently, in technical writing, you will need to qualify your nouns in various ways to be certain that your reader knows exactly which item is being discussed. Normal sentence structure calls for such qualifiers to follow the noun; for example, "the truck weighs 2 tons and has a capacity of 1 cubic yard of material." As technical writers have tried to reduce the number of words required, a tradition has grown up in which the qualifiers precede the noun, and here it is necessary to let the reader know which words belong together; for example, "it is a 2-ton, 1-cubic-yard truck." In this example, "2-ton" is considered as a unit and, since it modifies the word "truck," it is called a "unit modifier." Such temporary compounds, appearing before rather than after the nouns that they modify, are joined by hyphens.

Unit modifiers cause many report writers a great deal of confusion, but the principle is reasonably easy to understand. Keep in mind that whenever you want your readers to understand that you have joined two words together for the moment in order to qualify a noun, and when these words precede the noun, you join the words into a single unit with hyphens. The following examples compare typical modifiers in normal sentence structure and as unit modifiers:

the method is well known
it is a well-known method

the decision was clear cut
it was a clear-cut decision

the camera was pointed down range
a down-range deflection camera

the orienting mechanism has three axes
a three-axis orienting mechanism

Probably the most frequent form of unit modifier is the combination of a numeral and the unit of measurement. When these precede the noun that they modify, they are unit modifiers and are joined by hyphens; for example:

a 3-bedroom house   a 10-inch focal length

in 100-foot rolls   a 60-cycle alternating current

the 117-volt, split-phase synchronous motor

When two or more unit modifiers of this type have a common basic element and are separated only by a conjunction, they retain the hyphens, but the basic element needs to be included in only the last unit; for example:

all 2.75- and 6.50-inch rockets

the 10-, 12-, and 14-cc samples

a 2- by 4-inch timber

Note that, in the unit modifiers preceding the noun, the units of measurement are written in the singular (a 40-foot pile); whereas, in the normal sentence structure, the plural form is used (a pile 40 feet long). Keep in mind that the plural form of a unit of measurement is never joined to a numeral by a hyphen to make a unit modifier.

4-1.8.8. ADVERB AND ADJECTIVE

In general, do not use a hyphen to join an adverb and an adjective into a temporary compound. Since the adverb could not normally be considered to modify the noun, there can be no confusion in the mind of the reader and hence no need for additional punctuation. This is particularly true if the adverb ends in *ly*; for example:

a carefully prepared report   a rigidly enforced rule

a poorly designed motor   a newly developed fuse

As always, you should use punctuation marks when you need them and refrain from using them when you do not. Although the principle is to not use a hyphen to join an adverb and an adjective into a unit modifier (as in the examples above), you must use one occasionally to avoid momentary confusion in the mind of the reader. When he might think that an adverb is an adjective modifying the noun, the adverb and adjective should be joined into a unit by a hyphen; for example:

the most-dependable glue

a long-sought solution

the above-mentioned tests

4-1.8.9. NUMBERS WRITTEN OUT

Most writers of technical reports follow a style in which all but occasional numbers are expressed in numerals; however, when you wish to write out compound numbers, join the parts together with hyphens; for example:

twenty-one	one hundred and seventy-five
thirty-six	the forty-second annual meeting
eighty-two	nineteen hundred and sixty-two

4-1.8.10. FRACTIONS WRITTEN OUT

When you write out a fraction, hyphenate the compound; for example:

one-half   three-quarters   one-hundredth

However, do not use a hyphen between the numerator and the denominator if either one includes a hyphen; for example:

three ten-thousandths   twenty-eight thirty-seconds

forty-four fiftieths

4-1.8.11. CAPITALIZED WORDS

Capitalized words joined to form proper names usually do not need hyphens; the fact that they are capitalized is sufficient to avoid confusion. When the official designation of an item includes a hyphen, however, use it consistently. Following are examples of both situations:

New York City	Folding-Fin Aircraft Rocket
Jet Propulsion Laboratory	Variable-Offset Rocket Sight
Washington and Lee University	Three-Axis Tracking Mount
Wisconsin State Journal	Aircraft Fire-Control System Mk 6

4-1.8.12. PREDICATE ADJECTIVES

Use a hyphen when you join a noun and a past participle to make a predicate adjective; for example:

The steel was heat-treated.	The weapon was field-fired.
The tube was cold-worked.	The lens was plane-polarized.

4-1.8.13. DOUBLING A VOWEL AND TRIPLING A CONSONANT

Use a hyphen in compound words whenever writing the words solid would result in doubling a vowel or tripling a consonant. In this situation, the hyphen prevents a misreading that might otherwise cause the reader to falter; for example:

magneto-optical *is better than* magnetooptical

micro-organism *is better than* microorganism

ultra-atomic *is better than* ultraatomic

bell-like *is better than* belllike

anti-imperial *is better than* antiimperial

4-1.8.14 HYPHEN USED TO AVOID MISPRONUNCIATION

In addition to using hyphens in accordance with the suggestions given above, you will sometimes need to use them to indicate the pronunciation or interpretation of a word; for example:

re-use (meaning use again)	re-ice
re-treat (meaning treat again)	re-cover
bi-component	re-ink

4-1.9. Use of Numerals

Within any one report, follow a consistent style in handling numbers. The problem is when to use numerals and when to write the numbers as words. A drifting policy in this detail can quickly give your reader the impression that you have no style at all. If the organization for which you work has no established style in this matter, fix upon one of your own and follow it throughout all of your writing.

4-1.9.1. GENERAL PRINCIPLE

It is generally accepted that in technical reports most numbers should be expressed in the form of numerals rather than in words. Report readers are trained to expect this style and do not find numerals objectionable. Numerals permit quick comparison between related numbers; they are easily understood (for example, 22,849 is easier to comprehend than twenty-two thousand, eight hundred and forty-nine); and they can be readily located for reference because they stand out from the other text on a page. Since some problems arise in interpreting this general principle, the following sections are offered as a guide.

4-1.9.2. ISOLATED NUMBERS OF ONE DIGIT

Spell out isolated numbers from one through nine; for example:

> the university has *five* colleges
>
> there are *three* possible solutions
>
> only *one* sample was defective

4-1.9.3. ISOLATED NUMBERS OF TWO OR MORE DIGITS

Use numerals for isolated numbers of 10 or more; for example:

> the series consisted of 18 tests
>
> the questionnaire covered 42 subjects
>
> the meeting was attended by more than 50 delegates

4-1.9.4. FIRST WORD IN A SENTENCE

Try to avoid beginning a sentence with a number. If you must, however, write it out. Never begin a sentence with a numeral; for example:

> *Fifty* delegates attended the meeting.
>
> *One hundred and ten* samples were taken.
>
> *Thirty-three* cities were studied.

4-1.9.5. QUANTITIES FOLLOWED BY UNITS OF MEASUREMENT

A quantity immediately followed by the unit of measurement is expressed in numerals; for example:

16 tons	12 years, 6 months, 22 days
4 inches	185 miles
20 knots	34 rods

4-1.9.6. QUANTITIES SEPARATED FROM THE UNITS OF MEASUREMENT

Spell out quantities under 10 when they are separated from the units of measurement; for example:

the test went on for *two* or more hours

there were *eight* and possibly more miles to cover

But if you use numerals for one of a group of numbers, express all of the numbers in the group in numerals; for example:

not less than 5 nor more than 15 acres . . .

4-1.9.7. TEMPERATURE

Use numerals to express temperatures; for example:

45°F	−65 to 165°F
100°C	0.55°C
18°K	0, 50, 75, and 100°C

4-1.9.8. TIME

Express time in numerals; for example:

8:35 a.m.	3:30 p.m. or half past 3
0835 hours	12 years, 8 months, 9 days
8 o'clock or 8 p.m.	4 hours, 32 minutes, 18 seconds
5 days	8 months
6 weeks	12 years

4-1.9.9. PERCENTAGE

Use numerals to express percentage; for example:

5 percent	12½ percent	200 percent
0.25 percent	10 percentage points	100%
18%	5, 10, and 15 percent	2.25–3.25%

4-1.9.10. PROPORTION

Use numerals to express proportions; for example:

8 to 5	1:1,000	3-4-5
2 to 1	2:1	

4-1.9.11. FRACTIONS

Spell out fractions when they stand alone; for example:

the range is *one-half* mile wide

the series included *one-half* of the samples

the tolerance was only *two one-hundredths* of an inch

a space *one-fourth* inch wide separated the parts

the skin was *twenty-five one-thousandths* inch in thickness

Use numerals to express fractions that are part of a larger number. When you are working in typewriter typography, use the shilling mark. Do not use commas in any part of a fraction, regardless of the number of digits; for example:

12-1/4   6-1/2   4-3/4   25-33/1000

4-1.9.12 SERIAL NUMBERS

Express serial numbers in numerals. Do not use commas in numbers of more than three digits; for example:

Monograph 12	Technical Report 625	Memorandum 1274
Pages 133-158	Page 1449	the year 1960
Test 32	Run 208	Sample 1

4-1.9.13. ROUND NUMBERS

Spell out round numbers; for example:

a *million* dollars	increased a *hundredfold*
a *hundred* years	*fifty-odd* projects
a *thousand* rounds	*two or three thousand*

4-1.9.14. ORDINAL NUMBERS

In text, write out ordinal numbers from *first* through *ninth*; use numerals for ordinal numbers beginning with *10th*. In tables and leader-work, use numerals throughout. Examples of ordinal numbers used in text follow:

the *second* meeting	the 11th Naval District
the *fifth* firing	the *eighth* century
the 12th annual report	the 42nd test

Use numerals for military units (except Army and Corps); for example:

the 4th Infantry Division	the *Eighth* Army
the 50th Regiment	the VII Corps
the 198th Fighter Squadron	the 4th Task Force

When ordinal numbers are grouped and one of them is a numeral. show them all in numerals; for example:

the 1st, 8th, and 16th samples were selected

the 9th and 10th chapters were deleted

the 5th through the 20th tests were considered successful

the *third* and *fourth* rockets failed to fire

the *first* item off the line was discarded

4-1.9.15. LARGE NUMBERS

To express large numbers in straight text, use a combination of numerals and words; for example:

10 thousand	2 million	$1.5 billion, or $1½ billion
3 thousand		500 thousand, or 1/2 million

4-1.9.16. Two Series of Numbers in Same Sentence

When two series of numbers appear in the same sentence, spell out the numbers in one series and use numerals for the other; for example:

six 2.75-inch rockets	*twelve* columns 16 feet in length
four 10-foot lanes	*one hundred and ten* 12- by 12-inch tiles

4-1.10. Capitalization

A consistent style for the capitalization of words gives a professional touch to your report, whereas a lack of uniformity in this matter—as in other details of style—indicates to the discriminating reader a disturbing carelessness. Some organizations follow the "down" style favored by newspapers, in which as few words as possible are capitalized. For example, they would write, "John H. Smith, head, timber mechanics department, U. S. Forest Products Laboratory, reported that the new million-pound compression machine has been installed." In the "up" style used by writers in the advertising field, this statement would appear as follows: "John H. Smith, Head, Timber Mechanics Department, U. S. Forest Products Laboratory, reported that the new Million-Pound Compression Machine has been installed."

With this degree of variation appearing in print, it is impossible to set down any firm rules in regard to capitalization. Instead, the following sections should be taken as carefully considered suggestions, based upon accepted practice among major organizations producing technical reports.

4-1.10.1 Proper Names

Capitalize all words in proper names. This style indicates exactly to the reader the term that identifies the person, place, or thing. The problem of what is a proper name causes more indecision among report writers than any other phase of capitalization. It is suggested that you capitalize major items that are unique and relatively permanent. For example, the $10-million laboratory that is the hub of research activity at the U. S. Naval Ordnance Test Station is referred to as *Michelson Laboratory,* or *the Laboratory*. But within that building are many small laboratories, and these are identified as *the chem-*

istry laboratory, the optics laboratory, the materials laboratory, etc.

Similarly, the identifying name for a major piece of equipment is capitalized, while the names of minor or common equipment are not. For example, a massive launcher located at Morris Dam near Azusa, California, for the purpose of testing torpedos launched at various angles into water is known as the Variable Angle Launcher. In writing about this installation, authors refer to it as the Launcher. On the other hand, there are a great many relatively small pieces of equipment used to launch rockets and missiles from aircraft, ships, or the surface of the ground that are referred to simply as launchers, without any capitalization.

It is best to take a middle road in the matter of capitalizing proper names. The tendency is to over-capitalize. The item that you have been working with daily for a long time is likely to appear unusually important and unique to you, until it becomes "the Thing," while really it is only one of many similar "things." The capitalization habit will run away with you unless you consider proper names carefully to be certain that they are truly unique.

4-1.10.2. GEOGRAPHIC REGIONS

Capitalize descriptive terms used to identify geographic regions and localities (they are proper names); for example:

the East	the North Pole	the Pacific Northwest
the Midwest	the Orient	the Upper Peninsula
the Deep South	the Arctic Circle	the Eastern United States

But do not capitalize the terms used to describe mere direction or position (they are not proper names); for example:

> the arctic regions of the world
>
> the northern end of the range
>
> central Georgia
>
> the road ran north and south

4-1.10.3. OFFICIAL TITLES

Capitalize official titles used in full form following a name. Also capitalize the short form of a title or designation when it precedes a name; for example:

James J. Johnson, Vice President, Crown Container Corporation

Albert B. Carlson, Technical Director, Western Laboratories

President Eisenhower	Professor Wilson
Commander Jackson	Dean Withey
Queen Elizabeth	Chairman Coleman

4-1.10.4. NAMES OF GOVERNMENT ORGANIZATIONS

Capitalize the full names of government organizations and their short forms; for example:

United States Congress	the Senate	the House
Department of Defense	the Department	a department among many
Bureau of the Budget	the Bureau	a government bureau
United States Army	the Army	an army officer
United States Navy	the Navy	a naval shipyard
United Nations	the Council	a representative

4-1.10.5. TRADE NAMES

Capitalize each word in a trade name, and be careful to spell the name exactly as it is spelled by the owner; for example:

Fafnir Ball Bearing (product of the Fafnir Bearing Company)

Teletype (product of Teletype Corporation)

Computyper (product of Friden, Incorporated)

Durethene plastic film (product of Koppers Company, Incorporated)

Flex-Beam Guardrail (product of The Armco International Corporation)

Littlefuse (product of Littlefuse Corporation)

However, avoid the use of trade names in technical reports whenever a generic name will convey the same meaning or will convey the meaning more accurately. Do not use a trade name when you really mean a class of things that may be made by competing companies.

4-1.10.6. TITLES OF PUBLICATIONS

Capitalize the first word and all important words in titles of publications, including reports, books, articles, periodicals, historical documents, and legal cases. Follow this rule also when referring to parts, chapters, and sections of reports, books, and other publications.

As a guide to help you distinguish between important and unimportant words, the following practice is suggested:

> Do not capitalize the articles *a, an,* and *the.*
>
> Do not capitalize the prepositions *at, by, in, on, of, to, up, for,* or *per.*
>
> Do not capitalize the conjunctions *as, if, or, and,* or *but.*
>
> However, capitalize *to* when it is part of an infinitive, as in *To Connect, To Investigate,* and *To Prepare.*
>
> Do not capitalize the second element of a compound number expressed in words; for example, *Fifty-six, Three-fourths,* or *Seventy-two.*
>
> Do not capitalize abbreviations of technical units of measure; it might lead to confusion in interpretation of the abbreviation. However, retain capitalization when it is part of the abbreviation; for example: $°F, Mev, Mw, ft-L,$ or *Cal.*

Typical examples of recommended style in quoting titles of publications are as follows:

> "Scientific and Technical Abbreviations, Signs, and Symbols"
>
> "Graphs, How To Make and Use Them"
>
> "Definitive Report of the Commission on the Reform of the Nomenclature of Organic Chemistry"
>
> "The Use of Tensor Analysis To Obtain Trajectory Data"
>
> "Part 4. The Formulation of Data Reduction Problems in Tensor Notation"
>
> "Estimates of Variances and Covariances of Measurements Corrected by the Principle of Conditioned Observations With Applications to Data Reduction Problems"

4-1.10.7. DISPLAYED TEXT

Capitalize the first word (but no others) in a displayed series when each entry is identified by a number or letter; for example:

> Several types of courses are described, including the following:
>
> 1. Normal pursuit
>
> 2. Line-of-sight course
>
> 3. Constant-bearing course
>
> 4. Constant navigation
>
> 5. Proportional navigation

or

    The more common designs that have been applied to storage reservoirs include the following:

1. Circular wall acting as shells to resist internal bursting pressure
   a. Conventional types with tension steel in concrete
   b. A prestressed reinforcement type with tension steel outside the concrete
2. Retaining walls utilizing the weight of the impounded water to resist the outward pressure
   a. Cantilever
   b. Buttress or counterfort

Do not, however, capitalize the word definitions of mathematical symbols displayed in the form of a list with equals signs separating the symbols from the definitions; for example:

$$A = \text{an integration constant}$$

$$a = \text{half-length of slab}$$

$$C_a = \text{a fixed-end moment factor}$$

$$D_o = \text{center moment factor}$$

$$E = \text{modified modulus of elasticity}$$

$$I = \text{rectangular moment of inertia of a slab}$$

$$L = \text{span length}$$

Note that this practice differs from the style followed when a formal list of nomenclature is supplied, in which the equals sign is omitted; for example:

Notation

A Concentration at $y = 0$

C Constant

e Base of Naperian logarithms

f Weisbach-Darcy friction factor

h Total depth of fluid

4-1.10.8. SERIAL DESIGNATIONS

    Capitalize a common noun ("figure," "round," "test," etc.) or its abbreviation when it is combined with a number or letter to form a serial designation. Although styles vary in regard to this matter, the use of the capital letter helps to set off the designation from the other text matter and is a distinct aid when a report is used as a reference; for example:

Figure 16	Reference 8	Round 25
Fig. 22	Ref. 10	Sample 92
Table 12	Test 185	Appendix D

4-2. TABLES

4-2.1. Purpose

A table is a typographical device used to present in condensed form many pieces of related information for comparison, selection, or study. The entries in tables may be either numbers or words so arranged that their relationship is readily apparent. Tables play a major role in technical reports and, consequently, should be accurate, complete, and economical of space.

Although it would be impracticable, the information that is presented in tabular form could appear as running text. Your reader would soon be lost, however, and would have great difficulty in either grasping the point that you were trying to make or finding the specific detail for which he was searching. Successful tables are those that allow the reader to find and comprehend the information that he needs with the least difficulty. As a final cross check of every table that you prepare, try to use it as your reader will and see if you can find the information readily.

□ NOTE

Successful tables present a great deal of information in a small space. The relationship of the various entries must be clearly evident. Remember that a conglomeration of data neatly stacked in adjacent columns is not necessarily a usable table. □

The various types of tables will be discussed in the following sections. They may be used in the report proper or in the appendixes; the principles of preparing tables apply to those used anywhere in your report. Any technique or combination of techniques that is effective in improving the understandability of your report should be used freely; for example, you may find that the best method of presenting your material is to combine one or more figures with a table, and this is quite acceptable. Authors faced with unusually complicated problems in tabular presentation should call upon professional editors for help.

4-2.2. Types of Tables

This discussion is concerned with *formal tables* as differentiated from *text tables* (see Section 4-1.5). Formal tables are part of a numbered series; they have titles, subtitles, headnotes, and footnotes of their own; they frequently have vertical or horizontal rules; in hot-type composition they are set in a different (usually smaller) type face than the text. Text tables have none of these features. Formal tables may be moved about by the typographer to achieve the most workable page layout and may even be turned on the page; text tables must be printed exactly where they appear in the manuscript, and they may not be turned on the page. The problems of tabular presentation occur in formal tables, and it is with these that this discussion will be concerned.

Formal tables may be separated into *special-purpose tables* and *general-purpose tables*. Special-purpose tables serve to prove a specific point, emphasize a particular relationship, make a desired comparison, or accomplish some similar "special purpose." Distinguished from these are the general-purpose tables, which are used simply to record a mass of data in the most economical and usable form possible. In these, the author does not know the exact data that his readers will want at a specific time, but he knows that somewhere in the table the needed data will be available. A table of logarithms, for example, would be in this category. In order to accomplish their different purposes, the special- and general-purpose tables are designed differently.

Tables vary from the simplest form, in which you make a single comparison to prove a single point, to extremely complicated layouts in which relationships and cross-relationships are made between several groups of information. The fundamental principles of table construction are the same for both simple and complicated tables, however, because complex tables are devised by bringing into one arrangement several simple tables that are interrelated.

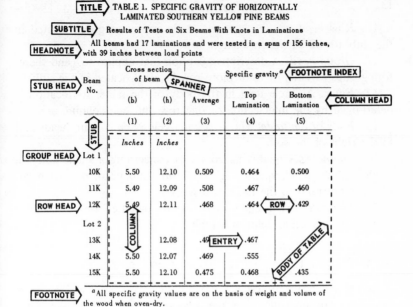

STUB HEAD → Beam No.	Cross section of beam SPANNER →		Specific gravity[a] FOOTNOTE INDEX →		
	(b)	(h)	Average	Top Lamination	Bottom Lamination COLUMN HEAD →
	(1)	(2)	(3)	(4)	(5)
GROUP HEAD → Lot 1	Inches	Inches			
10K	5.50	12.10	0.509	0.464	0.500
11K	5.49	12.09	.508	.467	.460
ROW HEAD → 12K	5.49	12.11	.468	.464 ROW → .429
Lot 2					
13K		12.08	.49 ENTRY .467		
14K	5.50	12.07	.469	.555	
15K	5.50	12.10	0.475	0.468	.435

TITLE → TABLE 1. SPECIFIC GRAVITY OF HORIZONTALLY LAMINATED SOUTHERN YELLOW PINE BEAMS

SUBTITLE → Results of Tests on Six Beams With Knots in Laminations

HEADNOTE → All beams had 17 laminations and were tested in a span of 156 inches, with 39 inches between load points

FOOTNOTE → [a]All specific gravity values are on the basis of weight and volume of the wood when oven-dry.

Figure 4-4. Terms used in discussion on tables.

4-2.3. Definitions

The following definitions will be used in this discussion; the items are keyed to Fig. 4-4.

1. *Title.* A brief description of the contents of the table. The title should be located above—not below—the table.

2. *Subtitle.* An expansion of the title, used to supply complete information about the table. Keeps the title from being too long.

3. *Headnote.* A qualifying comment concerning the entire table. Located between the title (or subtitle, if any) and the column heads.

4. *Column.* A vertical series of entries under a single heading.

5. *Stub.* The column farthest to the left.

6. *Row (or line).* A horizontal line of entries, aligned opposite a single stub entry.

7. *Column head.* A descriptive caption that applies to the entries in a single column.

8. *Spanner.* A descriptive caption that applies to the entries in two or more columns. (Hence, it "spans" the column heads in the related columns.)

9. *Stub head.* The descriptive caption for the stub column.

10. *Row head (or line caption)*. A descriptive caption, located in the stub, for all entries in a single row.

11. *Group head*. A descriptive caption that applies to (and therefore groups together) two or more row heads. Located in the stub.

12. *Entry*. A single item in the body of the table. Its location is determined by the intersection of one row and one column.

13. *Body of the table*. The area lying below the column heads and to the right of the stub.

14. *Footnote*. A qualifying comment concerning a single entry, a single column head, spanner, group head, stub head, or row head. (It does not refer to the table as a whole.)

15. *Footnote index*. The symbol, figure, or letter used to relate a footnote to a specific point in a table.

4-2.4. Factors That Influence Table Planning

Before you begin to design a table, review the comments listed below. They are not "rules" like the rules of grammar, but rather facts arrived at empirically through the construction of many tables in a wide variety of subject fields.

1. You are nearly always concerned with saving space in making a table; therefore, find out the exact measurements of the page on which your table will be printed. In extreme cases, count the characters that you have available and design your table to fit within the maximum. Remember that the binding takes space; there is no point in trying to force an 8-inch table onto an 8-inch page, for example, because you will lose a half inch in the binding, and you must allow at least an additional quarter inch on each side for margins.

2. Although a table may be continued from page to page, there is always one physical limitation that governs the design. You can achieve the effect of unlimited length and a fixed width by repeating the column headings at the top of each successive page, or you can have unlimited width by repeating the stub column on each page. But you cannot have both unlimited length and width in one table.

3. Normally, it is best to design a table with a fixed width. In such a table a column can hold more information than a row. Therefore, when you have a great many entries to make in a single category, enter them vertically in a column rather than try to force them into a horizontal row.

4. Since people are used to reading words set horizontally rather than stacked vertically, when you have entries in the form of comments put them in rows; for example, in a "Remarks" column that is wide enough so that you can get several words in each row. A "Remarks" column contributes greatly to the usefulness of many tables.

5. It is easiest to compare numerical entries when they are placed in a column, since readers are accustomed to scanning columns of figures. If two series of numerical entries are to be compared, place them in adjacent columns. The farther apart entries are, the harder it is to compare them. One of the most common faults in poorly designed tables is that entries that need to be compared are incorrectly placed in columns spaced far apart.

6. Column headings should be brief, but do not cut out words that are essential to understanding.

7. Abbreviations are useful for saving space, but be sure to use accepted forms. Do not make up abbreviations of your own that cannot be understood by a reader unless you use explanatory footnotes.

8. If you intend to refer to a table in the text, assign a number to it. (In this way, you can be certain that the reader looks at the right table when you refer to it.) And if you number one table in a report, number them all.

9. Row headings should be consistent in style, indention, punctuation, capitalization, and typography.

10. Word usage should be consistent throughout all of the tables in a report.

11. The use of vertical and horizontal rules makes it possible to get more data on a page.

12. If you do not use horizontal rules, vertical spacing (leading) makes long tables easier to read. If you have more than five rows of entries of similar items, insert vertical spacing so that the reader can follow a line across the page.

13. Normally, columns need not be numbered, but if you refer to individual colums of a table in your text, number all of the columns in a table. It is far easier, for example, to refer the reader to "Column 4" than to "the fourth column from the left."

14. When you have a long table with only three or four narrow columns, you can save space by "folding" the table, as shown on the following page.

TABLE 1. Title Centered

Stub	Col. 1	Col. 2	Stub	Col. 1	Col. 2
1	22	345	6	81	334
2	33	654	7	37	747
3	32	728	8	61	446
4	56	929	9	77	364
5	43	887	10	85	759

15. Tables are expensive. The cost of composing a page containing a table is much more than that of a page of text. Therefore, make every table worthwhile.

16. Once the type is set it is difficult to eliminate errors in a table. Always proofread the typed or printed page proofs against the original manuscript. Do not read final copy against an intermediate proof except to locate previous errors.

17. Vertical rules are expensive to set by machine and are avoided unless the table has many columns. They can be used at will in material for offset reproduction, where they can be put in by hand.

4-2.5. Steps in Making a Table

Tables should be designed so that they are easy for readers to use. In a special-purpose table, you want the reader to be able to compare the various pieces of information and arrive at a certain conclusion about them. A general-purpose table must be arranged so that the user can find the data or information he wants with the least difficulty.

It is usually necessary to try more than one arrangement of column heads and row heads. A good practice is to use 14- by 17-inch (or larger) crossruled paper (blue or green) to lay out tables in pencil. The rules make it easy to compute spacing, keep entries aligned, put in horizontal and vertical rules, etc. There is always a strong tendency to use the first arrangement that comes to mind, but it should be cross-checked and discarded if it is obscure or difficult to read.

To prepare a table, follow these steps:

1. Decide upon the purpose of the table. It is helpful to write this down so that you can keep it in mind and use it to check the table when it is complete. A statement of the purpose is not the same as a title.

2. Write down the two primary classifications to be used.

3. Decide which classification will go vertically and which horizontally (see items 2 through 5 in Section 4-2.4).

4. Make a detailed outline for each of the primary classifications. Check these outlines for consistency and logic.

5. Make a preliminary design and fill in the column heads and the stub. Insert enough entries so that you can test the design for ease of reading and effectiveness.

6. Consider alternate designs with an open mind. If another design appears possible, try it out. If in doubt, try the column heads in the stub and see if this makes the table more effective.

7. When you have decided upon a firm design, insert all of the entries in the body of the table.

8. Write the footnotes and key them to the proper entries or heads.

9. Write the title. This should be done after the table has been designed rather than before so that you can be sure of the contents. If the title appears to be too long, try to shorten it by introducing a subtitle.

10. Write any headnotes that may be required.

11. Check the table against the purpose as you set it down in step 1.

4-2.6. Table Titles

The title should be clearly descriptive of the information contained in the table. For a special-purpose table, the title should indicate that purpose. The biggest problem encountered in composing a title is making it definitive without making it intolerably long. Although readers of technical reports are accustomed to long titles, you should keep the number of words to a minimum.

Since formal tables should be sufficiently complete so that they may be moved about as a unit to suit the requirements of the typographer (or typist), the title—combined with the subtitle and headnotes, if any—must supply all of the information that a reader will need to understand the contents.

4-2.6.1. STYLE

Use a telegraphic style, rather than complete sentences. Verbs and articles are usually omitted. All words not required are deleted;

for example, such phrases as "A Table of" are unnecessary. Special care should be taken with the punctuation of table titles.

4-2.6.2. FORMAT

There are a number of acceptable formats in current use. In general, your format should be completely consistent in all tables in a single report or in all reports of a series. Choose a format that makes the title stand out clearly. This requires that you consider the possibility of subtitles and headnotes.

If you are working in typewriter typography, use all capital letters for the title; this permits you to use capital letters and lower case for a subtitle, and lower case for the headnotes. If you have no subtitle, you can use capital letters and lower case for the main title.

Place the title at the top of the table. Tables are read from the top to the bottom, so anything that applies to the table as a whole should be read first—title, subtitle, and headnotes.

A title of one line only is normally centered above the table. If it has more than one line, it may be set in an inverted pyramid, thus:

Table 28. Safe Resistance to Withdrawal of Common Wire
Nails Driven Perpendicular to the Grain Into
Seasoned Wood

or the second and following lines may be brought back flush left, thus:

Table 28. Safe Resistance to Withdrawal of Common Wire
Nails Driven Perpendicular to the Grain Into Seasoned
Wood

Some styles call for the table number to be centered above the title, thus:

Table 12

Standard Thicknesses for Hardwood Lumber

Because this style takes up more space on the page than is necessary, it is not recommended.

If you are working in hot type, you have the flexibility of using capitals and small capitals, boldface type, or italics. Any of these variations is satisfactory as long as it sets the title off clearly from the other parts of the table and permits variations of decreasing weight for the subtitles and headnotes.

4-2.7. Headnotes

A headnote is a comment by the author in answer to an anticipated question of a reader about the table as a whole. It is located between the title (or subtitle, if any) and the column headings. Many tables in technical reports are without headnotes only because the author has not put himself in the place of a reader to determine questions that might naturally be asked about his table and therefore answered by headnotes.

A headnote is an excellent device with which to indicate any unusual limitations to the data contained in a table. If there is anything that would affect the meaning of the data, it should be clearly stated. For example, anything unusual about the sampling, anything incomplete in the procedures used to get the data, a rounding off of the data for some reason, something in the materials used that would influence the results, or a repeating inconsistency in the operation of a computing machine should be mentioned in a headnote.

Use normal punctuation in headnotes, with one exception: it is standard practice not to end a headnote with a period, even though the note is otherwise a sentence. Use periods elsewhere in headnotes if there are sentences. If the report is composed in hot type, have the headnote set two points smaller than the table and enclose the entire headnote in brackets. In typewriter typography, have the headnote set in lower case letters and enclose in parentheses. Headnotes concerning unrelated ideas should begin on separate lines. Write your headnotes in telegraphic style and use the same abbreviations that you use in the remainder of the table.

4-2.8. Footnotes

Identify the footnotes that apply to each formal table in your report in a series of their own (distinct from the series of footnotes for the report as a whole), and place them immediately below the table. The typographer will then handle the table as a unit from the title through the final footnote.

Footnotes may be related to the proper points in a table by means of letters, numbers, or symbols. Because tables in technical reports frequently require many footnotes, the most satisfactory method is to use lower case letters in alphabetical sequence (see examples). On the rare occasions when you need more than 26 footnotes, you can

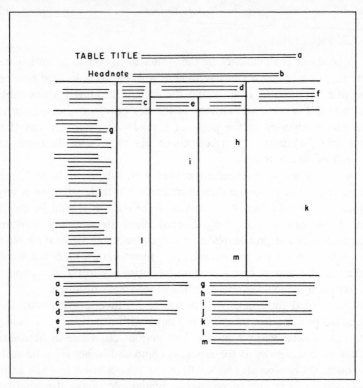

Figure 4-5. Preferred sequence for identification of footnotes in formal table.

start over with double letters. A raised lower case letter (in smaller type if set in hot type) will never be mistaken for an exponent. Place each footnote index immediately after the item in question (without a space) and raised above the normal line of type. If numbers are used as indexes they should be placed before, rather than after, figures. (If placed after an entry of figures, the footnote index may be mistaken for an exponent; for example, 32^2 might mean 32×32.) A different problem arises if you use symbols. There are so few symbols that you can use (*, †, ‡, §, ‖) that you soon find it necessary to double and triple them. In addition, readers have difficulty in keeping them in sequence, which leads to trouble in reading the table.

☐ NOTE

Use letters rather than numbers or symbols to key your footnotes in formal tables. ☐

Identify footnotes within tables sequentially from the top to the bottom and from the left to the right, starting with the upper left corner of the table (see Fig. 4-5). Read each line from left to right, starting with the title. As you encounter items to be footnoted, assign letters to them in sequence. When you have finished one line, move down to the next line and again read from left to right, etc. Obviously, you must assign index letters to your footnotes after the table has been completed. If you add a footnote after the letters have been assigned, change the identification of all following footnotes. The necessity for many footnotes usually indicates that the table is poorly designed.

4-2.9. Miscellaneous Comments on Tables

Every column should have a column head, and every row should have a row head in the stub. On the principle that a column of entries must be a column of "something," you will be able to contrive a head for each column. There is frequently an inclination to omit the head for the stub column, but a head of some sort will definitely assist the reader in quickly understanding the table.

If a column has no entries in it, delete it from the table. Often, you may plan to use a certain column and then find that you have no need for it. An empty column accomplishes nothing except to waste space; it does not belong in a proper table. Similarly, if a column has relatively few entries, try to combine it with another column or to put the information in a footnote.

If you find that all of the entries in one column have the same value or comment, delete the column and transfer the information to a headnote. Again, in the interests of conserving space, a simple statement in a headnote takes up less space than a full column of identical entries.

If you refer in the text to specific columns in a table, all of the columns should be numbered. Place these numbers in a row set off from the rest of the table by horizontal rules and located between the column heads and the first row of entries (see Fig. 4-4).

Entries of unequal length in the stub column should be aligned on the left and followed by leaders (a row of dots) to square the column. The leaders help to carry the reader's eye from the stub to the proper line of entries.

Identical word entries (one word or more than one word) in succeeding rows may be replaced with the abbreviation "do." This device can often save considerable space in a table. However, do not use "do." in place of figure entries; repeat the figures as often as you must. There are a number of rather complicated styles in use regarding the capitalization of "do." For example, some styles require that "Do." be used in the stub column and in the final remarks column, but that "do." be used elsewhere. Whatever style you select, be consistent. The intent is to let the reader know that one entry is identical with the one above it. The simplest style is to use the abbreviation without any capitalization in all columns.

Omissions are indicated by leaders (. . . . . .) entirely across the column, by an ellipsis (. . .) or (. . .), or by two or three hyphens (---). The ellipsis without spaces (. . .) is recommended. Do not leave a cell blank; the printer, the proofreaders, and the ultimate user may all wonder if an entry has been inadvertently left out.

Units of measure may be located in the column head, separated from it by a comma; or they may be placed below the horizontal line that separates the column heads from the body of the table. They are usually abbreviated if they are part of the column head and spelled out if they stand alone; thus:

Depth of ring, in.	Load on bearing, lb.	Depth of ring	Load on bearing
		Inches	Pounds
0.75	5,700	0.75	5,700
1.00	12,000	1.00	12,000
1.25	18,000	1.25	18,000

The maximum depth of the block of column heads is determined by the longest head. Center all others vertically within the limits of the block, as shown in the examples in Section 4-2.10.

Do not box, or close in, your tables with vertical rules at the extreme left and right edges of the tables. These rules are not necessary for clarity and they detract from the appearance of the table. Also, omitting the outside rules permits you to extend a table horizontally across two facing pages, in which case a lightweight vertical rule at the right edge of the left-hand page and the left edge of the right-hand page can be assumed by the reader to be the same vertical line, and he can read the table without difficulty; if you box your tables, he may be confused as to whether or not he should read across the gutter.

It is preferable to locate your tables within the text where you refer to them. This definitely makes the easiest reading. When your report is to be reproduced in hot type, the tables should always be inserted in the text as part of the discussion. Preferably, a table should appear as soon after the reference to it as possible. It should never be encountered by a reader before it is mentioned, or he will be confused. If a table is not more than a page in length, it should not be broken; for this reason, it may be necessary to place it on the page following the reference to it.

In typewriter typography, it is sometimes expedient to group the tables together at the end of the text. Often, when this is done, they are introduced by a half-title page labeled "Tables," or they are grouped in an appendix so labeled. This procedure is particularly useful when the text is typed by one typist and the tables are prepared by a second typist on another machine. Then, to ease the problem of pagination, the tables can be grouped at the end of the text and paginated as the last step in the process of composition. It is better, however, to interleave the tables throughout the text at appropriate places following the references to them. By this method, you do not have text and tables on the same page. The text is typed continuously; the tables are all prepared one to a page; they are interleaved into the text; and finally, all pages are numbered. This process makes it possible for more than one typist to work on a report during the production stage and still permits you to place the tables where they will be of the most benefit to the reader.

When tables are continued from one page to a following page, the column heads should be repeated on the new page for the benefit of the user, but the title and headnotes do not require repetition. Instead, simply identify the table by number and indicate that it is a continuation, thus: "Table 16 (Contd.)"

Frequently, there is confusion over such details as whether or not a zero should appear before a decimal point in an entry. In settling such matters of style, consider your readers' ability to understand your meaning without question, use your best judgment, and then be consistent.

□ NOTE

Repetition is better than confusion. If you have any doubt about whether you should use a zero before a decimal point, repeat an entry, or explain an entry with a footnote, do it. The few moments that you lose will be gained many times over by your readers. □

In this matter, there are several acceptable styles, as indicated in the following examples:

0.0123	0.0123	0.0123
0.6541	.6541	.6541
0.8275	.8275	.8275
0.9914	.9914	.9914
0.6395	.6395	.6395
0.9147	0.9147	.9147

Any one of the three styles is understandable, but once you have selected a style, stay with it throughout all of the tables in any report. If you vacillate, your reader wonders if the change in style indicates some obscure meaning that he has missed.

Alignment of figures in a column of entries is another problem that causes considerable concern. Keeping in mind, once more, that you must hold consistently to one style, you should find the following suggestions useful: (1) if all of the entries are in the same unit of measure, align them on the decimal point; (2) if whole numbers are mixed with fractions, align on the first digit with the fractions extending to the right; and (3) if the entries are in mixed units of measure, align them to the right.

Turnover lines in the stub column are indented. Each new row head begins flush left, and leaders extend from the last line of each stub head. This style leaves no doubt in the mind of the reader as to where the head for a new row begins and where to look for the column entries corresponding to any row head. Vacillation in matters of style can lead to complete chaos in a complicated table.

4-2.10. Examples

Each new table is a new problem that must be given individual consideration. Advice on some of the more common areas of trouble will be useful. When you are undecided about the treatment of a specific point, examine the following examples for suggested treatment and then adapt it to your own purpose. Remember that experts in this field are completely adamant in their points of disagreement; yet each is considered an authority. So use your common sense and keep your reader in mind, and you will not go far wrong. Here follow some examples:

TABLE 1. Test Configurations

Test no.	Grain chamber		Grain			Grain-face propellant		Nitrogen in chamber, psig	Total igniter charge, g	Burst diaphragm		Test no.
	ID, in.	Length, in.	Type	Diam., in.	Length, in.	Type	Wt., g			Material	Thickness, in.	
1	6.2	24.5	steel slug	5.2	4	583	16	type 424	...	copper	0.006	1
2	6.2	24.5	steel slug	5.2	4	583	15.2	N-5	...	copper	0.006	2
3	11.5	34.5	AJ	11	5.2	boron	63.0	none	3.4	cellophane tape	...	3
4	11.5	34.5	448-C	11	8.5	TB-12	136	none	3.4	plastic	0.050	4
5	11.0	34.5	AJ	11	8.8	583	80	77.7	3.4	brass	0.003	5
6	11.5	34.5										

Example 1. Note the following: use of spanners to group information; stub column repeated on the right side of the table; consistency in abbreviation of units of measure and capitalization; use of "none" as an entry; and alignment of entries on the decimal point.

143

TABLE 1. Pressing and Curing Schedule Used in Preparing Modified Wood

Type of material	Species	Initial curing conditions			Heating center of panel to curing temp.		Total heating time, min.	Cooling conditions		
		Temp. of platens, °F	Pressure, psi	Time, min.	Time, min.	Temp., °F		Cooling time (range), min.	Pressure, psi Max.	Pressure, psi Min.
		(1)	(2)	(3)	(4)	(5)	(6)	(7)	(8)	(9)
Normal laminated wood	yellow birch	310	250	10	40	285	30	none	225	25
	sweet gum	310	175	21	35	290	30	25-30	100	50
	Sitka spruce	310	150	3	20	316	28	15-20		
Impreg.........	yellow birch	295	270	...	24	315	70			
	sweet gum	300	245	...	20	320				
	Sitka spruce	295	200	10	18					
Semi-compreg	yellow birch	322	275	10						
	sweet gum	320	350	11						
	Sitka spruce	322	260							
Compreg.........	yellow birch	285	750							
	sweet gum	287								
	Sitka spruce	285								
Staypak.........	yellow birch									
	sweet gum									
	Sitka spruce									

Example 2. Note the following: use of a two-column stub; method of numbering columns in the body of the table; use of spanners to group information; and use of vertical spacing to make table easier to read.

144

TABLE 1. Test Configurations

Test No.	Grain chamber		Grain			Grain-face propellant		Nitrogen in chamber, psig
	ID, in.	Length, in.	Type	Diam., in.	Length, in.	Type	Wt., g	
1	6.2	24.5	steel slug	5.2	4.0	583	16.0	800
2	6.2	24.5	steel slug	5.2	4.0	583	15.2	800
3	11.5	34.5	AJ AN-2091	11.0	3.1	583 boron	60.0	725
4	11.5	34.5	steel slug	...	...	583	63.0	none
5								

(a)

TABLE 1. Test Configurations

Characteristic	Test number				
	1	2	3	4	5
Grain chamber:					
ID, in.............	6.2	6.2	11.5	11.5	
Length, in.........	24.5	24.5	34.5	34.5	
Grain:					
Type..............	steel slug	steel slug	AJ AN-2091	steel slug	
Diam, in...........	5.2	5.2	11.0	...	
Length, in.........	4.0	4.0	3.1	...	
Grain face propellant:					
Type..............	583	583	583 boron	583	
Weight, g..........	16	15.2	60	63	
Nitrogen in chamber, psig......	800	800	725	none	

(b)

Example 3. Two methods of presenting the same information. In (a), the test identification numbers are located in the stub and the characteristics in the column headings; in (b), these are reversed. Use the style shown in (a) if you are recording information for a large number of tests; use the style shown in (b) if your tests are few enough so that they can be arrayed horizontally on one page.

TABLE 1. Average Capillary Data and Their Source, for the Heartwood of a Softwood With a Swollen-Volume Specific Gravity of 0.365

Property or dimension	Symbol	Value	Source of value
Fractional void value and cross-sectional area:			
Filter cavities of dry wood....................	$\underline{A_d}$	0.722	$1 - \dfrac{\underline{g_d}}{\underline{g_o}}$
Filter cavities of swollen wood	$\underline{A_m}$	0.650	$1 - \left(\dfrac{\underline{g_m}}{\underline{g_o}} + \dfrac{g_m \underline{m}}{\rho}\right)$
Average cross-sectional area:			
Dry wood fibers...........	$\alpha_{\underline{d}}$	$1{,}000 \cdot \mu^2$	$\dfrac{1 - \underline{S}}{\underline{n_t}^2}$
Fiber cavities of swollen and dry wood............	$\alpha_{\underline{f}}$	$722 \cdot \mu^2$	$\dfrac{\underline{A_m}}{\underline{n_t}^2}$ or $\dfrac{\underline{A_d}(1 - \underline{S})}{\underline{n_t}^2}$
Swollen wood fibers.......	$\alpha_{\underline{m}}$	$1{,}111 \cdot \mu^2$	$\dfrac{1}{\underline{n_t}^2}$
Specific gravity:			
Apparent swollen-wood substance...............	$\underline{g_a}$	1.530	water displacement
Wood (dry-volume basis)...	$\underline{g_d}$	0.406	$\dfrac{\underline{g_m}}{1 - \underline{S}}$
Wood (swollen-volume basis)	$\underline{g_m}$	0.365	assumed value
Wood substance...........	$\underline{g_o}$	1.460	helium displacement

Example 4. Note the following: use of equations in a table; occasional word entries; use of group heads and vertical spacing between groups; and leaders from the turnover lines of the row heads.

TABLE 4. Fiber Length of Softwoods Determined by Different Methods of Measurement

(All values in millimeters)

Species	Direct microscopical				Electro-osmose			Hydro-static flow	Over-coming capillary rise
	Number measured	Min.	Ave.	Max.	Min.	Ave.	Max.	Max.	Max.
Yellow cedar, Alaska	...	...	...	...	3.1	3.3	4.8	4.5	4.5
Red cedar, western.	...	3.1	3.8	4.5	3.2	3.8	5.5	5.5	5.6
Douglas fir	900	...	3.2	...	3.5	3.8	5.2	...	4.9
Hemlock, western ...	...	1.8	3.1	3.7	3.1	3.8	5.5	...	...
Pine, ponderosa	...	...	...	...	3.2	3.8	5.7	...	5.5
Spruce, Sitka	...	2.3	2.8	3.7	3.2	3.8	5.5	...	5.3
	50	2.4	4.2	5.4					
	50	1.8	3.6	5.1					
	50	2.4	4.1	5.4					

Example 5. Note the following: use of brackets to group entries under a single row head; use of a headnote to eliminate repetition of units of measure in column heads; and vertical centering of column heads within boxes.

Air-line Distances Between Principal Cities of the United States
Prepared by Department of Commerce, Bureau of Navigation, Radio Division

(Distances in Statute Miles)

FROM/TO	Albuquerque, N. Mex.	Atlanta, Ga.	Baltimore, Md.	Boise, Idaho	Boston, Mass.	Brownsville, Tex.	Buffalo, N.Y.	Chicago, Ill.	Cincinnati, Ohio	Cleveland, Ohio
Albuquerque, N. Mex....	....	1273	1670	774	1967	838	1577	1126	1248	1417
Atlanta, Ga....	1273	....	575	1830	933	960	695	583	368	550
Baltimore, Md....	1670	575	....	2055	358	1525	273	603	423	305
Boise, Idaho....	774	1830	2055	....	2266	1610	1872	1453	1663	1754
Boston, Mass....	1967	933	358	2266	....	1881	398	849	737	550
Brownsville, Tex....	838	960	1525	1610	1881	....	1575	1234	1184	1402
Buffalo, N.Y....	1577	695	273	1872	398	1575	....	454	392	175
Chicago, Ill....	1126	583	603	1453	849	1234	454	....	249	307
Cincinnati, Ohio....	1248	368	423	1663	737	1184	392	249	....	218
Cleveland, Ohio....	1417	550	305	1754	550	1402	175	307	218	....

Example 6. Typical general-purpose table for presenting distances between cities. Note that cities are arranged alphabetically from top to bottom and left to right; that rules are used to separate cities into groups of five for easier reading.

148

4-3. ILLUSTRATIONS

4-3.1. Principles of Report Illustration

Illustrations play a part in technical reports equal to that of the text and tables. It usually takes all three forms to present your information as clearly and concisely as possible. Illustrations, therefore, should be treated as integral parts of a report when you are developing your basic plan (see Section 2-3).

Many concepts cannot be passed on to a reader without the use of illustrations. Typical of these are the structure of crystals (which you can show by reproducing a photomicrograph), the interconnections of parts in an electronic device (which can be "told" precisely by a schematic), and the results of a tensile-strength test (which can be conveyed instantly by a photograph of the broken end of the specimen). In other instances, the text can be greatly simplified if it is supported by illustrations (for example, a series of photographs that show the steps in the repair of a glider wing). In such portions of technical reports, the illustrations are considered essential to an understanding of the thesis being presented.

A careful writer leads his readers back and forth from text to illustrations, using one to support the other. Although you will never be able to present your information entirely by illustrations, you will find that they will greatly simplify your task.

□ NOTE

In modern reporting, it is not necessary that each illustration be able to stand alone when removed from the text. Rather, it is an integral part of the report, and neither text nor illustration is complete without the other. There is no need to say in words what is clearly evident in an illustration.   □

Illustrations that serve no specific purpose have no place in technical reports. Regardless of how much you may admire the artistry of a photograph, do not include it if its sole purpose is decoration. Such illustrations have two disadvantages: first, they "get in the way" of the reader who is in a hurry; and second, they tend to distract your readers so that they lose the thread of your discussion. The better the picture, of course, the more this is true. Note, however, that illustrations are used differently in technical reports than they are in technical brochures, which have another purpose.

In brief, then, illustrations are used to supplement the text, to substitute for text in complicated explanations, and to create a mental picture that cannot be given by words.

4-3.2. The Author and Report Illustration

A working knowledge of illustration techniques is essential if you are to get the most out of the illustrations in your report. The extent to which you will become involved in the actual preparation of the illustrations depends upon your own abilities, the facilities available to you, and the support that you have from professional photographers, draftsmen, and technical illustrators. If you are a competent photographer, you may actually take pictures yourself that will become part of your report. Most engineers and many scientists are capable draftsmen; if you are one, you may decide to do your own drafting. This takes time, but it is often the only way to obtain the illustrations that you need. Unless you are a professional illustrator or artist, however, photo-retouching and airbrush work will be beyond your capabilities. Before you plan your illustrations, determine who is going to prepare them and plan according to his talents.

You alone know which parts of your text should be illustrated. Regardless of the competence of the illustrator or draftsman who is working with you, he can do nothing until you tell him the points to illustrate and give him a rough sketch of what you have in mind.

This is equally true in regard to photographs. You are the only one who knows, for example, when your equipment is set up and ready to be photographed. You schedule the tests, so you know when a photographer is needed. Where the camera or cameras should be placed in order to get the most satisfactory photograph, when the results of a test are worth photographing, and which item should be the center of interest are additional questions that only you can answer.

□ NOTE

Work closely with your illustrators and photographers. Without your considered and patient advice, they cannot give you the high-grade illustrations that can greatly simplify your task of writing a report. □

Timing is particularly important when you wish to record a situation that would be very expensive to re-create. There may be times, for example, when you test a scarce or expensive item to destruction. Suppose you have been given five rockets to test, each costing $5,000. Then suppose that to get an additional rocket of the precise type that you need would take three months. It is evident that you must schedule your tests so that you have complete camera 'coverage, because you will not have the opportunity to come back later to shoot the picture "that you forgot." It is equally evident that you and not the photographer know when he should be on the scene.

As the author of a report, you will determine the type of illustration that is prepared. The writer—not the illustrator, photographer, or draftsman—makes the final decision concerning whether to use one or two views of an item he is describing, whether a single picture or a series is needed to illustrate a process, whether a photograph or an illustrator's rendering is most desirable, or whether details should be called out or not, and, if so, which they should be.

Finally, you are the person who must be satisfied with the final illustration. If a figure does not "tell" the story that you want, it is you who will reject it and ask for revision or improvement.

Therefore, as the author, you must be able to distinguish good illustrations from bad ones. You should be aware of the advantages and disadvantages of each medium and should know when to turn to one or the other to support your text. No attempt will be made here to teach you how to do the work of a photographer, draftsman, or illustrator; instead, the various forms of report illustration will be discussed so that you can realize maximum benefit to your report from the talents and materials available to you.

4-3.3. Types of Illustrations

The most common type of illustration is the line drawing (Fig. 4-6a). This is a figure made entirely of black lines drawn on a light background and augmented by words, numbers, or letters added in the same black tone. When it is reproduced, the image is black—that is, there are no gradations from light to dark. The effect of shading is obtained by various forms of crosshatching, dot patterns, or parallel lines of different thickness. The line drawing is fast, easy to make, and the least expensive to reproduce.

Figure 4-6. Types of illustrations available to report writers.

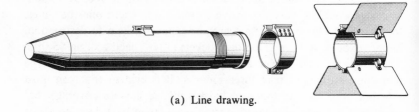

(a) Line drawing.

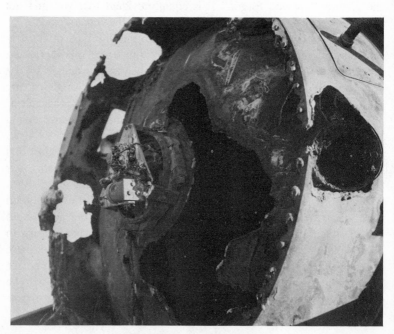

(b) Documentary photograph.

The next most common type of illustration is the photograph. A documentary photograph is shown in Fig. 4-6b, in which the item under discussion was photographed exactly as it appeared in place. In Fig. 4-6c is shown an example of a studio shot; all extraneous matter has been removed from the background, and the lighting has been adjusted to get the maximum benefit of display. If you have even the most elementary camera available, you can take pictures that will add greatly to the impact of your report and simplify your problems

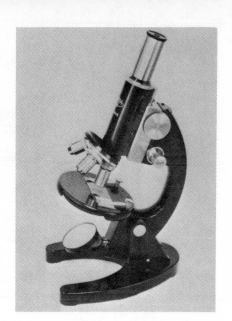

(c) Studio photograph
(catalog type).

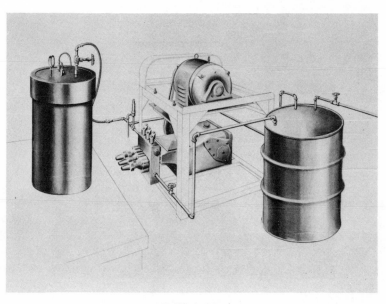

(d) Wash drawing.

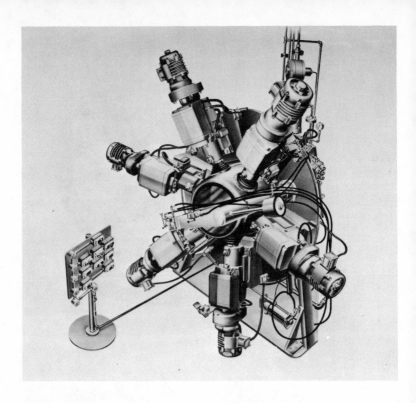

(e) Airbrush rendering.

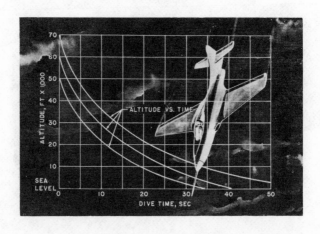

(f) Combination line graph and wash drawing.

154

of communication. If you have the services of technical photographers and a complete photo laboratory, you can make excellent use of this type of illustration.

Wash drawings (Fig. 4-6d) and airbrush renderings (Fig. 4-6e) require the assistance of skilled illustrators. Each has its distinct advantages, which will be discussed in the following sections. These illustrations may be considered intermediates between line drawings and photographs. They combine the flexibility of the drawing with the reality and pleasing appearance of the photograph and are often well worth the additional time and expense required. If you do not have qualified illustrators in your organization, there are an increasing number of technical illustrating firms that will contract to prepare one or a series of illustrations.

Graphs and charts are basically line drawings, but they may be combined with photographs or airbrush art (Fig. 4-6f) to suit your needs.

4-3.4. Color

Color is seldom required in technical illustrations. It does, of course, lend interest to a report, but the extent to which it aids reader comprehension is not fully known. In some instances, color is necessary to prevent confusion with regard to separate functions in a complex graph or flow chart. Colored illustrations (particularly colored photographs) are very expensive, however, and it is wise to resist the urge to use them, unless there is a true need.

□ NOTE

The use of color in report illustrations is expensive and time consuming. Do not use it purely for decoration. Be sure that it is functional or otherwise justified. □

4-3.5. Photographs

If you want your reader to know exactly what something "looks like," your most effective means is to show him a photograph of it. The more unusual or complicated the item is, the more a photograph will help. For example, you communicate more successfully if you show your reader a photograph of a new tooling machine in operation and supplement the picture with a minimum of words than if you must describe it entirely with words. On the other hand, avoid photographs of ordinary things with which your reader is already familiar; for example, a truck, a conventional building, a quonset hut, a small boat, or the rear view of a black box. Be sure that your photographs are really informative.

Photographs are well suited for illustrating such things as a facility, an actual test setup, or the results of physical tests. In addition, they are useful as illustrations in reports intended for nontechnical readers, who are accustomed to seeing photographs in newspapers and magazines, but who may not be able to read other types of illustrations so well.

4-3.5.1. DOCUMENTARY PHOTOGRAPHS

Photographs taken of your subject in place (for example, in the laboratory or on the test range) are called documentary photographs. These are the least expensive photographs, so long as you do not later have to have them retouched in order to emphasize your subject or to subdue unwanted background clutter. Their big advantage is that they are convincing in showing a reader the exact physical conditions when certain work was performed.

□ NOTE

If you are striving for a documentary effect in a photograph, do not permit any retouching. If a reader can detect the least trace of retouching, the value of the photograph as an honest illustration of the actual experiment is lost. □

4-3.5.2. CALLOUTS

Because most laboratory setups and similar subjects that lend themselves to documentary photographs are located amid other machines, pipes, pieces of equipment, etc., it is often necessary to use callouts to identify special items. For example, Fig. 4-7b is considerably easier to read than Fig. 4-7a, because the points of interest have been called out. In general, the technique of using letters to identify points on a photograph and explaining them in its caption is most useful when you have a considerable number of points to call out, when the callouts are long, or when the callouts might obscure an im-

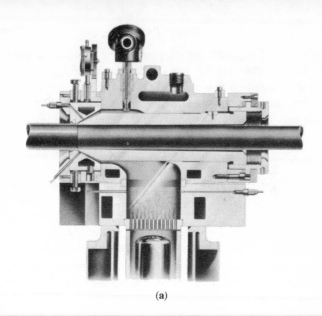

(a)

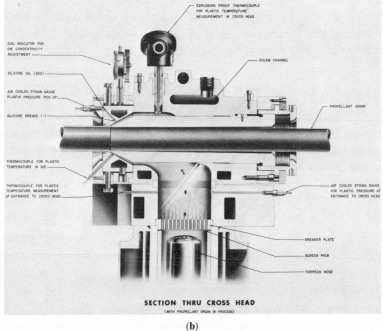

EXPLOSION PROOF THERMOCOUPLE
FOR PLASTIC TEMPERATURE
MEASUREMENT IN CROSS HEAD

DIAL INDICATOR FOR
DIE CONCENTRICITY
ADJUSTMENT

SILICONE OIL (200)

STEAM CHANNEL

AIR COOLED STRAIN GAUGE
PLASTIC PRESSURE PICK UP

SILICONE GREASE (—)

PROPELLANT GRAIN

THERMOCOUPLE FOR PLASTIC
TEMPERATURE IN DIE

THERMOCOUPLE FOR PLASTIC
TEMPERATURE MEASUREMENT
AT ENTRANCE TO CROSS HEAD

AIR COOLED STRAIN GAUGE
FOR PLASTIC PRESSURE AT
ENTRANCE TO CROSS HEAD

BREAKER PLATE

SCREEN PACK

TORPEDO NOSE

SECTION THRU CROSS HEAD
(WITH PROPELLANT GRAIN IN PROCESS)

(b)

Figure 4-7. Example of the technique of identifying items by the use of callouts.
(a) Without callouts. (b) With callouts.

portant detail. The technique of placing the callout on the photograph with an arrow leading the eye to the specific point is feasible when you have only a few items to call out; it has the advantage of placing the information where it is most effective. Either letters or numerals may be used to key points to their definitions in the caption.

4-3.5.3. STUDIO PHOTOGRAPHS

Studio photographs are most satisfactory for presenting a clear, well-lighted picture of your subject, but they look obviously posed. The benefits of careful positioning, proper angle, optimum lighting, and an uncluttered background make a studio photograph superior to the "in-place" photo in many situations. Although they are more expensive to take, they may save money in the long run through the elimination of airbrush retouching. As in documentary photographs, the value of studio photos may be greatly increased by the addition of callouts. You can help materially in obtaining effective photographs if you work with the photographer while he takes them and advise him as to the purpose of each photo and the important features that need to be emphasized.

4-3.5.4. CROPPING

Most photographs can be improved by judicious cropping. A photograph is said to be "cropped" when portions of it are cut or masked off by the engraver or photolithographer. Figure 4-8 demonstrates how a photograph can be cropped to eliminate undesirable portions and to emphasize the subject. As the writer, you know which feature should be the center of interest of a photograph and which parts must be included. You will protect your interests if you mark your photographs in such a way that necessary items will not be cropped out in the processing.

□ NOTE

If there can be any doubt as to the information that must or must not be included in a photograph used as an illustration, mark one print with the maximum limits of permissible cropping on all four sides.   □

Figure 4-8. Example of the technique of cropping a photograph to emphasize the subject and eliminate unwanted clutter. The final illustration would include only the area within the dotted lines.

4-3.5.5. RETOUCHING

Retouching can often greatly improve the communication of a photograph. Because of a variety of circumstances (such as non-availability of photographers), you frequently have to "make do" with a photograph that is less than ideal. By careful retouching, poor photographs can be turned into good illustrations. A typical example of the benefits of retouching may be seen in Fig. 4-9. Dirty equipment can be cleaned up; confusing background can be eliminated; unexpected signs (for example, the ubiquitous "No Smoking" sign) can be removed; distracting watches and rings can be made to disappear from arms and hands. Such retouching is expensive, but it is often well worth the cost. If you are supported by illustrators or other persons skilled in retouching, or if you can hire them, you can do much to improve your report and ensure maximum communication.

4-3.5.6. OTHER TECHNIQUES

There are many tricks of the trade, so to speak, that can be used to improve your photographs. For example, if you are illustrating a process, include personnel actually performing the steps. A re-

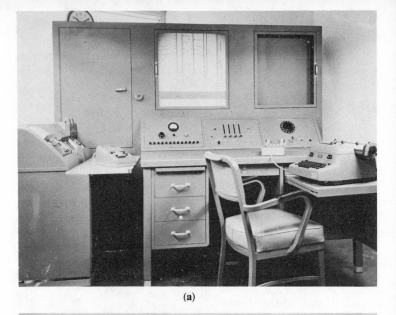

(a)

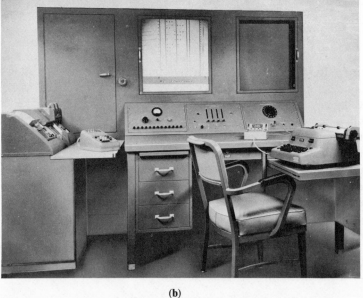

(b)

Figure 4-9. Example of a photograph improved by retouching. (a) original photograph. (b) Retouched photograph. Note that the clock and window have been removed, the machine at the left has been cleaned, the fourth leg has been added to the chair, the floor has been cleaned, and the dark areas have been lightened.

port that is intended for casual or nontechnical readers needs people in most of the photographs. If you wish to show the size of an item, include something in the picture that is readily recognized by your readers (a ruler will do, but use a hand, a match box, a few coins, or some similar item occasionally to break the monotony). To emphasize your subject in a documentary photograph, throw the background slightly out of focus. And so on. A few variations are shown in Fig. 4-10.

☐ NOTE

Many people "read" a report by thumbing through it looking at the pictures, but skipping the text. Every illustration, therefore, must serve a purpose and be as interesting as you can make it. A successful photograph will stop a "thumber" and make him read the caption; a successful caption will lead him into the text.   ☐

4-3.5.7. HANDLING OF PHOTOGRAPHS

Glossy prints of photographs are usually preferred for reproduction purposes. It is essential, however, that they be handled carefully. Two prints of each photograph are required: one for editing and marking, the other for use by the artist, engraver, or lithographer. In handling the latter, take the following precautions:

Do not use paper clips to hold prints together. The clips will leave marks that may show in the final reproduction.

Do not staple through a glossy print. The holes will show.

Do not attach overlays with adhesive tape. When the tape is removed, it may tear the glossy surface, and adhesive left on the print will pick up dirt and appear as a smudge.

Do not fold, bend, or dog-ear a print. Cracks in the surface will show.

Do not write on the front or back of the print. The indentation will reflect light and be picked up in the final reproduction.

Do not write on a piece of paper on top of a glossy print. Many a grocery list has appeared mysteriously in the reproduction.

Do not stamp an identification form on the back with a wet stamp. The ink (particularly red ink) is likely to creep through to the front of the print and spoil it.

(a)

(b)

(f)

Figure 4-10. Some methods of adding interest to photographs to be used as illustrations. (a) Choose a dramatic moment. (b) Show a man

162

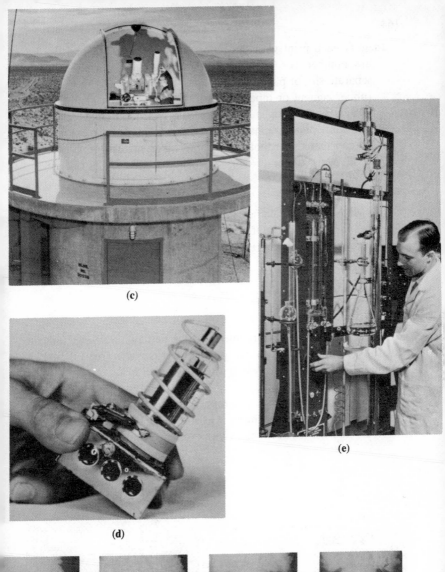

(c)

(d)

(e)

at work. (c) Select an unusual angle. (d) Use a hand to emphasize a
small item. (e) Put people in your picture. (f) Show a series of events.

163

Identify each print with the report number (or title) and the figure number (or caption). Either type this information on a separate slip of paper and attach it to the back of the print with rubber cement or tape, or mark the identification in the margin outside of the crop marks (preferably on mounting board).

If you mail photographs, protect them from damage with pieces of corrugated cardboard or some other material that will not bend. Mark the outer envelope "Photographs. Do not bend!"

4-3.6. Drawings

Drawings may be classified into line, wash, and airbrush types (see Fig. 4-6 for examples). Of these, the line drawing is the most common, probably because it is the easiest to prepare and the least expensive to reproduce.

4-3.6.1. LINE DRAWINGS

Line drawings have the following advantages:

1. By the use of various line and dot patterns, you can indicate the different materials of which your subject is made (see Fig. 4-11). Standard codes have been established in several fields.

2. You can give dimensions of as many features as are necessary with complete confidence that your reader will understand you. If you wish, you can show tolerances in as much detail as you need.

3. By the use of sectional views, you can show your reader the

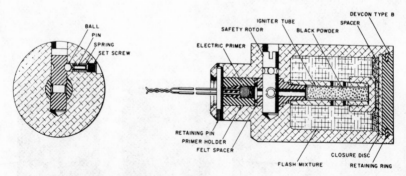

Figure 4-11. Line drawing illustrating the use of line codes to indicate different materials.

interior construction of an item, with enlargements of particularly complicated portions.

4. You can identify many more features on a line drawing than you can on any other type of illustration. It is relatively easy to add callouts to a line drawing because they are put on at the same time that the drawing is made.

5. Notes of considerable length may be placed within the limits of a line drawing in order to explain limitations of various items or to describe the operation of the piece illustrated.

6. Corrections and revisions can be made more easily on line drawings than on any other type of illustration. This is most important when the design of an item is undergoing rapid development during the time that you are preparing your report, and you are anxious to include the latest version. Changes in any other form of drawing are quite expensive.

☐ NOTE

Shop drawings do not make good report illustrations and should be avoided. They are wasteful of space, so the principal item is too small in the final reproduction, and they are usually cluttered with irrelevant detail. Compare the effectiveness of Fig. 4-12a, which is a typical shop drawing, with that of Fig. 4-12b, which is the same subject reworked for an illustration. ☐

The most satisfactory reproductions are obtained from line drawings prepared in ink. All lines remain clear when reduced, and there is no fading out of important callouts. Ink drawings, however, are about twice as expensive as pencil drawings and take considerably longer to prepare. For routine reports, you can obtain satisfactory results with pencil drawings if the draftsmen take care that all lines are solid, firm, and black. It is essential that all lines and callouts be of equal intensity. There are also various substitutes for ink, such as lines of different dot or dash patterns in the form of adhesive tape, that can be used on graphs, schematics, and charts.

4-3.6.2. WASH DRAWINGS

Wash drawings are prepared by using a hair brush to wash color onto an artist's board in the same manner that watercolor paintings are made. The color is usually India ink mixed with water. These

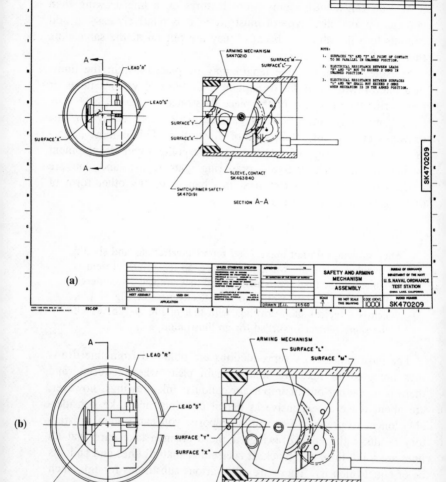

Figure 4-12. Comparison of (a) a shop drawing and (b) an illustration prepared for use in a report. By eliminating detail required for production but unnecessary as part of the discussion in a report, the principal items are shown larger on the page and in a form more easily understood.

drawings are intermediate between line drawings and airbrush drawings. They are reasonably fast to prepare and have the advantage of giving a realistic appearance to a figure by adding depth. Although they are not used to a great extent in technical reports, they add to the appearance of a report and should be considered when you are preparing a report for a nontechnical audience. Many readers can understand a wash drawing more easily than a detailed line drawing containing many dimensions, notes, and callouts.

There are times when you wish to give your readers a realistic picture of something that cannot be photographed. Typical of this situation is a piece of equipment that has not passed the drawing-board stage. Perhaps a clear visual impression of the piece will help you to sell your project. If so, a wash drawing prepared from blueprints will be your solution. Another example is a picture of a new missile exploding against a target aircraft flying at Mach 1.5. It is obvious that you could not get a photograph, but you could have a wash drawing prepared. Such drawings require a skilled illustrator.

4-3.6.3. AIRBRUSH RENDERINGS

An airbrush rendering is the highest form of technical illustration and also the most expensive. It is not unusual for a complicated airbrush drawing to cost from $500 to $1,000. These drawings, however, combine the advantages of the line drawing with the complete realism of the photograph. They can be prepared to precise dimensions, and portions can be cut away, revolved, enlarged, etc., following the same techniques used in line drawings. To this flexibility is added the full three-dimensional effect of a photograph without the problems of lighting or distortion encountered with a camera. Figure 4-13 is an airbrush rendering of a machine made long before it had been manufactured. Like the wash drawing, airbrush drawings require highly skilled illustrators.

4-3.6.4. EXPLODED VIEWS

An excellent means of showing the parts of a complicated item, such as a machine or piece of equipment, is the exploded view (Fig. 4-14). All of the parts are shown in the sequence in which they are put together, but with each part slightly removed from the others. By using an exploded view, you can identify every part and indicate its relation to the others. This method is most satisfactory if the parts are arrayed along one or more natural axes, rather than being scattered at random around the illustration or placed in groups of similar parts. Exploded views can be prepared as photographs, line drawings, or airbrush drawings, depending upon the talents and facilities that you have available.

4-3.6.5. CUTAWAY DRAWINGS

Two examples of cutaway drawings are shown in Fig. 4-15. In such an illustration, you "cut away" a portion of an item so that you can let your reader see how it is put together on the inside. This

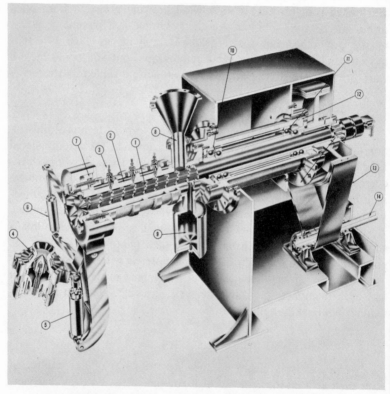

Figure 4-13. Airbrush rendering of a machine, prepared before the machine had been made. Developed from engineering drawings, such illustrations greatly simplify the task of describing items that are still in the planning stage.

can save a great deal of complicated verbal explanation. A cutaway is usually a drawing—either line or airbrush. It is normally prepared from design blueprints by an artist. A single illustration of this type can save your reader the trouble of working back and forth through a number of blueprints and virtually sketching the item out for himself if he wants to have some idea of what it looks like.

Cutaways can be made from photographs in either of two ways. One method is to saw one of the items in question in half and then photograph the section. For small, simple, and inexpensive items, this is not too difficult, but for large and expensive items or items in short supply, it is practically out of the question. With these, it is best to make a clear, well-lighted photograph of the item and to turn this over to an artist, who proceeds, with the aid of blueprints, to re-

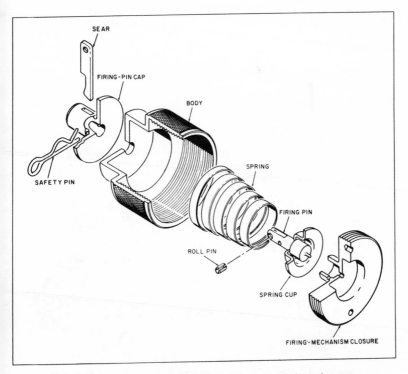

Figure 4-14. Typical exploded view of a piece of equipment. This technique is excellent for showing parts that would otherwise be hidden and the relation of these parts to each other.

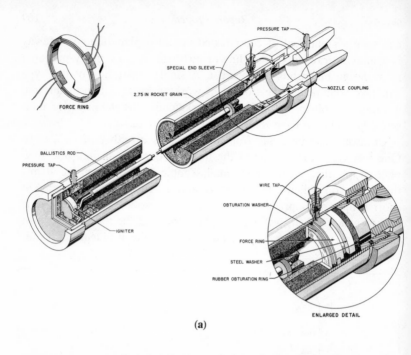

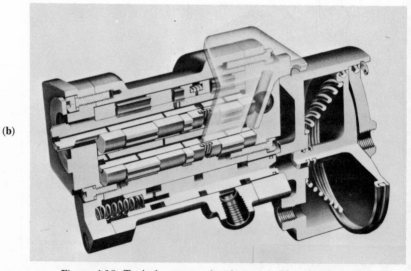

Figure 4-15. Typical cutaway drawings. (a) Line drawing. (b) Airbrush rendering. Illustrations of this type make it possible for you to inform your reader of the internal arrangement of complicated parts better than any other technique.

170

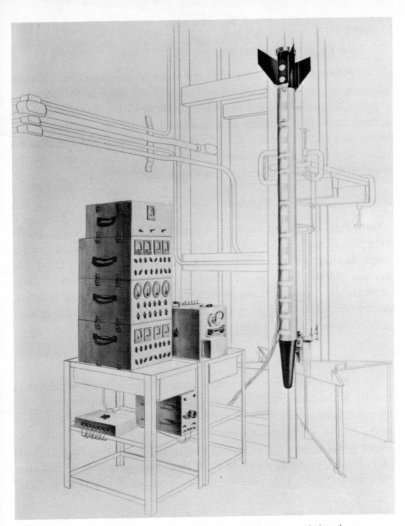

Figure 4-16. Example of combination of two types of drawings. Here the important items have been done in wash, while the related pieces have been subdued by showing them in line.

move the outer shell at the critical point and draw in the internal parts as though they had been actually cut away. This method often takes considerably less time than having the artist work up the entire item from blueprints, because the basic outside proportions are already determined for him. The result is a technical illustration of high quality.

4-3.6.6 COMBINATIONS

Combinations of the different types of drawings can be quite effective in certain situations and should be considered whenever possible. Figure 4-16, for example, illustrates what can be done by combining a line drawing and a wash drawing in one illustration. When you understand the advantages of the different types of illustrations, you will find an increasing number of variations that can be worked out to give maximum communication.

4-3.7. Graphs and Charts

Probably the fastest method of presenting data is to use a graph or a chart. Technically trained readers are as much at home with a graph as they are with words, and even the general public today has become accustomed to understanding simple graphs and charts through their frequent use in newspapers and popular magazines. A clear and well-designed graph can be used most effectively in support of or in place of verbal description.

4-3.7.1. LINE GRAPHS

By far the most common form of graph used in technical reports is the line graph, in which the interrelationship between two or more parameters is symbolized by a series of points, a curve, or both. Figure 4-17 is a typical graph showing the relationship between pressure and time. By measuring the pressure along the axis of ordinates (vertical axis) and the time along the axis of abscissas (horizontal axis), it is possible to plot a series of points determined

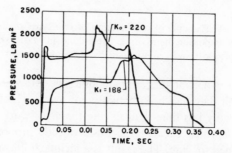

Figure 4-17. Typical line graph.

either mathematically or empirically. A curve can then be laid through these points so that for any desired time a corresponding value of pressure can be obtained, and vice versa. It is assumed that all users of this handbook have been trained in the basic principles of the construction of line graphs. The following discussion will be confined to indicating techniques for achieving various effects with graphs and pointing out common pitfalls that should be avoided.

The selection of the proper scale is probably the most important factor to consider. Although you will normally have prepared rough graphs on standard graph paper during the accumulation and study of your data, consider the advisability of redrawing these graphs when you prepare them for illustrations in your report. Figure 4-18 shows what can be done by the simple device of changing scales. In Figure 4-18a the information has been presented in the manner in which it was first put down. By decreasing the horizontal scale in Fig. 4-18b,

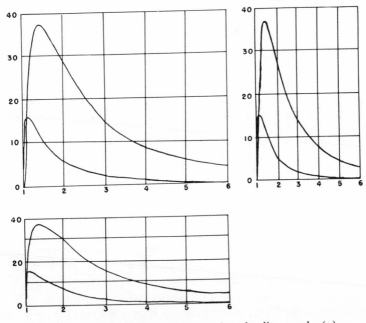

Figure 4-18. Effect of changing the scales of a line graph. (a) Original graph. (b) Slope of the curves is increased by shortening the horizontal scale. (c) Slope of the curves is decreased by shortening the vertical scale.

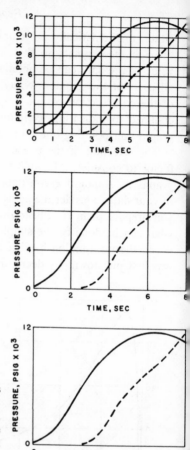

Figure 4-19. Effect of spacing of grid lines on reading accuracy of a line graph. (a) Close grid lines make for accurate reading. (b) Widely spaced grid lines require some estimating. (c) No grid lines at all permit only a comparison of trends.

the slope of the curve has been exaggerated, and it is easy to convince your reader that he should be alarmed over the situation. In Fig. 4-18c, however, the slope has been reduced by reducing the vertical scale, and your reader will probably decide that there is really nothing to get excited about. Your choice of scales, of course, will be dictated by the purpose of your report.

The more accurately you want users of your report to be able to read a graph, the closer you should put your grid lines. Figure 4-19a, for example, is easy to read with great accuracy, but Fig. 4-19b requires some degree of estimating, and you cannot be sure that all readers will get identical values from the graph. If you do not expect your readers to take specific values from your figure, but only want to show them general relationships and trends, you do not need grid lines at all, as is shown in Fig. 4-19c; here grid lines would only confuse the picture and should be omitted.

☐ NOTE

Too many conflicting curves on a single graph can make it unreadable. To remedy this situation, separate them into similar parts grouped on one page (see Fig. 4-20). ☐

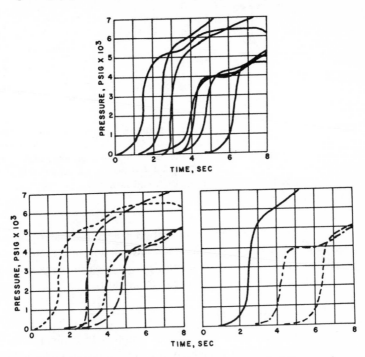

Figure 4-20. Method of simplifying an overcrowded line graph. (a) Original graph difficult to read. (b) Graph made easier to read by separating the lines into two groups and using various line codes.

It is frequently necessary to show two or more relationships in a single graph. The problem is to indicate the various scales in such a way that they can be read without confusion and so that the user can be instantly certain which curves are governed by which scales.

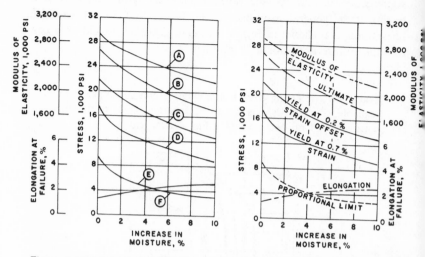

Figure 4-21. Method of simplifying a line graph with several groups of related information. (a) Three vertical scales on the left make for complicated reading. Curves called out by letters force the reader to look from the graph to the legend and back to the graph. (b) The graph has been made easier to read by placing vertical scales on both right and left and identifying the curves on the graph.

Figure 4-21 presents a comparison between a graph that is difficult to read and one that contains the same information in a more usable form. Whenever you plan your graphs, put yourself in the position of the user, and be sure that he can read them easily.

4-3.7.2. Bar Graphs

The most common use of a bar graph is to compare two or more discrete items of the same kind at various times or under various circumstances. Figure 4-22 shows a typical bar graph, which compares the population of the city of Los Angeles in 10-year intervals between 1900 and 1950. As may be seen in this figure, there is no attempt to indicate that the increase in population is a straight-line function between any two bars; the graph states only that on certain specific dates the city had a population as shown. However, the reader can see at a glance that the population is steadily increasing and can make a quick comparison between the values at different dates; for example, in 1950 there were about 50 percent more people in Los Angeles than there were in 1930.

Extending this principle, it is possible to show similar comparisons for other cities at the same periods and thereby to compare, for example, the rate of growth of several cities, as shown in Fig. 4-23. Note, however, that bar graphs soon reach a saturation point, and if you attempt to include too many items, you lose the benefits of quick comparison by confusing your reader.

Bar graphs can be designed horizontally (Fig. 4-22) or vertically (Fig. 4-23). In deciding upon which way to set up a graph, consider the format of your text. If you are using a two-column format, design

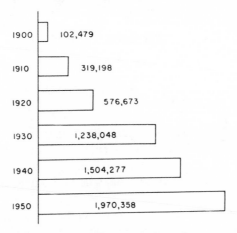

Figure 4-22. Typical bar graph.

a vertical graph to fit one column or a horizontal graph to spread across two columns. Next, consider your scale—a long bar is better set vertically on a page. Finally, determine the descriptive matter that must be included in words; a long description can be handled better in a horizontal line than stacked vertically.

For the usual technical audience, you can rely on the standard bars in your graphs. Nontechnical readers, however, may find graphs more interesting if you make them more elaborate by replacing the bars with rows of symbols. Here you can let each symbol represent a certain unit of measure, say, 100,000 people. It is possible to make a graph even more elaborate by printing the bars or rows of symbols

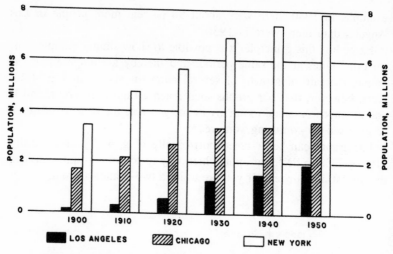

Figure 4-23. Bar graph typical of those used to compare several items at various dates. Such graphs are useful to show trends and to give quick comparisons. They are readily understood by nearly all readers.

over a background made of a photograph that is representative of your figure title. There are many variations of this type of illuminated graph, and, when you are competing for readership, they can be definite additions to what might otherwise be a rather dull statistical report.

In designing bar graphs, use as few grid lines as possible. Since you do not expect your readers to read a bar graph with great accuracy, you can space the lines far apart. If, as is occasionally necessary, you want your readers to know the exact figure represented by a bar, show the figures in the bar or at the end of it (see Fig. 4-22).

☐ NOTE

Use bar graphs to compare quantities of the same kind, place, or type. Compare only a limited number of values. For maximum effectiveness, keep bar graphs uncomplicated. ☐

A variation of the bar graph can be used to show changing proportions of a whole, as in Fig. 4-24. The same items are converted to percentages of the whole at different times, in different places, or

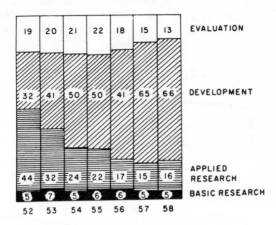

Figure 4-24. Variation of the bar graph used to compare relative proportions of a whole. Here, although the total may vary from year to year, the proportions are shown as percentages making quick comparisons easy. In this example, it is readily apparent that effort is increasing on development work and decreasing on applied research, while the percentage of effort expended on basic research remains about the same.

under different circumstances. By using various line or dot patterns, each major item can be readily distinguished. Each bar represents 100%. These graphs serve as excellent supporting material for statistical discussions and are easily understood by most readers.

4-3.7.3. PIE CHARTS

A familiar tool of the author of financial reports is the pie chart, in which 360° represents 100%, 180° represents 50%, 90° represents 25%, etc. (Fig. 4-25). These charts offer an easily understood means of showing the breakdown of 100% of such items as money, manpower, or time. Like the bar graph, a pie chart can be understood by nearly all readers. Because it is difficult for untrained readers to estimate the portions of the pie with any accuracy, it is best to include numerical values within each section. Variations can be made by adding a third dimension, or by using something other than a simple circle—a coin, for example—for the basic element.

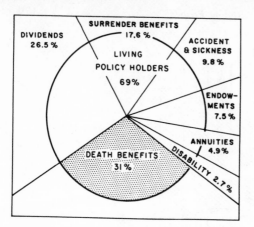

Figure 4-25. Typical pie chart. These charts are familiar to most readers and are useful to give a quick picture of the breakdown of any total figure on a percentage basis. (Courtesy of New York Life Insurance Co.)

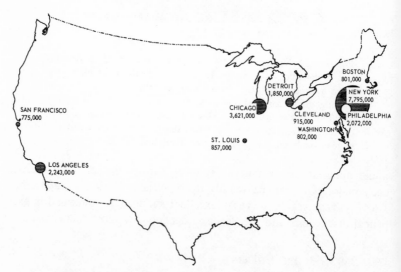

Figure 4-26. Typical map graph. Here the population of the cities is indicated by the size of the circles, and the location is shown in the proper position of the map. Without the figures, however, exact comparisons could not be made.

4-3.7.4. Map Graphs

When your discussion is concerned with the geography of an area, it is good practice to introduce a map as early as possible. Map graphs can be used to compare quantities while at the same time giving the geographical location of those quantities. Fundamentally, these are prepared by superimposing an area diagram on a map. The quantitative comparison between the various values is indicated by the size of the circles or other symbols located at the proper points on the map. Thus, in Fig. 4-26 the population of the ten largest cities in the United States is indicated by a map graph. Note, however, that because the symbols are some distance apart, it is difficult to distinguish between values that are approximately the same size.

Map graphs should be prepared with care to bring out the proper emphasis. The tendency is to show too much detail on these graphs. It is better to prepare a new map with only pertinent points on it than to attempt to make use of a standard map by adding additional information to what is apt to be already a confusing array of information.

□ NOTE

Standard road maps are designed to include as much information as possible, because the designers cannot know what use will be made of them. They definitely are not designed to be the foundation for a map graph. In addition, most maps are copyrighted and should not be used in publications without permission of the copyright holder. □

Show no more than is necessary and eliminate all superfluous details. If mountains are unnecessary, dispense with them. Do not include railroads, unless they have a bearing on the information that you are presenting. Treat all other details in a like manner.

Every map graph should contain a scale of miles (or feet) if the distance between points is of any interest, and, of course, it is customary to include a north point. Do not overlook the fact that north is located traditionally at the top of the page.

4-3.7.5. Flow Charts

Among the more useful devices for explaining a process is the flow chart (Fig. 4-27), which offers a means of showing visually a fixed series of steps or events. A flow chart is particularly useful if the process that you are explaining is complex, because you can present all of the major steps in one figure. You can guide the reader through it by numbering the steps, adding directional arrows to be sure that he follows the proper sequence, or indicating simultaneous events by the introduction of line symbols or color codes.

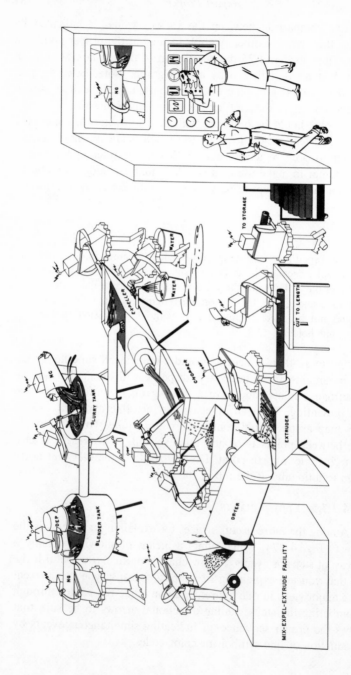

Figure 4-27. Typical flow chart used to illustrate the steps in a process. Here interest has been added by the use of stylized robots. Flow charts should be kept compact in order to convey the maximum information in the space available.

The major problems encountered in preparing flow diagrams are to be sure that they are logical, to include all necessary steps or events, and to design them so that they make the best use of the space available.

□ NOTE

Flow charts are among the limited number of illustrations that may justify the use of color in technical reports. When flow lines overlap, color will keep the reader from getting lost and carry him surely from one step to the next in the proper sequence. □

Schematic flow charts are prepared by indicating the steps in boxes joined by lines—with direction arrows if there is any question about the sequence. Such charts may be varied and interest added by replacing the boxes with drawings or photographs of the events or equipment to be found at each step. Cartoons or stylized figures may help to lend interest to an otherwise routine flow chart.

Another type of flow chart makes use of a floor plan, area map, or cutaway drawing to serve as the framework on which the steps of the flow are shown. This device has the advantage of helping the reader to picture the actual chain of events.

4-3.7.6. ORGANIZATION CHARTS

When it is necessary for you to explain an existing or proposed organization to your readers, an excellent device is the organization chart. This is a graphical representation of organizational units arranged to indicate the relative importance of each unit and showing the administrative lines of responsibility. Figure 4-28 is a typical organization chart.

□ NOTE

Organization charts traditionally read down and across. Place the unit (or office) with prime authority and responsibility at the top of your chart and the units with the least authority at the bottom, and array the other units in levels of decreasing authority from top to bottom. □

In designing an organization chart, locate the boxes so that units of equal rank are aligned in a horizontal row. The illusion of equal

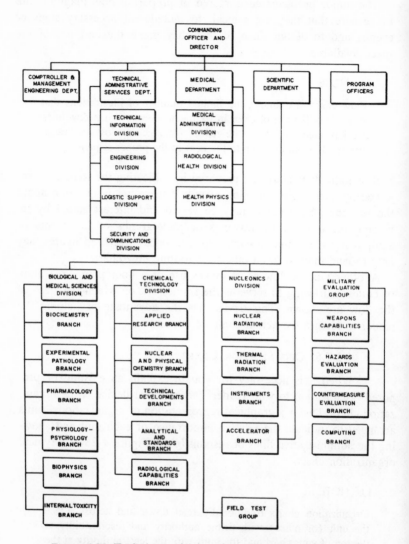

Figure 4-28. Typical organization chart. Economy of space has been achieved in this example by dropping the organizational units of the scientific department into a position below the units of the other departments, thereby making a compact chart out of a structure that would otherwise be excessively spread out.

rank will be improved if all of the boxes are of equal size (at least of equal width). The lines of authority are clearly indicated by a single line drawn from the bottom of one box to a box in the row below it or to a spanner from which lines drop to two or more boxes below. This process is followed from top to bottom of the chart until the bottom row is reached.

Variations of this basic style may be devised for the more complicated organizations. You will have little difficulty if you follow the principle that units have authority over those below them and take direction from those above them.

Organization charts are most effective if they are not too complicated. If you find that your chart is a mass of boxes, or if your lines of authority become difficult to follow, try a series of charts in which the first (or control) chart shows the relationship among the major organizational units and the organization of each of these units is indicated with a separate chart. You can direct the reader to the proper supplementary charts by a short statement at the bottom of each box in the last row of the control chart.

Depending upon the need, you can elaborate on the basic organization chart by including the names of the officers, descriptions of the duties of each unit, the number of employees in each unit, the money budgeted for each unit, etc., in the appropriate boxes. It is also possible to make such charts more attractive by adding pictures to each box; for example, photographs of the officers or of the buildings or equipment most characteristic of the units.

4-3.8. Comparison of Advantages and Disadvantages of Various Types of Illustrations

4-3.8.1. TO SHOW DIMENSIONS

A simple line drawing serves best when you want to give the dimensions of a part, a piece of equipment, a plot of ground, or similar items. By including a plan, elevation, or side view as needed, or by showing an isometric drawing with dimension lines precisely in place, you can be certain that your reader knows exactly all necessary dimensions. You may include as many dimensions as you need and show tolerances if they are significant. On a line drawing you can also add necessary short comments so that the reader will be certain to see them when he studies the illustration.

While dimensions can be added to other types of illustrations, the limits are less apparent, and such detailed callouts tend to detract from the normal advantages of the other mediums.

4-3.8.2. To Create a Mental Image

A photograph of an item serves most satisfactorily when you need to be sure that your reader has the same image in his mind that you have in yours. This is particularly true when you are describing something new to your readers. Usually, a studio shot with the background dropped out is the most effective.

An airbrush drawing of an item is about as effective in creating an exact mental image, but it is much more expensive. There are times, however, when it is impossible to photograph your subject, and you must resort to using an airbrush rendering regardless of the cost.

4-3.8.3. To Record Test Results

The most effective means, by far, of recording actual test results is with a documentary photograph. Such a photograph will prove your written statements and save you many words of text. The photograph should be made as soon as the test is completed, without any rearrangement of materials or equipment (see Fig. 4-6b).

4-3.8.4. To Indicate Materials

When you need to indicate a variety of materials from which component pieces of an item are made, use a line drawing with different styles of crosshatching, stippling, etc. (see Fig. 4-11). The proper symbols have been set down by such organizations as the American Standards Association.

If you must distinguish between only two or three materials, you can do so reasonably effectively with an airbrush drawing with the materials clearly called out with words and arrows.

4-3.8.5. To Show Steps in a Process

A series of photographs, either studio or documentary, is the most satisfactory way to explain a sequence of steps in a process (see Fig. 4-29). The photographs should be close-ups, each showing only what is necessary to illustrate one step. Be sure that the accompanying legends clearly identify each step and that the figures lead the reader logically to the end product.

If photographs cannot be taken, line drawings are adequate substitutes. They are best, however, when the process is a simple one. They usually require a skillful artist, and they cost considerably more than the photographs.

□ NOTE

Retouching of photographs used to illustrate steps in a process is an acceptable practice. Everything should be done to make these illustrations as clear as possible; there is no need to try for a documentary effect here. □

4-3.8.6. TO CALL OUT PARTS

Line drawings—either simple or shaded—are useful when you must call out many items on an illustration. It is possible to arrange the callouts in such a way that they can be easily read (see Fig. 4-11). The identifying arrows can be carried to the precise points being called out with a minimum of confusion. Complicated areas can be enlarged, and sectional views can be included to reach all sides of an item.

If there are only a few items to be called out, you can use an airbrush drawing to advantage, especially if you wish to cut away a portion of the piece.

Although they are not so effective as line drawings for this purpose, photographs are also frequently used with callouts. The callouts should be placed on an acetate overlay when prepared for offset reproduction so that they can be reversed if necessary. With photographs, it is best to use letters or numbers to identify the points on the picture and explain them in the legend. In working with overlays, be sure that the words, letters, or arrows are placed so that they do not conflict with important areas on the photograph.

□ NOTE

If you are in doubt as to whether a callout on a photograph can be read, reverse it (white letters against a gray background). □

4-3.8.7. TO SHOW A TEST SETUP

An over-all picture of a test setup is best conveyed by a photograph. Such a photograph is generally documentary, showing

(a)

(b)

Figure 4-29. Example of method of explaining the steps in a process by a series of photographs. Show no more than is necessary to demonstrate each step; keep the photographs in proper sequence; integrate the text, legends, and photographs.

(c)

(d)

(e)

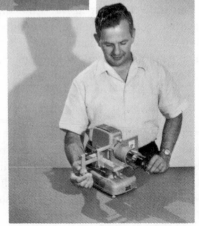

(f)

189

the equipment actually in place and ready for a test to begin. It is frequently necessary, however, to subdue extraneous pipes, wires, other pieces of equipment, etc., by use of overlays or airbrushing.

A line drawing should occasionally be used in combination with such a photograph in order to make clear the interlocking of several pieces of equipment or to serve as a key for callouts and comments.

4-3.8.8. To Give a Visual Impression of an Event

A wash drawing will effectively convey to a reader an impression of some action that cannot be photographed. Where precision is not required, a wash drawing is just as effective as an airbrush drawing and much less expensive. For this purpose, it is considerably more realistic than a line drawing.

4-3.8.9. Cost Comparison

A documentary photograph is normally less expensive than a photograph made in a studio. However, if an "in-place" photograph requires a great deal of retouching in order to bring out pertinent parts and subdue others, it may become the more expensive in the long run. Consider the use that you plan to make of a photograph before you decide that a documentary picture will do.

Of the types of drawings, a simple line drawing done in pencil is the least expensive. An airbrush drawing is the most expensive; such illustrations often run to several hundred dollars. Wash drawings are comparatively inexpensive. Line drawings become increasingly expensive as they are made more elaborate. To ink a simple line drawing will nearly double the cost of a pencil rendering. The addition of line patterns on overlays again increases the cost, but not so much as when the hatching or shading is done by hand.

4-3.8.10 Time Comparison

An unretouched documentary photograph is less time consuming than a studio shot, but a retouched photograph takes the longest time to prepare. Line drawings done in pencil take the least time of any of the drawings. Wash drawings and drawings shaded with overlays are next, and airbrush drawings take the longest time to prepare.

5

Supplementary Matter

5-1. APPENDIXES

5-1.1. Purpose

An appendix in a technical report is an additional part that supplements the report proper. It carries information that is intimately related to the main thesis but not essential to it. Whether certain information is assigned to the report proper or removed to an appendix depends largely upon the characteristics of your primary audience and the purpose of the report. Consider your readers and the amount of information they need to understand the material that you are presenting and to react to it as you want them to; their background determines the amount that you need in the report proper. Information that is in support of your theme and of sufficient interest to your readers to be included is put in an appendix.

□ NOTE

Be sure that the report will serve its primary purpose without the information in its appendixes. Since many readers do not read beyond the closing section, essential information relegated to an appendix may never be read. □

191

Appendixes are useful adjuncts to the main body of the report when you expect your report to be read by more than one group of readers. By removing bulky information to an appendix, you can tell your story quickly in comparatively few pages and still supply more detailed information for a group of your colleagues who might be interested in the actual data upon which you based your conclusions.

5-1.2. Typical Appendix Material

As a guide to the kinds of material that might logically be placed in the appendix rather than in the main body of your report, the following suggestions are offered:

1. *Detailed test data.* There are occasions when it is useful to include bulky test data in a report. Perhaps you know that some of your readers will be extremely interested in specific results, but you cannot be sure who or how many they may be; or possibly you want to record these data in the report so that you and your immediate co-workers will have them ready for future work on your project. Masses of minute detail, however, have no place in the main body of a report, for they tend to interrupt your presentation; readers begin to skip pages and may pass over important points before their attention is recaptured. Use a summary of the data in the main body of the report and put the detailed data in an appendix.

2. *Photographic records of many similar tests.* Frequently, the results of a series of tests are recorded photographically. Any one of these photographs may serve to make your point in the report, but you may want to prove that the photograph chosen was actually typical and not just an individual shot selected because it served your purpose. If this is the situation, support your statements with as many photographs as you think are necessary, but put them in an appendix.

3. *Procedures.* In reports concerned primarily with the use of equipment, detailed procedures for making adjustments may be needed by some of your readers and not by others. For example, in a report on the calibration-range procedures for a Bowen camera, the instructions on how to read the betascope vernier scale were placed in an appendix.

4. *Detailed mathematics.* In reports that present a mathematical analysis of a problem, the detailed work may be of interest to many readers, but if it were included in the body of the report, it would

seriously interrupt the discussion. The essential mathematics must appear in the report proper, while the extended calculations should be removed to an appendix. For example, in a report presenting an analysis of the yawing motion of tangent-finned rockets, the following material was placed in the appendixes: (a) the components of acceleration measured by accelerometers, (b) analog computations, (c) aerodynamic forces and moments, and (d) numerical constants for computer solutions.

5. *Detailed specifications.* When you have been given a project for which very careful specifications were defined, you will probably want to include them in your report. Usually, however, only the major points need to be mentioned in the report proper, while the complete set of specifications can appear in an appendix.

5-1.3. Format

The format for appendixes usually follows that of the report proper. Each appendix should be considered a major section. In long-form reports, it is customary to start each appendix on a new page, with the heading treated as a first-order heading. For example, if your first-order headings are centered, you might begin an appendix as follows:

Appendix 3

FRACTIONAL FACTORIAL DESIGNS, TYPE A

The text for this appendix would then begin here with normal paragraph indention, and with the text composed to normal measure . . .

If your report is particularly formal, you may wish to use a half-title page (see Section 3-2.3) to introduce the appendixes as a group, or you may employ a half-title page before each appendix when they are unusually long. A half-title page is also useful if the report proper ends on a left-hand page and it is necessary to begin the appendix on a left-hand page—for example, when the appendix consists of a table that extends horizontally across two pages. Since it is not good form to have a blank right-hand page in a report, you can introduce the appendix with a half-title page with the beginning of the appendix on the reverse side.

Normally, the numbering of all series should continue consecutively from the report proper through all appendixes. This includes the numbering of pages, figures, tables, equations, footnotes, and references. The only exception to this practice occurs in an unusually long formal report in which the material is presented in chapters. Here, you may use the technique of identifying the individual appendix and starting over with the number 1 with each appendix; thus, Figure A-1, Table B-6, or Equation C-22 would identify, respectively, the first figure in Appendix A, the sixth table in Appendix B, and the twenty-second equation in Appendix C.

5-2. NOMENCLATURE LISTS

5-2.1. Purpose

A list of the unusual or new nomenclature that you have used in your report will often help your readers. When many symbols are used, they should also be listed and identified. If you include a considerable amount of mathematics in your report, the reader must understand the value of each symbol. Using an undefined symbol is analogous to introducing a foreign word without translating it. If most of your readers know the language, do not translate; if they are not familiar with the language, you had better translate your terms if you want them to understand you.

A special list is not required when you have only a few terms to define, for these can be explained in the text the first time that you use them in some such manner as this:

... The formula in present use is

$$E = 0.067 \frac{V^2}{r}$$

in which E equals superelevations, in feet per foot of width; V equals velocity, in miles per hour; and r equals radius, in feet.

or this:

... Problems involving the determination of true bearings may be solved by applying the formula

$$\cos Z = \frac{\sin a}{\cos h \cos \phi} - \tan h \tan \phi$$

in which

$Z =$ the azimuth of the sun
$a =$ the declination of the sun
$h =$ the altitude of the sun
$\phi =$ the latitude of the point of observation

It is customary to define your terms in this manner as you proceed through your report. When the section involving mathematics is relatively short, this is sufficient. Your reader will be able to remember the terms that you are using, or he can turn back a page or two to refresh his memory.

As your discussion becomes more involved, however, it is increasingly difficult for the reader to keep your nomenclature in mind. In addition, he may lose time and be distracted from the theme of your argument if he has to turn back and forth through the pages to find the various places where you have defined your terms. Therefore, if you have more than a few terms and symbols to define, or if your discussion spreads out over more than a few pages, gather all of the terms and their definitions into one list, headed "Nomenclature" or "Notation."

5-2.2. Location in the Report

The traditional location of the list of nomenclature is at the back of the report, between the text (including any appendixes) and the bibliography. It is easy to find and, therefore, easy to use in this location, and readers are trained to look for it there.

However, placing it before the mathematical discussion, rather than after it is helpful if, for example, you expect a majority of your readers to be unfamiliar with your symbols or definitions. It is also useful if you wish to eliminate the need to break into your discussion with a definition each time that you use a new symbol or term. When you offer the reader a list of nomenclature at the beginning of your discussion, you are free to move directly from equation to equation without defining your terms. On such occasions, locate the list of nomenclature in the preliminary matter or insert it as the first page of the section in which your mathematics begins—usually, immediately after the opening section.

5-2.3. Order of Entries

Arrange your entries in the list of nomenclature in the following order:

> English letters
> Greek letters
> subscripts
> superscripts
> special notes

The English and Greek letters are listed alphabetically (see Fig. 5-1). For the convenience of the reader, insert vertical spacing between groups, as shown in the illustration.

NOMENCLATURE

B	Magnetic flux vector
c	Radius of the bow shock
e_r, e_θ	Unit directional vectors in r and θ directions, respectively
E	Internal energy
M_s	Shock Mach number, based on sonic speed of 332 in/sec
p	Pressure
T	Temperature
V	Velocity
γ'	Effective specific heat ratio
Δ	Standoff distance
ρ	Density
σ	Electrical conductivity

SUBSCRIPTS

b	Body
c	Bow stock
0	Stagnation point
1	Ahead of the traveling shock wave
2	Behind the traveling shock wave
3	Bow shock layer

Figure 5-1. Typical list of nomenclature. The symbols are grouped with English letters first in alphabetical order, followed by the Greek letters. Subscripts are listed separately.

5-2.4. Format

List the symbol or term first, followed by the definition. Align the symbols to the right and the definitions to the left. Leave a small space (two or three spaces on a typewriter) between the symbols and the definitions. If you allow a wide space, the reader will have trouble in relating the correct definition to each symbol. If it is necessary to give the units of measure, place a comma after the definition and follow it with the unit, as illustrated in Fig. 5-1. When most of your definitions are short, you can save space by arranging the list in two columns, even though you may be using a single-column format elsewhere in the report.

> ☐ NOTE
>
> Do not assign more than one meaning to any symbol. If a symbol means one thing at the beginning of your report and another at the end of it, you are certain to confuse your readers.   ☐

Try to use standard symbols whenever they exist. For example, it is better to let P represent pressure and T represent time than arbitrarily to select X and Y to represent these factors. It is also helpful to check with your printer before you introduce an unusual symbol in order to determine whether or not he will be able to print it for you. Frequently, you can save considerable trouble for him if you adjust your selection of symbols to fit the type that he has available. If he must have a special piece of type made because you have chosen an unusual symbol, it is both expensive and time consuming.

5-3. REFERENCE LISTS

5-3.1. Purpose

A reference list is a tabulation of the bibliographic information of the publications to which the author refers in the text of his report, as distinguished from a bibliography, which includes information concerning not only the publications mentioned in the report but also any others that the author thinks will be of interest to his readers. Such lists customarily are located at the end of reports. (The only exception to this practice is made when a distribution list is included; then the distribution list is the final item in the report.) Readers are in the habit of turning to the back of a report when they want to find the references, and to locate the list anywhere else will cause confusion.

□ NOTE

A reader should be able to obtain a copy of any item included in a reference list so that he may study it. Therefore, list only publications that have actually been released and are available. Any other documents should be described in footnotes throughout the text. □

As you write your report, it is often desirable to suggest to your readers that they find additional information in other publications. Frequently, you can eliminate the need to include lengthy discussions by directing your readers to other publications in which this information is available in detail. Sometimes you will wish to give proper credit to colleagues, by mentioning the documents in which their work has been recorded. Or you may be preparing a report for more than one group of readers and may wish to tell your secondary audience where to look for information that, since it is already well known by your primary audience, should not be included in detail in your report. In these and similar circumstances, you make reference throughout your text to the works of other authors. To supply the complete bibliographic information in the body of the text, however, would be distracting to your readers. Therefore, use a simple key (such as "Ref. 6," or just the number in parentheses, or the number as a superscript) at the point of reference and then supply complete bibliographic information in the reference list.

The information contained in an entry in a reference list is the same as that in an entry in a bibliography. Entries in a reference list are arrayed in the order in which they are mentioned in the text, while the entries in a bibliography are listed in alphabetical order, without regard to the order in which they have been mentioned in the report.

Most technical report writers use a reference list rather than a bibliography. Occasionally, an author believes that his readers will be interested in more information on the subject and includes a bibliography. Under rather unusual circumstances, an author will use both a reference list and a bibliography in the same report; this is acceptable but seldom desirable.

5-3.2. Information Required

When you prepare a reference list, keep in mind that your reader should be able to procure a copy of each publication from the data that you supply him. If the information is incorrect or incomplete, he may not be able to do so, and the purpose of your reference will be defeated. A great deal of time has been lost and irritation generated by people searching for publications without the necessary data. Care in the preparation of your list of references will save time for everyone who uses the list. It is necessary, then, that you know what information is required. A complete bibliographic reference should include the following data:

Authors. Give the name of the author or authors. Take this information from the title page of a copy of the original publication. Be careful with the spelling and the initials. Publications are catalogued in libraries according to the way in which the author's name is spelled in the publication, regardless of any other spelling that he may use elsewhere.

Title. The full title and any subtitles should be recorded. Do not change word order, spelling, or punctuation from that used on the title page, even though you may think that it is incorrect.

Name of publisher. If you are referring to another report, use the name of the releasing organization (for example, U. S. Naval Ordnance Test Station). If you are referring to a book, give the name of the publishing company (for example, Prentice-Hall, Inc.).

Place of publication. This is the name of the town or city in which the item was published. If it is a well-known city (New York, Philadelphia, Boston, London, or Paris), you do not need to give the name of the state or country. If it is not easily recognized, however (China Lake, California), or if there are two or more cities with the same name (Madison, Corona, or Portland), include the name of the state as well.

Date of publication. This can be found on either the front or the back of the title page. Most reports include the month and even the day of publication, whereas books usually give only the year.

Series number. Most reports carry an identifying series number, such as "NOTS TP 2134," which should be listed. Many libraries file reports by series number.

Edition number. Each time that a book is revised, it is assigned a new edition number. If, for example, you wish to refer your reader to the third edition of a certain book but neglect to indicate the edition, he may pick up the first or second edition and not find the information that he wants.

Volume and issue numbers. If you are referring to an article in a journal, give the volume and issue number in which the item may be found.

Classification. When you refer to a publication in the classified literature, indicate its classification so that the requester will know whether or not he is cleared to read it and if he must establish his "need-to-know" in order to obtain it.

Number of pages. Although it is not necessary to give the number of pages in the publication referred to, this may be useful information for the reader. By indicating the size of the publication, you give an idea of its scope. Many authors show this figure for books but not for reports.

Illustrations. When you refer to a book (as opposed to a report), it may be helpful to let the reader know whether or not it is well illustrated. If it is, place the abbreviation "illus." at the end of the reference.

Page numbers. Occasionally you will want to refer your reader to a specific page or two in a publication so that he will find the needed information without delay. If so, give the page numbers in the reference. This is frequently done in referring to an article in a journal.

□ NOTE

The guiding principle in preparing a bibliographic reference is to supply the reader with all of the data that he will need to find the publication with a minimum of effort. It is better to give too much than too little information. □

It is good practice to make adequate notes for a bibliographic reference when you are using a publication in gathering the material for your report. Any time that you take notes from a report or book, identify the source and be sure that you have all of the data that you will need later. There is a danger that publications that you have used during the course of your project will be unavailable to you when you write your report.

5-3.3. Problem References

While you can help your readers by directing them to publications that will supply them with additional information about your subject, you should select your references with care. You will waste your readers' time by referring them to publications that they cannot obtain. The following types of references should be included in your lists only after careful consideration of more satisfactory alternatives.

5-3.3.1. AUTHOR'S OWN PUBLICATIONS

If you have published a number of reports on earlier phases of your work, it is inevitable that you will refer your readers to some of your own publications. When they contain the latest or most significant information on your subject, this is quite in order. There are, however, certain dangers that should be avoided.

If your reference list is made up only of your own publications, you indicate a conceit that is in bad taste. In effect, you are telling your readers that you think you are the only one who has written anything worth reading on your subject, which probably is not true. In addition, you show a narrowness in your background, because you apparently have not bothered to search the literature for supporting information.

5-3.3.2. OBSOLETE REFERENCES

Try to refer your readers to publications that contain up-to-date information. You will accomplish nothing by including references to books and reports that have been superseded by later publications. Some authors, under the illusion that a long list of references will impress their readers, list every publication that they have ever read on their subject. Actually, all that they accomplish is to make it difficult for their readers to discover the references that will be of real value to them.

5-3.3.3. INCOMPLETE REFERENCES

There is nothing more frustrating than to attempt to locate a publication with only part of the necessary information. When you supply a defective reference, you put your readers and their secretaries and librarians to much needless work in trying to piece together enough data to locate the right report or book. The information that is required is detailed in Section 5-3.2 and should always be furnished.

5-3.3.4. PADDED REFERENCE LISTS

A proper reference list should include only those publications that will, in fact, benefit the reader. To include more than these only confuses the situation. Some authors, however, think that the longer their list, the more convinced their readers will be that they know a great deal about their subjects. In their enthusiasm, they pad their lists with many publications that have little or no bearing on their subjects. In the long run, however, several pages of references that are only slightly related to your report will cast doubt upon your sincerity; if the reader doubts your intentions in one part of a report, he may doubt your presentation in other parts. It is best to list all of the publications that your readers may need, but no more.

5-3.3.5. OBSCURE REFERENCES

There are times when a reference may be obscure even though you apparently have supplied all of the required information. For example, you may refer to a foreign publication that is not available in this country, or you may refer to a very old publication of a company no longer in business. Perhaps the publication is out of print, or it may now be available under a different title. Any of these circumstances would make it hard for a reader to obtain a copy of your reference. Unless you are reasonably certain that a publication is available, it is unwise to list it as a reference.

5-3.3.6. UNPUBLISHED REFERENCES

Do not include unpublished works in a reference list. Unless a publication is off the press and some copies are available, your readers will not be able to obtain copies for their own use, and the whole purpose of your reference will be defeated. There is a strong temptation to refer to publications that your colleagues are working on at the same time that you are preparing your report. Although it is reasonable to assume that the reports or papers will be completed, they still do not exist in fact; and, unfortunately, circumstances change at the last moment just often enough so that sooner or later you will include a publication that never sees the light of day. When this happens, you start a chain of queries from readers to publishers and authors, followed by explanations as to why the report is not available, that will go on as long as your report is used. Even when another report is actually being processed, it is best to exclude it from your reference list.

When it is necessary for you to refer to an unpublished report, article, or book, give the information in a footnote (see Section 4-1.4.3) and mention that it is "in process." In such a note, it is best to indicate the subject of the proposed publication rather than to show a precise title, because the title may be changed.

5-3.3.7. Secondhand References

When you list a reference, it is assumed that you have, in fact, used that reference in gathering the information or background material for your report. Always take the bibliographic information for your entry from the title page of a copy of the publication that you intend to list—do not take it secondhand from some other source. From time to time, an author will draw on abstract journals or similar listings for the data necessary to prepare an entry for his reference list. With very little effort, it is possible by this process to prepare a long and impressive list. It is not a sound policy, however, even if you have used the publication but neglected to record the data. The danger, of course, is that an error was made by the person who prepared the list you are using and that you will copy and perpetuate this error. Frequently, too, you will be forced to use a defective entry, because the man before you did not supply all of the information that should be given. Also, avoid the practice of reading one report and incorporating all of the publications referred to there as part of your own list, unless you verify for yourself that they are worth mentioning.

□ NOTE

When you prepare an entry for a reference list, be sure to take all of the bibliographic information from the title page of an actual copy of the publication. Do not trust information obtained by someone else by using a secondhand reference. □

5-3.4. Format

There are many different formats for reference lists in use by reputable publishers today, and each can be justified; but because there are many, it is impossible to say that one is right and all others are wrong. They differ mainly in matters of punctuation, order of items, and selection of type faces. Any organization that does considerable publishing of reports will have established a style that best suits its needs. If you work for such an organization, you need only to learn that style and follow it. If, however, you are publishing your own reports or are working in an organization that has no set style, you must decide upon a format of your own.

Fundamentally, the basic principle is to be sure that you supply all of the information that a reader will require in order to obtain a copy of the item. This material has been discussed in Section 5-3.2. If you do not wish to get involved in deciding whether to use a comma, a period, a semicolon, or a colon at a given point in the entry, you will not go wrong if you simply string the data out, item by item, and insert a comma after each item; for example:

> Hunt, K. W. and R. W. Lucas, "Tests of Navy Bureau of Ordnance Rocket Models," Northrop Aircraft, Inc., Hawthorne, Calif., April 1947, Report No. A-WTM-18, Unclassified.

or

> Mayo, Elton, "The Social Problems of an Industrial Civilization," Division of Research, Graduate School of Business Administration, Harvard University, Boston, 1945, 150 pp.

Although your readers would have no difficulty in obtaining copies of these publications from the entries as they stand, a few minor changes would make it even easier for them. It is useful to group some of the items, as follows: the authors, the title, and any facts about editions, parts, or revisions in the first group; the name of the publisher, the place of publication, and the date of publication in the second group; and all other information in a third group. In addition, if you put the name of the publication in italics (underscored in typewriter typography), you make it stand out from the other data in the entry so that it can be seen immediately by the readers. The entries given above would then appear as follows:

Hunt, K. W. and R. W. Lucas, *Tests of Navy Bureau of Ordnance Rocket Models.* Northrop Aircraft, Inc., Hawthorne, Calif., April 1947. Report No. A-WTM-18, Unclassified.

and

Mayo, Elton, *The Social Problems of an Industrial Civilization.* Division of Research, Graduate School of Business Administration, Harvard University, Boston, 1945. 150 pp.

The order in which the data are given in these two examples is fairly standard and logical, and is recommended for use. The name of the author is given first because publications are normally catalogued and filed according to authors, and therefore this is the information that is needed first when a reader begins his search.

However, the entries in a reference list appear in the order in which they are mentioned in the text—not alphabetically by authors, so it is not necessary to give the name of the author first for purposes of making the list. Some organizations, therefore, place the title of the publication first on the theory that it is the item of primary interest to the reader in deciding whether or not he wants to see a copy. The entries would then take the following form:

Tests of Navy Bureau of Ordnance Rocket Models, by K. W. Hunt and R. W. Lucas. Northrop Aircraft, Inc., Hawthorne, Calif., April 1947. Report No. A-WTM-18, Unclassified.

and

The Social Problems of an Industrial Civilization, by Elton Mayo. Division of Research, Graduate School of Business Administration, Harvard University, Boston, 1945. 150 pp.

When an entry begins with the name of the author, give the surname of the senior author first, followed by a comma, and then his initials. Give the names of additional authors in normal order (initials preceding the surname), because nothing can be accomplished by inverting the order. For an author who has two or more given names, use only the initials. If an author has only one given name, however, spell it out as insurance against two authors having given names beginning with the same initial. Include such abbreviations as "Jr." when an author has used them on the title page of his report.

When two or more titles by the same author appear in sequence, substitute a solid line 1 inch long for the name of the author in the second and all following entries. This line takes the place of everything in the second entry that is identical with that in the first entry.

When you cite an article or paper that was published in a journal, in proceedings, or in some other larger publication, show the title of the article in quotation marks and the title of the publication in which it appears in italics, thus:

1. Speyer, Edward, "Interference Spherometer," *Rev. Sci. Instruments,* Vol. 14. Nov. 1934, pp. 336-38.
2. Textor, C. K., "Wood-Fiber Production With Revolving Disk Mills," *Forest Prod. Res. Soc. Proc. for 1948,* pp. 89-99.

Each reference is listed only once in a reference list, regardless of the number of times that it is cited in the text. The same index number is used to relate a text statement to an entry in the list each time that it is cited.

Except for the title of the publication listed (which should be given in full exactly as it appears in the original publication), bibliographic data are abbreviated as much as is possible without making them obscure or unintelligible. The names of states and the months of the year can be abbreviated. If you are in doubt about an abbreviation, follow the style given in your dictionary. Such words as "Incorporated" and "Company" are abbreviated to "Inc." and "Co.," but avoid abbreviations of the names of industrial organizations—several companies may have similar abbreviations.

Although it is common practice to refer to various universities, colleges, and government activities by initials that are virtually symbols (for example, ARPA, NASA, NOTS, NOLC, NRL), such symbols should not be used unexplained in reference lists. Consider the confusion that arises from the use of "CIT," which variously stands for California Institute of Technology, Carnegie Institute of Technology, and Case Institute of Technology. It is also better to use "Univ. of Wis." rather than "UW," which might mean University of Washington or University of Wyoming, as well as University of Wisconsin. The names of journals, magazines, proceedings, and similar publications are customarily abbreviated whenever possible. Some useful abbreviations that indicate acceptable forms are as follows:

Acad.	academy	Jour.	journal
Agr.	agriculture, agricultural	Lab.	laboratory
Am.	American	Lit.	literary
Anal.	analytical	Mag.	magazine
Ann.	annual	Math.	mathematical, etc.
Assoc.	association	Mem.	memoir, memorandum
Biol.	biologic, etc.	Met.	metallurgical
Bot.	botanic, etc.	Micr.	microscopic
Bull.	bulletin	Min.	mineral, mining
Bur.	bureau	Misc.	miscellaneous
Chem.	chemical, etc.	Mon.	monograph
Coll.	college	Mtn.	mountain
Comm.	commission, committee	Mus.	museum
Cong.	congress	Nat.	natural, national
Cons.	conservation	Pamph.	pamphlet
Dept.	department	Philos.	philosophical
Devel.	development	Polytech.	polytechnic, etc.
Div.	division	Proc.	proceedings
Econ.	economic	Prof.	professional
Eng.	engineers, engineering	Pub.	publication
Exper.	experiment	Quart.	quarterly
Fac.	faculty	Rec.	record
Gen.	general	Rept.	report
Geog.	geographic, etc.	Rev.	review
Geol.	geologic, etc.	Sci.	science, scientific
Govt.	government	Ser.	series
Hist.	historical, etc.	Soc.	society
Ind.	industrial, etc.	Sta.	station
Inf.	information	Tech.	technical, etc.
Inst.	institute, institution	Trans.	transactions
		Univ.	university
		U.S.	United States
		Vol.	volume
		Zool.	zoological, etc.

5-4. BIBLIOGRAPHIES

5-4.1. Purpose

A bibliography is a list of publications that relate to the subjects covered in your report and that may or may not have been cited in the text. If your readers would benefit from reading supporting or collateral material or would understand your discussions better if they had additional background, include a bibliography as the last section of your report.

If you do not cite in the text of your report any of the publications listed in the bibliography, there is no need to number the entries. If you cite one or more of the entries, however, number all of them so that you may refer to them by number and the readers will be able to locate them in the listing.

5-4.2. Format

Since not all of the entries in a bibliography are cited in the text, the normal method is to list them alphabetically by the surnames of the authors. For this reason, the name of the first author is inverted. Follow each surname with a comma and the author's initials. Enter names of additional authors in normal order with the initials preceding the surname; for example:

> Sherman, T. A., *Modern Technical Writing*. Prentice-Hall, Inc., New York, 1955.

or

> Walker, Helen M. and W. N. Durost, *Statistical Tables, Their Structure and Use*. Bureau of Publications, Teachers College, Columbia Univ., New York, 1936.

or

> Arkin, Herbert and R. R. Colton, *Graphs, How To Make and Use Them*. Harper & Brothers, New York, 1940.

Note that when an author has only one given name, it is spelled out, but if he has more than one, only the initials are used. If the author is a woman, her first name is spelled out regardless of whether or not she has more than one given name.

The entries in a long bibliography may be divided into groups by subjects to assist the reader in locating publications that are of special interest to him. For example, in his book entitled *The Economics of Transportation in America* (The Ronald Press Co., New York, 1940), K. T. Healy has grouped the bibliographic entries under the following subjects: Early History, Railroads, Street Railways and Urban Transit, Highway Transportation, Air Transpotation, and Current Periodicals.

In the comparatively short bibliography found in most technical reports, however, there is no need to separate the entries into groups because the reader can make his selection by merely scanning the list.

In all other respects, the techniques of preparing a bibliography are the same as those recommended for the preparation of a list of references. See Section 5-3 for detailed suggestions.

5-5. SUBJECT INDEXES

5-5.1. When to Use a Subject Index

An index in a technical report is the exception rather than the rule. Most reports proceed in an orderly fashion from one subject to another until they come to the end—the author does not discuss the same subject in a number of places, nor does he refer in one section to an item mentioned in another section. The table of contents, therefore, serves adequately to help a reader find the information that he is looking for.

In addition, most research and development reports are reasonably short—75 pages or less, many of only 20 or 30 pages. In such short reports, the table of contents will normally lead a user to within a page or two of the item he is seeking and quick scanning will bring him to the specific paragraph that he wants. Again, there is no need for an index.

In a long report, however, one in which the same subject is mentioned in a number of places, or one that covers a large number of subjects (as a catalog), a subject index can be helpful to the readers. This is especially true if the report is to be used as a reference work.

A subject index is a listing arranged in alphabetical order of the various subjects that the report covers. Each subject is accompanied by the number of the page or pages on which it is mentioned. Primary subjects are listed alphabetically, and these are subdivided into subordinate categories when such a breakdown will be of assistance to the readers.

The most critical problem in preparing a subject index is the selection of subjects to be indexed. A carefully prepared index can be a distinct addition to a report and may be the determining factor in whether or not it is used as fully as the author intended it to be.

5-5.2. Selection of Subject Headings

Since the choice of the subjects to be indexed is of primary importance, you must give careful consideration to each entry. The first step is to select major headings. Flag these subjects immediately after you have completed the final draft. Arrange them in alphabetical order and type them in columns on 8½- by 11-inch paper. At this point in the preparation of your report, you will be most familiar with its contents and able to recognize any gaps in your list of major subjects. However, this is not the time to paginate your list of entries.

When—and only when—your report is in final form, you can proceed with the detailed indexing. If your report is to be in typewriter typography, you cannot do any indexing until after the final typing. Because you should not mark the reproduction copy, have your typist make a carbon copy, or have a copy made by some office duplicating process.

☐ NOTE

Do not make a detailed listing of index entries until your report is in final form. Listing of entries by pages before the final pages have been set results in chaos from which you may never recover. ☐

Make a separate reading of the report for the sole purpose of selecting all items to be indexed. This is a step that cannot be combined with any other if you expect it to be complete. Check each item in the text with a colored pencil. Then begin again at the beginning of the report and prepare a 3- by 5-inch card for each entry that you have marked. Depending upon the length and complexity of your report, you will have several hundred or even several thousand cards. Cards for major subject headings that do not have subheadings would appear as follows:

HANGAR CONSTRUCTION 9

HEAT-BARRIER MATERIALS 37

HEAT-TRANSFER STUDIES   38

HOUSING   10

Cards for subheadings should be related to your major headings as shown in the sample below:

INSTRUMENTATION
  ballistic test equipment   180

INSTRUMENTATION
  cameras, tracking   233

INSTRUMENTATION
  cinetheodolite evaluation   246

When you have a card for each item that you checked, sort them into alphabetical order. Items that are mentioned several times in your report will have several cards that differ only in the page numbers. Replace each of these groups with a single card identified by the item with all of the pages on which it is mentioned listed in numerical order. Number each card from 1 to 1,000 or more when you have sorted them into the final order.

□ NOTE

There is always the danger that a file of cards may be dropped or otherwise disarranged; if your file is numbered, you will not have to re-sort the cards when this happens.   □

Next, edit the numbered cards in order to eliminate unnecessary words. Index entries should be as brief as possible but still intelligible. On cards with subheadings under major headings, cross out the major headings; they have served their purpose of identifying subheadings and will not be repeated for each subheading. Eliminate unnecessary prepositions and articles. Indicate the order (value) of the entry on each card; that is, first-, second-, or third-order heading. This can be most easily done by using a color code, such as black for first-order entries, red for second, and green for third. Mark a red numeral 2 on each card intended to be a second-order entry, and a green numeral 3 on each card intended to be a third-order entry. Other devices in use are to mark an em quad (□) before each second-order entry and a double em quad (□□) before a third-order entry or to place a single dot before a second- and a double dot before a third-order entry.

When the cards have been sorted into final order and edited, your index is complete, but it may not yet be in final manuscript form. The file of cards will serve as manuscript if you are working closely with the typist or compositor who is setting final copy for you. For typed reports, you can usually give the cards to your typist, and she can work directly from them. If you can personally deliver your file of cards to your printer, the linotype operator may be able to use them for manuscript. This needs to be worked out with your printer, for it depends upon the skill and experience of the operator. When you are working with a printer who is at some distance from you so that you will have to mail the manuscript to him, it is best to copy the entries from the cards in column form on 8½- by 11-inch paper (one column only), with the proper indentions clearly indicated for the subentries and the sub-subentries. Proofread this manuscript against the card file with great care.

5-5.3. Problems in Indexing

This section contains suggestions for handling some types of entries that cause trouble for the inexperienced indexer. No attempt is made to give all possible solutions, because there may be several in use by leading publishers, each of which adequately serves its purpose. These suggestions, however, are defensible, workable, and in use today. Entire books have been written on the art of indexing (see the Bibliography). If your report is unusually complicated and you do not have the services of a professional indexer, study one of these books before you prepare your index.

1. Entries consisting of *letter symbols* (ARPA, NOTS, NASA, AAA, etc.) should be listed at the beginning of the entries under the first letter of the symbol.

2. Entries beginning with *numerals* should be alphabetized according to the letters in the first word of the entry after the numerals (that is, disregard the numerals in alphabetizing).

3. Names beginning with *Mac, Mc, O', von,* etc., should be listed where they would normally fall among the other entries rather than grouped at the beginning of the entries under each letter.

4. Entries should not be comprised of *adjectives* only. To justify indexing, an entry should include a noun or its equivalent.

5. *Cross references* should be used to eliminate repetition of entries. For example, you might have as entries "Concrete, aggregates for" and "Aggregates for concrete." Under the first you could list the various aggregates discussed in your report; then, following the second, you would write *"see* Concrete, aggregates for."

6. *See also* references can be useful to your readers when you suspect that they will be interested in reading discussions on collateral subjects. For example, after an entry of "Fungi, control by eliminating host" you might write *"see also* Fungicides."

7. *Page numbers* may be placed immediately after the entries but separated from them by commas, or they may be aligned at the right-hand edge of the column with a row of leaders between each entry and the corresponding number.

8. *Greek letters* preceding the first word of an entry should be ignored. For example, "β-trinitrotoluene" would be listed under the letter "T".

9. In arranging your list, *alphabetize* the entries on a *letter-by-letter basis,* rather than on a word-by-word basis. Thus, entries would fall in this order: a, ab, aba, abab, abbb, ac, aca, acad, etc.

10. *Phrases* should be edited so that the key word is placed first and the entry is listed according to that word; for example, "Hulls, fabrication of"—not "Fabrication of hulls."

5-6. GLOSSARIES

5-6.1. Purpose

A glossary is a partial dictionary in which special terms are listed alphabetically and defined or explained. It is a useful adjunct to a report that contains a number of words your readers may not understand. A glossary may be needed because you wish to be understood in a restricted sense, because you have had to create a new terminology, or because you are writing for readers who are outside your specialty.

Although, in general, it is best not to use too many terms that will be unfamiliar to your readers, there are times when to restrict yourself to simple terms known by all possible readers will be so unnatural that your report will lose all interest to your primary audience. In this situation, write in the language of your field and supply a glossary for the use of those who are not familiar with it.

If you have only a few terms (less than ten, for instance) that need to be explained, a separate glossary may not be justified. Instead, you can define the terms in parenthetical statements inserted in the text at the points where they occur. Or you can actually incorporate the definitions into the text and, by doing so, make certain that they are not overlooked by the readers.

If the definitions are long, however, they tend to distract the readers, particularly those who are already familiar with the terms. This problem can be solved by defining the terms in footnotes at the bottom of the pages where they occur. While these methods are satisfactory when you are concerned with only a few terms, it is best to prepare a glossary when you have ten or more definitions.

5-6.2. How To Prepare a Glossary

It is most satisfactory to prepare the glossary as a separate step after your manuscript has been completed. Read your report through and record on 3- by 5-inch cards each word or term that you think requires special definition or explanation. Then sort the cards into alphabetical order, eliminating all duplications.

To each card add the proper definition or explanation. Be sure that you use in these definitions only words that your readers can reasonably be expected to know. Then copy the list from the cards onto manuscript paper.

5-6.3. Format

The terms being defined should be set off typographically from the definitions. One method of doing this is illustrated in Fig. 5-2. Other styles are satisfactory, as long as the terms stand out on the page and are easily found by the users. If the list is long, separate

<u>GLOSSARY</u>

Cross break
  To place the grain of layers of wood at right angles in order to
  minimize shrinking and swelling and consequent warping; also the
  layer of veneer at right angles to the face plies.

Cross grain
  (See grain)

Cup
  The distortion of a board in which the face is convex or concave
  transversely.

Decay
  Disintegration of wood substance through the action of wood-
  destroying fungi.

Defect
  Any irregularity occurring in or on wood that may lower its strength.

Density
  The mass of a body per unit volume. When expressed in the c.g.s.
  system, it is numerically equal to the specific gravity of the
  same substance.

Density rule
  Rules for estimating the density of wood based on percentage of
  summer wood and rate of growth.

Diagonal grain
  (See grain)

Diamond
  A distortion in drying that causes a piece of wood originally
  rectangular in cross section to become diamond shaped.

Diffuse-porous woods
  Hardwoods in which the pores are practically uniform in size
  throughout each angular ring, or decrease slightly toward the
  outer border of the ring.

Dote
  "Dote," "doze," and "rot" are synonymous with "decay," and are
  any form of decay which may be evident as either a discoloration
  or a softening of the wood.

43

Figure 5-2. Typical glossary. The terms are set off typographically from the definitions. Prepare the definitions in words that your readers are sure to understand. (Definitions taken from *Wood Handbook* by Forest Products Laboratory, Forest Service, USDA, Washington, D.C., 1940.)

the terms into groups by first letters. As a final step, review the list and delete any terms that appear unnecessary.

A glossary is usually part of the supplementary matter and is located after the appendixes but ahead of the bibliography. Occasionally, however, it should be situated early in the report, either as part of the front matter or immediately after the introduction. This is useful when you know that a majority of your readers are unfamiliar with your terms and that you must define them early or your text will not be understood.

In a formal report, begin your glossary on a page of its own, rather than at the end of a page with other material on it.

5-7. ABSTRACT CARDS

5-7.1. Purpose

Abstract cards printed on card stock or other heavy paper and bound into reports provide useful tools for the individual report user as well as for librarians. These cards, which are designed to fit into 3- by 5-inch card files, can be printed four to a page; some organizations include two identical pages of abstracts in a report, thereby making eight copies available for each addressee.

Individual readers usually file these cards in subject-matter files in their desks or some equally handy place. Each user can thus build up his file of abstracts tailored to his own needs. Since no two men work in quite the same way, such individualized subject-matter files prove to be extremely useful. It is also possible for a man to add comments of his own to cards in his private file, indicating the quality, coverage, detail, authoritativeness, and other characteristics of each report to aid him in selecting the most profitable reports to review when he needs information in a special area of his work.

Libraries require several cards, depending upon the local policies. For instance, they may file cards on one report in subject-matter files, author files, company or organization files, and serial-number files. If there are several authors, a library may file a card under each. If a report deals with more than one subject, a card may be filed under each major subject.

Since it is far more economical to reproduce these cards on a printing press than to force each of the users to copy the information by hand, include the cards in reports whenever possible.

5-7.2. Content

The problem is to produce abstract cards that will be used. Individual scientists, engineers, and administrators tend to file the cards in whatever form they may appear. But there is no such willingness among librarians to accept different styles of abstract cards, and they often re-do them. Nor is there yet any agreement among librarians as to the most desirable format for abstract cards. Nonetheless, abstract card users are drawing closer together in their demands.

In general, an abstract card should contain all of the bibliographic information needed for quick and easy retrieval of the document to which it refers. It should also contain an adequate abstract of the information contained in the report so that the potential user can determine whether or not he wants the report. If the capsule information that can be included in an abstract serves to refresh the user's memory on a particular point, he may be able to use only the card, and not need to recall the full report.

In addition to the bibliographic information and the abstract, an increasing number of abstract cards contain lists of suggested descriptors to aid those who intend to file cards in more than one subject-matter file. These are useful and can save a great deal of time for librarians who would otherwise be forced to scan the report to decide upon the proper descriptors.

5-7.3. Format

Typical abstract cards are shown in Fig. 5-3. If your organization does not have an established format for these cards, you may use one of the cards shown in the figure as a guide, or decide upon your own variation. The following features are pointed out for your special consideration.

More and more the face (or front) of each card is being divided into two portions, as shown in Fig. 5-3. This permits the descriptors to be shown on the right side, where they can be readily seen. These are located far enough down on the card to leave space for the librarians to add their particular code markings.

The bibliographic information appears at the top of the left portion on the front of the card. The order of this information is not set, but a typical listing is shown.

Since abstract cards are frequently secured in drawers by means

Naval Research Laboratory. Report 5277
INFRARED DISPERSION AND THE DETERMINATION OF ABSORPTION
COEFFICIENTS, by R. E. Kagarise. 20 pp. and figs.
March 23, 1959

1. Organic liquids--
   Refractive index

I. Kagarise, R. E.

    The retroactive indices of liquid carbon tetrachlo-
ride, tetrachloroethylene, methylene iodide and acetone
have been measured using the interferometric method.
In the case of the latter three compounds, the orders
of interference were established by studying the materials dissolved in CS_2. By gradually increasing the
concentration of solute, it was possible to extrapolate
the known orders of interference in CS_2 to the pure
solute.
    The dispersion in the neighborhood of the 13μ ab-
sorption band of CCl_4 and the 9μ band of CH_2I_2 has been
analyzed in terms of classical dispersion theory. The
so-called oscillator strengths obtained from such analyses were found to be in good agreement with those obtained directly from integrated absorption coefficients.
                                                   (over)

    Finally, it has been shown that the two classical dispersion equations can
be used to predict the ratio of the integrated absorption coefficients for the
liquid and vapor states. The expression thus obtained is identical to that
obtained by Polo and Wilson using a different approach.

Figure 5-3. Typical abstract card. Bibliographic information is
placed at the top left. Descriptors are listed at the right side of the
front of the card.

of metal rods, it is useful to print the fronts and backs of the cards in the manner known as "head to foot"; that is, the top of the front of the card is at the same edge as the bottom of the back of the card. This style permits the card to be read from one position without removing it from the file.

6

Variations of Reports

6-1. SHORT-FORM REPORTS

6-1.1. Comparison with Long-Form Reports

In principle, the short-form report serves the same ends as a long-form report. Its readers fall into the same classes, and, with the possible exception of serving to record information for future use, it may be put to the same uses as the long-form report.

Usually, however, the information that it contains is less permanent. It is more often used to transmit information to readers in increments as quickly as it is available. Frequently, the contents of a number of short reports issued during the progress of a project are gathered together at a later date and published in a long-form report, which can be given the editorial and typographical care justified by a report that will remain in the literature for some years.

Speed and low cost are the outstanding advantages of the short-form report. Although there is no definite line that separates long-form and short-form reports, it is convenient to consider 10 pages as the limit of the short-form report. In reports that have more pages, the formality of the long-form report is useful. With a short-form report, however, all of the steps of report preparation are simplified, including the writing, reviewing, illustrating, and reproduction. When you have information that you must distribute as soon as possible, or when you have limited funds, the short-form report fills your needs best.

Short-form reports should be planned with the same care as long-form reports. The planning takes less time, however, because there is less information to be considered. But, just as with all other types of reports, the short-form report should be designed to be put to a particular use by a particular group of readers, and an outline should be prepared before the writing is begun (see Section 2-3).

□ NOTE

Since short-form reports should be prepared with as little delay as possible, it is important that you reach complete agreement with your line reviewers as to the purpose of your report before you start to write. Do not waste effort. □

6-1.2. Usual Parts of a Short-Form Report

6-1.2.1. FRONT MATTER

Keep the front matter of a short-form report to a minimum. A title page is usually all that is necessary. Unless you expect the report to get rough handling, you need not use covers; if you do require covers, it is best to use preprinted window covers or plain covers on which the title information can be added with a typed label.

If you use a title page, you may want to back it up with a brief foreword or preface. It is equally effective, however, to place the title page information at the top of the first page of text (see Fig. 6-1). Thus the title, the name of the author, and the name of the organization appear at the top of the page. Immediately below them you may place a brief abstract; this should be only a few lines, because the entire report will have only a few primary points to make.

An acknowledgment, if you need one, may be placed in a footnote to the name of the senior author on the first page (see Fig. 6-1).

A table of contents is not necessary in a short-form report. Such a table indicates the pattern of a report to a potential reader and keys special sections for the benefit of the person who uses the report as a reference work (see Section 3-8). These ends can be achieved

THE EXPLOSIVE PRESS AS A RESEARCH
TOOL IN MATERIAL BEHAVIOR AND
FORMING

by Edward W. LaRocca*
and John Pearson

Weapon Development Department
U.S. Naval Ordnance Test Station

ABSTRACT

Small, explosively activated presses have been used as
research tools in the study of the behavior of powdered materials under impulsive loads. Both single- and double-action
presses have provided positive retention of the test specimen.
The double-action press, which is of sandwich-type construction,
uses two explosive charges fired simultaneously to drive two
opposed pistons together into a central steel cylinder in which
the specimen material has been placed. Estimates of the pressures that can be obtained are on the order of several million
pounds per square inch. By modifying the working faces of the
pistons, materials can be formed into various shapes by the
actions of the press. Operation of these presses and their
application to the study of several materials are described.

INTRODUCTION

Explosive charges have been used for a number of years to study the
effect of impulsive loads on the behavior of metals (Ref. 1). Internally
loaded cylinders, metal-explosive sandwiches, externally loaded rods,
and the like have been used to study stress waves, fracturing, plastic
flow, and other features. In most of these studies, the explosive charge
has been placed in close contact with the specimen. This technique lends
itself to those cases where the specimen is fairly large so that recovery
is not a serious problem. On the other hand, materials that are in a
lowdered form or materials where only small samples are available are
difficult to study because of the lack of specimen recovery.

To overcome the recovery problems that exist for most metal-explosive
systems and still retain the inherent simplicity for generating high

---

*The authors wish to acknowledge the assistance given by L. A. Burkhardt
of this Station.

Figure 6-1. Page 1 of a typical short-form report. This page includes the material normally found on the title page, abstract
page, acknowledgment page, and page 1 of a long-form report.
The abstract is made to stand out from the text by setting it in
slightly different format (here it is set in narrow measure). By
combining four pages into one, you can achieve a marked saving
in processing time.

by simply thumbing through the few pages of a short-form report; a table of contents, adding to the bulk unnecessarily, hinders the use of the report.

6-1.2.2. BODY OF THE REPORT

A short-form report should have an opening section and a closing section, but these should be brief—a few paragraphs, instead of the several pages in a long-form report. The remainder of the report proper should also follow the same pattern as that of a long-form report, but again the sections should be brief. You may, for example, have sections on materials, equipment, procedures, and results, followed by a section in which you discuss these results.

You should use headings in a short-form report, even if you have only a few pages. The heading structure is not so complicated, however, as it is in a long-form report; one or two orders of headings are adequate to take care of most situations.

6-1.2.3. SUPPLEMENTARY MATTER

Appendixes are seldom used in short-form reports, and rather than listing any special nomenclature or definitions separately, you can explain them in the text as they occur. Bulky tables of data or pages of graphs detract from the advantages of this style of report and tend to convert it into a long-form report. Occasionally, you may want to take a mathematical derivation from the text and put it in a short appendix in order to leave the main thread of your report clear, but it should be only a page or two.

You may need a list of references or a short bibliography in a short-form report. The references are normally listed on the last page after the report proper, rather than on a separate page, in order to conserve space. It is even possible that you can give your references as bibliographical footnotes (see Section 4-1.4.3) placed at the bottom of the pages on which they are mentioned.

Abstract cards serve the same purpose for a short-form report as for a long-form report and should be included (see Section 5-7).

A distribution list, if required, can begin on the last page of the text; or, if you are using covers, the list can be placed on the inside of the back cover.

☐ NOTE

The guiding principle throughout the preparation of a short-form report should be to conserve space wherever possible. If you can save a page, do so.   ☐

6-1.3. Illustrations in Short-Form Reports

The modern trend in short-form reports is to make as much use of illustrations as possible to cut down on the amount of text that is needed. Unretouched photographs are especially useful to aid in the description of test setups and to show actual test results. They are inexpensive and can usually be quickly produced.

Reproduction of photographs in quantity, however, requires photo-offset reproduction facilities, so include only photographs that help to get across your message. Never use a frontispiece in a short-form report, and do not use two pictures where one will do; illustrations always add to the cost of a report and to the time required to produce it.

Line drawings, which can be made rapidly and easily, are useful. Virtually all engineers and many scientists have had training in drafting and are capable of preparing quite acceptable line drawings themselves if they do not have the support of draftsmen or illustrators. Line drawings have the added advantage of being reproducible on diazo process machines in limited quantities—usually sufficient for short-run reports. If they are not too elaborate, they can even be drawn on stencils or hectograph masters and reproduced economically and rapidly.

The time and expense required to prepare airbrush drawings usually precludes their use in short-form reports. Sometimes such drawings are available because they have been prepared for another purpose, but do not delay the release of a short report in order to include a specially prepared airbrush drawing.

6-1.4. Repeating Patterns in Short-Form Reports

Short-form reports released at frequent stages in a long project often follow identical patterns. For example, a series of tests might be made in which the test equipment and test procedures varied only slightly as a series of similar items were tested. The customer, however, might very well want to learn as quickly as possible how each material fared in the program. In this situation, the pattern of all of the short-form reports would be the same; once it was determined for the first test, it could be used again each time. Frequently, you can actually set up and preprint pages that are the equivalent of forms on which the headings are already printed (see Fig. 4-1). On these, it is necessary only to fill in the information that is pertinent to the particular test, add photoprints of a figure or two, and the report is completed. When you are producing a series of short-form reports, it is not necessary to change the plan just for the sake of variety. But preprinted forms can be dangerous.

□ NOTE

Never try to force a report into a predetermined plan that was not developed to accomplish the specific purpose that you have in mind. There is no single plan that can be used for all reports. Make your plan suit your need.   □

6-1.5. Format Suggestions

The format of short-form reports should be as simple as possible, in order to hold processing time to a minimum. The arrangement best suited to this type of report is to place all the text first, followed by all the tables, and finally by all the illustrations. With relatively few pages, the reader has no difficulty in referring to tables and illustrations, even though they are grouped at the end of the text.

Under usual circumstances, place each figure on a page of its own without attempting to combine text and figures on the same page. Cut-in figures or combinations of figures and text increase the processing time, thereby adding to the time and expense of production. When two or more small figures follow in sequence, however, they may be combined on one page with no additional effort.

Whereas long-form reports are normally bound on the left side (by staples or fasteners), is is often useful to bind short-form reports at the top when they are printed or typed on only one side of the page. If your report consists of only a few pages, a single staple in the upper left corner will be adequate.

Short-form reports are generally prepared on a typewriter. Greek letters and other symbols not found on standard typewriters can be inserted by hand. Although this is not so attractive as other methods of composition, it is satisfactory for reports with limited distribution that are to be reproduced by carbon copies or on office duplicating machines. Cold-type or hot-type composition takes considerably longer to prepare and requires more elaborate methods of reproduction. Do not attempt to justify (align) the right-hand margins of the text in short-form reports—again, in order to save time.

6-2. PROGRESS REPORTS

6-2.1. Purpose

A progress report is a history of an undertaking over a fixed period of time. It is written for a specific group of readers, normally at the request of these readers. The subjects covered in a progress report have usually been agreed upon by the author and the readers, as has the period covered by the report.

The purpose of a progress report is to inform the readers of advances that have been made in a project from the time of the preceding report until a specific date. It serves as a vehicle to keep management informed of the latest developments in a program and makes possible intelligent decision by management in matters of money, manpower, equipment, and materials. Assuming that a project is intended to accomplish certain results in a predetermined time or for a fixed amount of money, it is imperative that the men with primary responsibility for the success of the project know whether or not it is progressing according to plan. Only if they are fully informed, can they make such decisions as moving up equipment that will be needed for the next step, adding more men to the force, bringing in men of different talents, or supplying additional funds.

Because the progress report is an essential tool, as vital to the success of a project as men or materials, it is mandatory that it be prepared with complete honesty.

□ NOTE

When you report progress, show only progress that has actually occurred by the end of the period covered. Under no circumstances should you attempt to mislead the readers. To act wisely, management must have a completely accurate picture of your project. □

Any progress report is but one of a continuing series of reports that does not end until the project is completed. Together, the individual reports make up a history of the entire project.

6-2.2. Content

It is useful to relate the current progress to the general status of the work by including an introductory section. The extent and detail of this first section depends upon the readers and the degree of their familiarity with the work. Describe the previous work in the past perfect tense: "These things had been done before the beginning of the reporting period." In this section you remind the readers of the purpose of the project, the steps that had previously been taken, and the accomplishments that had already been made.

The basic—and longest—portion of a progress report is a description of the activities within the limits of the reporting period. Write this section in the past tense: "These things happened."

In most circumstances it is wise to let your readers know the direction of your work by telling them something of your plans for the future. Such plans should be discussed in the future tense: "We shall do these things in the next period if all goes well."

□ NOTE

Avoid stating categorically that something "will be done" in the next period or by a certain date. Too many things can happen to upset your plans, even at the last moment. Instead, state that you intend, or plan, or expect to do something, or that something is scheduled to happen by a given date.   □

The outline of a progress report should be carefully worked out in advance by you and the men to whom you are reporting. Normally, it is built around the project plan, subdivided in such a way that the reader can determine immediately how closely the work is following the plan. Figure 6-2 is a simple progress report; it has within it all of the elements of a satisfactory progress report. Reports vary from this one-page report to full-scale books of several hundred pages, but they are all constructed on the same principle.

Progress reports can be divided into short-form and long-form reports in the same manner as other types of reports. The short-form progress reports may actually be so stylized that they simply require

GREAT NORTHERN DREDGE & DOCK COMPANY

Milwaukee, Wisconsin

Job No. 1876　　　　　　Place: Ludington, Michigan　　　　Superintendent: T. S. Severson

CUMULATIVE DAILY PROGRESS REPORT

Job started: May 1, 1960　　　　　　　　　　　Schedule completion date: 1 November 1960

Date	Piles		Timbers		Tie rods	Excava-tion, yd.	Back-fill, yd.	Remarks
	60'	40'	12 x 12	2 x 12				
May 1	—	12	—	—	—	6000	—	Drove first pile at 2:00 p.m.
2	—	46	—	—	—	6250	—	—
3	—	42	—	—	—	5900	—	Will start timber crew tomorrow
4	16	23	86	—	—	6120	—	—
5	30	—	110	60	10	3000	—	Rain and high wind. Shut down 2 hours.
6	38	—	94	50	8	5600	—	Rain stopped Wind continued
7	43	—	102	64	16	5850	2000	—
Total	127	123	392	174	34	38,720	2000	

Figure 6-2. Typical one-page progress report. This report contains all the elements needed in a progress report. It identifies the job, shows daily progress in important areas of work, and allows comments that might influence future planning by the man on the job.

filling in a preprinted form day after day, with the progress indicated quantitatively, as so many cubic yards of concrete poured or so many board feet of lumber used. There is very little that the compiler of such reports can do to vary them. These are not very imaginative reports, however, and they give the readers a minimum of information. Interpretation of the facts is often as valuable to management as the facts themselves. The man on the job is in a better position than anyone else to analyze the implications of variations in progress. He is also in a position to make specific recommendations, based upon the information in the report. Even the daily routine report is a more satisfactory vehicle if it is designed to permit the author to comment on the progress shown whenever he believes that such comments are justified.

A great many projects are served best by a series of progress reports prepared on a monthly or biweekly basis. These cover a period long enough for some progress to have been made, yet they are sufficiently frequent for the reader to keep up to date on the project. They normally have the following parts:

Cover	Progress (subdivided to give a major section to each major item in
Title page	the project plan)
Introduction and background	Future plans

The cover and title page may be one item. Note that the short-form progress report does not include an abstract, since the title itself is all the abstract that is needed. Because the report is short, neither a table of contents nor an index is necessary. Reference to other publications should be made in bibliographic footnotes, rather than in a separate bibliography. It is assumed that your readers are completely familiar with your subject, so there is no need for a glossary and rarely a need for a list of nomenclature.

One of the major problems in the short-form progress reports is fast production. This type of report enables management to make rapid adjustments to compensate for deviations from the project plan or to accommodate new developments in the project. This can be done only if the necessary information reaches the managers shortly after it takes place. Production of the report, therefore, becomes a serious problem. It is best to work out a set pattern for your reports and to follow it from period to period. Review procedures that will keep the production line moving should be agreed upon.

□ NOTE

Alternates for writers and reviewers of short-form progress reports should be designated in advance, so that absence of one or the other will not delay the report production. Processing schedules must be maintained exactly if the reports are to be successful. □

Illustrations should be kept to a minimum in these reports, for the preparation of either drawings or photographs takes an appreciable amount of time. On the other hand, there are times when an illustration can eliminate the need for a long description and can thereby speed up production. When they are used, illustrations should be interleaved between pages of text or gathered in a block at the end of the report in order to obviate the need for time-consuming book design.

6-2.3. Style

Since you can assume that a short-form progress report will be read as soon as it is received, you need not be concerned with developing a "style" to make it readable. There is no need to induce the reader to continue reading by the smooth and mellifluous wording of your prose; he will read on whether you want him to or not because it is important to him to know what you have to say. Nevertheless, you can make the task considerably more palatable for him by writing in a cl ar, succinct, and factual manner.

Transmission of information—not the creation of a mood—is the point. Above all, you must be clear, so that there is no confusion in the reader's mind about the information that you are recording. Keep your sentences and paragraphs short and to the point. You can use abbreviations at will, and the use of technical jargon is far more permissible in these than in any other reports. You know your readers and, therefore, whether or not they are familiar with any "shop talk" that you might use.

6-2.4. Long-Form Progress Reports

Long-form progress reports are prepared when projects are planned to continue from year to year, or they may be designed to record the progress made by an organization on its many projects during a 3-, 6-, or 12-month period. Such reports are made to a parent organization, to stockholders, to voters, or to similar audiences. A subcommittee may make such a report to its parent committee.

Progress reports of this type are longer, more formal, and frequently far more elaborate than routine short-form progress reports. Although speed is a consideration in long-form progress reports, it is not the primary factor. In a semiannual report, for example, some of the information would be 6 months old even if you could release the report the day after the period ended. Such a report, then, does not bring "news" to the readers who have been following the projects closely over the months, but rather provides them with a history and permanent record of the happenings and achievements during the period.

Most long-form progress reports are intended for a variety of readers. Ostensibly, they are written to readers who are vitally interested in the project or the organization, and these should be considered your primary audience. In addition, you expect such reports to be read by men and women with only a casual knowledge of your projects. Although they may have a definite interest in the progress of your work, they by no means have kept abreast of the latest developments over the reporting period. This secondary audience has a strong effect upon the outline of the report and upon the language and style of writing as well; here you must define unusual terms, avoid obtuse abbreviations, and eliminate jargon as much as possible.

You must go into considerable detail in giving the background necessary to understand the discussion on actual progress, or the readers will not be able to comprehend your statements in the sections that describe progress.

Since speed is not so important here as in the short reports covering a brief period, you have much more flexibility in the manner in which you illustrate your report. Special photographs can be taken and elaborate artwork can be prepared to help you in your presentation. Maximum use of graphic aids should be made.

The long-form progress report has much the same structure as the long-form research and development report, as follows:

Cover	Opening section
Title page	History of the project or organization
Foreword	Fiscal report (optional)
Table of contents	Project reports (divided into subdivisions according to the phases of the project or to the various projects in progress in the organization. Each subdivision is divided into sections on previous status, progress during the reporting period, and future plans.)
	Appendixes
	Bibliography

Long-form progress reports can be expected to be retained in the permanent files of the reporting organization, of the parent organization, and of most of the major related organizations and individuals who receive copies. They are usually produced in considerably larger quantities than the short-form reports—often in thousands of copies —and given wide distribution. For these reasons, among others, they should be planned, written, edited, and produced in the same manner as other major publications and permanent contributions to the literature. Errors in fact, obscure passages of text, ambiguities, and similar weaknesses in reporting will seriously reflect upon the reputation of the releasing organization, so take care to eliminate them.

In writing the report, consider each section a complete report of its own on a small scale. Each should include its own subsection giving background information and bringing the reader up to date on the status of the project at the beginning of the period. This is followed by a subsection on progress during the period, and the section is concluded with comments on future plans for the project. An approximate breakdown of space allotted to these three subsections that has proved to be acceptable is (1) background, 30%, (2) progress, 60%, and (3) future plans, 10%.

In a long-form progress report, you are at liberty to refer to other publications in the text as you do in normal long-form reports and then to collect the bibliographic information about these references in a bibliography or list of references at the end of the report. Another useful style is to supply a bibliography for each major section of the report covering the references in that section, rather than to use only one complete list of references at the end.

Although each section and subsection of a progress report is written in narrative style, you cannot assume that a reader will start at the beginning of your report and read through section after section to the end. Instead, readers will skip through the report, stopping to read only those sections in which they have a particular interest. There is no need, therefore, to be concerned with working out transitions from one section to another. You may depend upon your system of section headings to serve as keys to the individual sections and to be all of the transition that is necessary.

The major phases of work performed by the organization make up the major parts of the report. It is advisable to introduce each of these major parts with an over-all introduction that indicates any changes in emphasis from the work as reported in the preceding issue. Similarly, you may wish to close each major part with an over-all closing section that discusses possible future trends in the work as a whole. Thus, the body of a long-form progress report is comprised of major parts, each handled as a separate report, and, in turn, these parts are made up of minor sections in the nature of small, but complete, reports.

6-2.5. Variations

There are two styles followed in presenting information in progress reports. The first is to show an entry in every issue of the report for each heading and subheading in the over-all outline, whether there has been any progress to report or not. The second is to include a heading only if there has been some progress that can be reported; otherwise to omit the heading completely. Each has advantages and disadvantages.

Under the first method, it is customary to cover items on which there was no progress by listing the heading in its regular sequence and following it with the statement, "No progress to report during this period." Some writers prefer to qualify this statement by giving a brief explanation as to "why" there was no progress, thus: "No progress was made on this project during this reporting period because the work was set aside to accommodate the testing program on Project A, which has higher priority," ". . . because the material that was scheduled to be supplied by the Metropolitan Plastics Co. was not received until too late to complete the tests. It is expected that the results of these tests will be available before the end of the next reporting period."

If the simple "no progress" statement is used, the report tends to be filled with unproductive statements that, in addition to making a lengthy report, can give a definitely negative impression to the work. While the inclusion of explanations can be a help to the readers, the longer they are, the more difficult they make the task of finding the actual progress.

On the other hand, the report that simply ignores projects in which no progress was made can also give a distorted picture. To omit comment on a project without any explanation can leave the readers in the dark about what is happening. There is the added danger that a project will quietly disappear altogether without any record of the reason. When a project is discontinued, it should be noted in a progress report so that all parties are aware of it. Parallel to this is the principle that the start of a new project should be recorded at the time that work first starts on it—this in itself is progress. A sudden report that a project is partially completed when there has been no previous mention of it can be completely confusing to the reader.

□ NOTE

Record the beginning of each new project or phase of a continuing project and the closing out of any work that has been completed or discontinued. □

The outline for reports in a continuing series needs to be adjusted from time to time to keep it in line with the changing work program of an organization. There is a tendency for outlines to become frozen, and after 6 months or a year they no longer present the material in the proper order or under current groupings. At regular intervals, review your outline and make the adjustments necessary to keep your reports up to date.

A summary sheet at the beginning of a progress report can be a useful addition when the report is to be sent to a group of readers who want to be kept generally informed of major accomplishments or developments but do not have time to read the detailed information in the body of the report. Such a summary may be printed on colored paper to make it easy to find or designed in a special format for easy reading.

Charts are particularly useful in progress reports to present statistics indicating accomplishments. For example, charts comparing actual and planned progress by dates can show a reader at a glance whether a project is on schedule or not. These can be designed in such a way that they can be added to for each period with very little trouble.

6-3. HANDBOOKS AND MANUALS

6-3.1. Purpose

Handbooks and manuals are technical publications that contain information regarding the manufacture, installation, operation, maintenance, or use of a piece of equipment, a machine, a material, or a product of some kind. A manual is concerned with the effective use of a product for a given purpose. It may furnish manufacturing procedures, instruction on how to install, operate, or service some equipment, how to inspect it, or how to maintain it.

Manuals contain supporting information only when such information is essential to the successful performance of the procedures described in them. Manuals and handbooks are designed for specific users; examples are a handbook for pilots describing the use of a new fire-control system, a handbook for craftsmen on the repair of wood aircraft structures, a handbook for ordnancemen instructing in the handling of a new weapon, or a manual for warehousemen on the assembly and storage of electric motors. The man who prepares such a publication knows exactly who will read it, and, therefore, the information it must contain and the language that should be used.

6-3.2. Style

Handbooks and manuals are written in a direct and straightforward style. Florid or elaborate writing has no place in a manual, and everything possible should be done to make the text clear, crisp, and understandable. Avoid involved sentences and complicated paragraphs, because the user must be able to follow the steps easily, without the need to keep one finger on the book.

Language that requires a specialized knowledge should be avoided unless you know that your readers have that knowledge. When it is necessary to use a term you think might not be understood, be sure to define it precisely. In the presentation of operating procedures, use the imperative mood; for example, "Taper the hole evenly to the outer circle with a chisel, knife, or rasp. Prepare a circular tapered patch to fit the prepared hole. Glue the patch into place with face grain direction matching that of the original surface."

Be consistent in the use of nomenclature throughout any manual or handbook, as well as throughout related publications. Particularly, be sure that your nomenclature is consistent between your text and your illustrations.

Manuals and handbooks call for extensive use of illustrations and tables wherever possible. Information presented in tabular form is easily understood, and the tables can be quickly located by the user.

Line illustrations are helpful in describing parts to be made or steps to be followed. Make frequent use of callouts (see Section 4-3.6) in such illustrations. A series of drawings combined with a step-by-step description in the text is an excellent method of presenting a procedure.

6-3.3. Usual Parts

The preliminary matter of a handbook or manual is much the same as that for a report. It may include a title page, an acknowledgment (optional), a foreword (or letter or transmittal), a table of contents, a list of illustrations, and a list of tables. The separate lists of illustrations and tables are useful in this type of publication because often the user wants to refer only to a particular illustration or table and is not concerned with the text that supports it. After the first reading, a handbook or manual is used for spot reference and is not read in a narrative fashion. The separate lists, therefore, make it easy for a user to find the item he needs. Normally, an abstract is superfluous in a manual; the title itself tells the reader all that he needs to know about the publication.

Like a report, every handbook or manual should open with an introduction that describes the product in question and indicates the contents of the book. Give the scope of the publication, and define the people who are expected to use it. Explain anything unusual about the manual; for example, if it is to be kept up to date by supplying the users with change sheets (see Section 6-3.4), this procedure should be stated.

Handbooks and manuals do not require closing sections as do most other publications. Since they do not lead up to conclusions or recommendations, such sections do not apply. Although it might be possible to summarize the important points in a handbook, to close with a summary section is quite pointless, for the user is concerned with the individual bits and pieces of information presented throughout the publication, rather than with an over-all summary of the subject.

The items of supplementary matter depend upon the size of the manual and the type of people who will use it. The following suggestions should be considered:

Glossary. Not required if the handbook is short and the language well known. Useful in a long book in which a term might be defined on page 20 and used again occasionally through the next hundred pages.

Bibliography. Useful only in such books as manuals on the design and manufacture of a product. There is no point in including a list of references in a book to be used by enlisted men on a destroyer, for example; they would have neither the opportunity nor the inclination to look them up.

Index. Not required in most handbooks or manuals. However, an index can be useful if many items are mentioned in a variety of places throughout the publication. The longer the book, the more likely the need for an index. A manual that explains how to put a collapsible rowboat together would not require an index (the table of contents is sufficient); however, a manual that describes the use of wood in shipbuilding would require an index, for the subject is complicated and the cross references would be many.

Distribution list. Usually not required. Handbooks and manuals are normally produced in large quantities and supplied to anyone who might have a need for them. If they contain classified information, however, a distribution list may be required as well as useful.

6-3.4. Format Variations

Thoughtful design of handbooks and manuals can add greatly to their usefulness. Consider the men who are going to use them and the circumstances under which they will have to work. If a manual is to be successful, it must be used, and it will not be used unless you make it easy for the men who need it. For example, you cannot expect a pilot to carry around an $8\frac{1}{2}$- by 11-inch, hard-covered, 200-page manual on how to fire a new weapon. Instead, give him a soft-covered booklet that will fit in his pocket. The following suggestions will be helpful:

Size. If a man is expected to use the handbook in the field, make it a $5\frac{1}{2}$- by $7\frac{1}{2}$-inch pocket-sized book. If he will use it at a desk, a full-sized, 8- by $10\frac{1}{2}$-inch or $8\frac{1}{2}$- by 11-inch book will be easier to read.

Foldouts. Foldouts are workable only if the book is to be used on a desk or table where they can be supported. If the handbook is to be used outdoors in wind or rain, foldouts are completely impractical.

Type size. Use a type face large enough to be read under the most difficult circumstances that can be reasonably expected. There is frequently a tendency to print manuals—particularly the tabular material—in small type (8 point, or less) in an attempt to get a maximum amount of information on a page. This is a prime example of false economy. If manuals are given hard use, they get dirty and the pages soon become dog-eared and coffee-stained. As often as not, the users must read them in bad light, and small type is an imposition. Even though large type (12 point is not too large) may require a few extra pages, as an aid to quick and accurate reading, it is more than justified.

Binding. If your manual is to be left open to a desired section, while the user performs the steps in a process, for example, it will be most useful if the binding permits it to lie flat. There is nothing more frustrating than to have a handbook flip shut when you have both hands busy with tools and are trying to read at the same time. A small handbook can be bound by saddle-stitching it (see Section 7-4). Books of 40 to 100 pages can be bound with plastic or spiral binding. Another very useful type is the looseleaf book in a multiple-ring binder. Side-stitched books or books bound with screws will not ordinarily stay open and are practical only for large manuals that will be opened for a moment and then put back on the shelf.

Covers. Because good handbooks or manuals receive continuous use, they should have sturdy covers. Simple paper covers will soon wear and tear and should be avoided for any handbook that will get much use. If possible, leatherette, vinyl, or some similar material serves best. As a rule, hard-backed covers should not be used.

Changes. Many manuals deal with subjects that are constantly changing. Frequently, some features are obsolete by the time the manual is off the press. These can be kept up to date only by the device of issuing change pages at frequent intervals. Such pages should be identified with the original publication and dated. Manuals that are planned for the addition of such pages must be bound in such a way that pages can be removed and inserted. Give consideration to this problem in the early planning stages so that the original book can be properly bound. Manuals of this type should include in the preliminary matter a page on which to record the changes as they are received by the users. New sets of change pages should be transmitted as enclosures to covering letters that clearly state the changes that have been made, the numbers of the new pages, and what should be done with the old pages. As a guide, when about 50 percent of the pages of a manual have been changed, it is time to reissue the manual with all of the changes incorporated into a revision and then to start over with the change-page procedure.

Cartoons. Manuals and handbooks are virtually the only type of technical publications that can be helped occasionally by the use of cartoons. At best, the subject matter makes dull reading, and cartoons (if well done) can help to inject some interest into the material (see Fig. 6-3). Line drawings of a cartoon character performing the var-

Figure 6-3. Example of a cartoon used in a handbook. Cartoons add interest to this type of publication and, if well done, help to emphasize important points. Here the reader was admonished not to stand in front of a rocket launcher during loading operations.

ious steps of a procedure described in the text can often help your description—especially if your readers are not trained to learn by reading. Be very careful to keep the cartoons in good taste. The temptation to introduce something "just a little off color" in the hope of "giving some life to the book" should be consistently resisted; bad taste in print will haunt you long after the subject matter of the handbook is forgotten.

Numbered paragraphs. Most manuals and many handbooks use numbered paragraphs. This device helps a reader to look up a point from the table of contents or the index, to relate the various sections, subsections, and sub-subsections, to make changes as new material is supplied, or to refer to a specific section for any reason whatever. Policies vary as to what is considered a "paragraph." Some require that a number be assigned to each actual paragraph; others use the word in a generic sense to include sub-paragraphs intimately related and concerned with a single subject.

One method is to assign an Arabic numeral to each major section (or chapter) of the manual, say, "3" for the third major section. The subsections and sub-subsections are numbered in series within each section. Thus, paragraph "3-1.4.2" would be the second paragraph within the fourth sub-subsection within the first subsection in the third major section. There are, of course, various other numbering systems, and as long as they are logical they are acceptable. For example, "11.6.c(1)(a)" indicates five orders of importance; or paragraph 4.133 indicates the third sub-subsection within the thirteenth sub-section in the fourth major section. These variations, however, tend to become complicated either for the writer or the reader, and the method originally described is recommended for your use.

Running heads. A large manual can be made easier to use if, in the running head at the top of each page, you show the numbers of the paragraphs or sections covered. These should appear at the outer edges of the pages. Sometimes numbers may be replaced with short titles of the subjects covered on the pages. There are many possibilities for helping the readers in this manner.

6-3.5. Military Manuals

The preparation of manuals to accompany the great mass of equipment, ordnance, and other "hardware" prepared for and used by the branches of the Department of Defense is rapidly developing into a major business. The specifications for most of these manuals are spelled out in complete detail. Since they specify everything from the size and style of type to the content and order of the various sections, there is no need to discuss them here. It is sufficient to point out that these specifications do exist and that you will be expected to follow them to the letter when you are involved in the preparation of such manuals.

7

Reproduction Processes

7-1. AVAILABLE PROCESSES

Some report writers are intimately concerned with the reproduction of their reports, others only casually, but until your report has been reproduced in the required quantity, your job is unfinished. In support of the basic principle of this handbook, that a report is intended to achieve a certain purpose with a predetermined group of readers, your manuscript is not a report until it is in the hands of your readers.

The circumstances in which a single copy of a report will serve all needs are so rare that they can be disregarded. Two to five copies are the least that a customer normally requires. In addition to these, you will want one for your own files (two are better); your line management will want one or more copies; and it is wise to have two or three spare copies for unexpected requests. This defines a minimum of eight to ten copies. The usual number of copies of a research and development report is more likely to be between 25 and 250 copies. Reports of general interest on unclassified subjects may well be reproduced in runs of 1,000 to 5,000 copies. It is reasonable, then, to assume that any report you write will have to be reproduced by one means or another.

As the author, you have information that may influence the method of reproduction that is used, and this information should be made available to the reproduction staff. For example, you know whether the report is of temporary interest or is expected to remain an active part of the technical literature for some years. You know the audience that you had in mind when you wrote the report, and, therefore, you can make the most accurate estimate of the number of copies that should be prepared. You are the only one who knows the critical points that must appear in the final copies in order to make your presentation complete; for example, a reproduction of an X-ray that shows a delicate flaw in a piece of metal, a photomicrograph of the crystalline structure of a material, or the variations of an oscilloscope tracing. You know the relative importance of the different items discussed and, therefore, the relative size of reproductions of illustrations. You know which figures or tables must appear on facing pages, which must appear on right-hand pages, the maximum reduction that schematic wiring diagrams can stand and still retain their readability, and a great variety of similar requirements that will dictate the type of reproduction permissible. You are more aware than anyone else of the manner in which your primary audience will react to the physical appearance of your report, and you know how the report will be used—at a desk, in the field, in a shop, etc.

Finally, you—the author—are the person who must ultimately be satisfied with the reproduction of your report. Your name appears on the title page, and the publication will be known as your report. You will want the physical appearance of the report to reflect favorably on your work.

While many large research and development organizations—both government and private—support their authors with complete publishing units, including captive print shops, the majority of report writers must become involved in the reproduction processes to a greater or lesser extent. You may need only to coordinate the activities of clerks, typists, photographers, and others; you may be involved in proofreading masters and discussing the preparation of illustrations with artists; or you may be operating the reproduction machines yourself and "walking around the table" collating the pages late at night, so that you can hand-staple some copies to have ready for that ever-imminent "meeting" the next morning. Regardless of the extent of active participation that you currently take in the reproduction of your reports, the information on the following pages will be of interest to you if you are to have the background you need to be sure that the reproduction of your work is the best possible under the prevailing circumstances.

Factors that must be considered include the time available, the amount of money that can be afforded, and the equipment that can be used. Keep in mind that printing and reproduction services are available on a job basis. These range from small reproduction shops to full-scale letterpress and offset printers. Every city of reasonable size has offset printing shops, which can handle the reproduction of a single oversize illustration or a complete report. If satisfactory printing facilities are not readily accessible in your organization, establish contact with a good print shop. Once you have worked out basic specifications for your work, you will be able to send and receive your material by mail. For men who write reports only occasionally, arrangements such as these are far less expensive and more satisfactory than buying the necessary equipment or trying to use inadequate machines.

First, however, familiarize yourself with all of the reproduction equipment that is available in your own organization. Learn the abilities of the operators and the physical limitations of the machines; then try to get the most out of them. For example, if the maximum width of paper that can be handled by your press is 19 inches, plan your illustrations and extended tables to fit within those limits. Or, if you do not have facilities for halftone reproduction, prepare your illustrations as line drawings. This type of cooperation between the writer and the reproduction staff is essential for a successful report.

7-1.1. Typewriters

The simplest method of reproducing a report is to prepare the text and tables on a typewriter and add the illustrations in the form of diazo prints or blueprints of the line drawings and ad-type photoprints of the tone figures. If necessary, you can type your own text and make your own blueprints. Then you need only to purchase prints of your photographs. It is more probable that you will have typists or stenographers available to do your typing and a clerk to make the blueprints. This method of report reproduction is known to all and requires no special equipment or trained personnel outside of your own office. It is fast and you have absolute control over it. When you are hard-pressed to make a deadline, this method of preparing advance copies should not be overlooked.

7-1.1.1. CHARACTERISTICS

Quality of product. The first copy is sharp and clean. Each additional copy is harder to read, until after the 10th copy (unless a copper platen is used) the product is unsatisfactory. Except for the first copy, the paper is thin and hard to handle.

Color of image. The original is black, as a general rule, but it can be in other colors if special ribbons are used. The copies are usually black or blue.

Permanence. Indefinite.

One-side or two-side printing. One side.

Size limitations. Normally 8 by $10\frac{1}{2}$, or $8\frac{1}{2}$ by 11 inches. Typewriters are available with carriage widths up to 16 inches, however.

Number of copies. 1 to 10. If a copper platen is used, as many as 20 copies can be made, but the last copies are difficult to read.

Type of master. No intermediate masters are required.

Changes. Changes can be made up to the last minute. The typewriter is the most flexible of reproduction machines. If necessary, you can write in corrections by hand on each copy.

Reduction or enlargement. None.

Speed. This is the fastest method of obtaining a few copies at the same time that the original is prepared. Any other method requires a second step.

Cost of equipment. No special equipment is required.

Level of operators. A skillful typist is all that is required. If the report is in a specialized field—particularly mathematics—the typist should be experienced in handling such matter.

Comments. One of the big advantages of this method of reproduction is complete control of all copies. If the report contains highly classified information, the entire report can be prepared by two or three people—even by the author alone, if necessary. There are no run-off pages or other scrap to be destroyed (except the sheets of carbon paper).

The principal disadvantage is that the copies are difficult to handle and appear to be preliminary. Carbon copies do not create a favorable first impression. To obtain additional copies with the same equipment requires as much work as the preparation of the first set of copies.

7-1.2. Diazo Process (Ammonia)

The diazo process of reproducing a report is usually available to engineers and often to scientists and administrators, because this is a standard method of reproducing engineering drawings. This process is well suited for the reproduction of oversize tables and line artwork; it operates on an endless belt, so there is no limit to the length of the page to be reproduced.

In this process, the master (translucent paper with an opaque image) is placed in direct contact with a paper that has been sensitized with a diazo chemical compound. These are fed into the machine, where they are exposed to ultraviolet light, which bleaches out the diazo emulsion. The exposed sheet is then developed in ammonia vapor, which converts the unexposed portion to a visible aniline dye image. A typical machine is shown in Fig. 7-1. The process is fast,

Figure 7-1. Diazo machine. (Courtesy of the Ozalid Division of General Aniline and Film Corporation.)

dry, and clean; but the ammonia fumes usually must be vented out of the building.

Although this process is most frequently used for reproducing line illustrations, it is also possible to reproduce text and even halftone illustrations when a screened positive transparency (see Section 7-1.5) is used for the master. Excellent reproductions of photographs can be produced, and this possibility should be considered when you do not have facilities for printing by offset reproduction.

7-1.2.1. CHARACTERISTICS

Quality of product. With an experienced operator, the end product can be excellent, depending upon the quality of the master. Weak pencil lines may be dropped out, and patches made with tape will leave a solid image. However, badly damaged and patched originals can be replaced with new originals by this process. Once the proper exposure has been determined (which may take one or two trial runs if the operator is inexperienced), every copy that is made is equal in quality to the others; there is no limit to the number of copies that can be made.

Color of image. Usually dark blue on a white background. It is also possible to use dyes that result in any of a variety of colors including black, which is very similar in appearance to that obtained by the offset process. The cost of this paper is slightly more than that of the blue-image paper.

Permanence of image. With normal usage, the image will last many years. If it is exposed to the sun, the image will fade.

One-side or two-side printing. Usually one side, but two-sided papers are available. With two-sided papers, there may be a problem of registering the images on the front and back when this is required. Also, these special papers are more expensive and have a shorter shelf life.

Size limitations. Office machines will handle paper up to 16 inches in width. Larger machines will handle masters up to 54 inches in width. There are no limitations with regard to length.

Number of copies. This process is best suited economically for reproducing from 1 to 50 copies of a report, but there is no limit to the number of copies that can be reproduced.

Type of masters. Translucent or transparent masters with an opaque image. Text typed on vellum or onionskin and backed with an orange carbon gives good results. Pencil drawings on vellum or ink drawings on linen make excellent masters. For halftone reproductions of photographs, a screened positive transparency is needed.

Reduction or enlargement. None.

Speed. Average speed of these machines is about 500 copies per hour with a top speed of 1,000 copies (standard page size) per hour. This depends upon the skill of the operator, the quality of the masters, and the size of the masters.

Cost of equipment. The office-type machines cost in the neighborhood of $1,200; the large machines cost as much as $10,500.

Level of operators. While office machines can be operated by unskilled operators with very little instruction, all diazo machines should be operated by trained and experienced operators for efficient production.

Comments. If necessary, you can have complete control of the copies turned out by this process; only one or two test sheets are required.

It is possible to make additional masters by this process so that special information can be added to the secondary masters without damaging the original. The process is also good for providing review copies of a report. Suggestions can be marked on these copies, and accepted changes can be made on the original, from which final copies can be made by this process; or the corrected originals can then be used as reproduction copy for the offset process.

7-1.3. Spirit Process (Hectograph)

The master used in the spirit process carries an aniline-dye image in reverse on the back of the master, the image having been picked up from a special aniline-dye carbon backing when pressure (by typing or drawing) was applied to the front. The master is placed on a drum, the image facing the outside. Slightly moistened paper is then passed between the master and a pressure roller so that a direct image appears on the printed sheet. Each time that a sheet is pressed against the master, a portion of the dye is transferred from the master to the sheet. Thus, as the dye is removed, the image becomes progressively lighter, until at last there is not sufficient dye to produce a legible image.

7-1.3.1. CHARACTERISTICS

Quality of product. The quality of the product depends upon the skill of the operator and the quality of the master; it can be clear and bright, or it can be fuzzy and faint. There is a tendency for small letters to fill in or to fade out. The paper is satisfactory and easy to write on with pen or pencil. It stands up well under handling.

Color of image. The usual color of the image is purple, but, with the proper masters, such colors as red, blue, yellow, and green are possible. To get more than one color on a print, each color is added to the master by using a different colored backing. Therefore, close registration of multiple colors can be obtained. The most difficult color to obtain is black, which is normally avoided.

Permanence. Since the image is reproduced in an aniline dye, it is not permanent and will fade. If it is kept out of direct sunlight, it will serve well for a number of months. If the image is kept out of the light most of the time (for example, in a file cabinet), it may last for several years. However, it is not satisfactory for reports that are to be used in the open, for the image will fade to illegibility in a few weeks when it is used in direct sunlight.

One-side or two-side printing. Normally one side.

Size limitations. Masters are available in sizes from 3 by 5 inches to 14 by 20 inches.

Number of copies. The practical limit is about 200 copies. If the masters are incorrectly made or run, the number of copies may be only 150. With care, you may get considerably more than 200, but this figure is best for planning purposes.

Type of masters. Special master sheets prepared by typing or drawing on special paper backed up by a patented aniline-dye carbon paper. These are easy to proofread because the image is direct on the face of the master.

Changes. Corrections can be made quickly with a little practice. Additions can be typed onto a master after some copies have been run off, which makes this method useful for preliminary drafts that are revised until a final version of a report is developed.

Reduction or enlargement. None.

Speed. About 75 copies per minute.

Cost of equipment. From about $350 up.

Level of operators. A good typist and an average draftsman will be able to prepare text or drawings on the masters. If you are not concerned with time, you can type your own masters and draw your own illustrations. This, of course, depends upon your own skill and the quality of the product that you will accept. With very little training, anyone can be taught to run the machine.

Comments. The machine is easy to operate (Fig. 7-2). It has very few controls to adjust and can be operated by clerical help after brief

Figure 7-2. Spirit process (hectograph) machine. (Courtesy of DITTO Inc.)

instructions. Although many users are not too happy with the results, this machine is a workhorse that will make it possible for you to get out a limited number of copies of a report when you need them in a hurry. With a minimum of maintenance, it can be kept working for years.

7-1.4. Stencil Process

In the stencil process, the master is a stencil on which a protective backing has been removed from the image. The stencil is secured over an ink-pad covering on a perforated drum, and the ink flows from inside the drum to the pad and from there through the stencil.

When the paper rolls between the stencil and a pressure roller, ink is forced through the openings in the stencil where the protective coating has been removed and prints the image on the paper. An ink-absorbent paper is required. A stencil duplicator is shown in Fig. 7-3.

Figure 7-3. Stencil duplicating machine. (Courtesy of the A. B. Dick Company.)

7-1.4.1. CHARACTERISTICS

Quality of product. Fair to good. The ink-absorbent paper tends to spread the image. It is most satisfactory for line drawings and typing; halftone illustrations are impracticable. With proper handling, however, the image of typed material can be quite good.

Color of image. Normally black. Other colors can be used, but, for each color, the ink cylinder must be removed from the machine and a new cylinder installed.

Permanence. The image will last for as long as 10 years, but the paper tends to discolor, eventually turning yellow. After about 5 years the oil in the ink begins to spread through the porous paper, and the letters tend to fill in.

One-side or two-side printing. Best for one side only, but two-sided printing is reasonably satisfactory, particularly if it is not intended to last too long. After several years, the show-through makes reading difficult.

Size limitations. Up to $8\frac{1}{2}$ by 14 inches.

Number of copies. 5,000 copies is the usual maximum. It is possible to make a first run (2,000 copies, for example), store the masters for a matter of months or years, and then make a second run of another thousand or two.

Type of masters. Special stencils are required. They can be prepared by typing (without the ribbon) or by drawing with a stylus. Simple forms and line drawings can be made, but detailed drawings or forms with handwritten entries filled in are not practical.

Changes. Corrections of letters or words can be made by using a prepared fluid that restores the coating. Corrections of more than a line are difficult, and it is usually easier to remake the stencil. Corrections cannot be made after a stencil has once been run.

Reduction or enlargement. None.

Speed. 100 per minute.

Cost of equipment. From $250 for table models up.

Level of operators. These machines can be run by clerks, and, if necessary, you can run your own machine. Experienced operators, however, will give a better product.

Comments. Because these machines normally duplicate in black ink, they give a product that looks more like printing than the product of the spirit process, typewriter, or diazo process. The machine is easy to run, so if you put out only an occasional report, you do not need to hire a trained operator. On the other hand, this machine is rugged and will stand up under continuous operation for years. With a capacity of several thousand copies from each stencil, one set of masters is adequate for most reports.

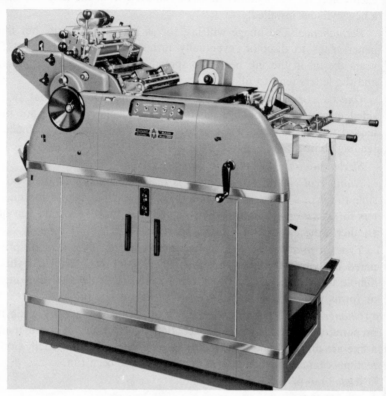

Figure 7-4. Offset printing machine. (Courtesy of the Addressograph Multigraph Company.)

7-1.5. Offset Process

Offset printing (Fig. 7-4) involves two steps: transferring the image from an inked plate onto a rubber blanket (in reverse) and from there onto the paper (in positive). The plate, which may be metal or paper, is chemically treated so that the image is ink-receptive and all the rest of the plate is water-receptive. The plate first passes water rollers, which cover everything but the image with a film of water. It then passes ink rollers, which leave a layer of ink on the image. This ink then passes from the plate to the blanket and finally to the paper. Since the paper does not come in contact with the image, there is so little wear that the image will last for thousands of copies.

Photographs and other illustrations made up of various tones can be reproduced by the photo-offset process. Here the illustrations are photographed and the tones broken up into patterns of dots of different sizes. The negatives are then placed in contact with metal plates and exposed to light, which forms the image by hardening the coating with which the plate has been treated. The plate is then washed and the coating removed, except where the image has been fixed by light action.

7-1.5.1. CHARACTERISTICS

Quality of product. Good to excellent. With skillful operators, the product of the offset press compares favorably with that of the best letterpress work. High-grade papers can be used, including coated stock, Bristols, and cover stocks.

Color of image. The image can be any color that is desired. The control of the machine is such that experienced operators can print up to five colors on a page and get excellent registration. Normally the printing is black.

Permanence. Indefinite. There is no fading of the image when it is exposed to sunlight, and the image neither creeps nor shows through the page with age. Offset paper will stand up with no more discoloration than any other good paper.

One-side or two-side printing. Two sides.

Size limitations. Direct-image offset plates up to 10 by 15 inches, with an image area of 9 by 13 inches. Photo-offset up to 48 by 54 inches. The size depends upon the machine and the copy board. The usual office-size machines handle paper up to $9\frac{3}{4}$ by 14 inches.

Number of copies. Direct-image plates are practical from 25 to 5,000 copies. Metal plates will produce from 25 to 25,000 or more copies. Using special plates, commercial printers can get more than one million copies from a single plate. When properly treated, plates can be stored and rerun as desired.

Type of masters. The reproduction copy from which photo-offset plates are made can be as simple as a typed page of copy, or it may be a combination of type proofs, line drawings, tone drawings, and photographs. "Repro copy" for photo-offset reproduction should be prepared by trained specialists. The amateur soon finds himself beyond his depth, and the results are far from what he expects.

Direct-image paper masters can be prepared by typing or drawing directly on the plate. A special ribbon, pencil, or pen is required.

Changes. On direct-image paper plates, corrections of a letter, a few words, or even a line can be made if done with care. These plates are easily damaged, however, and will show thumb prints, surface breaks, or bad erasures. Instructions for making corrections should be followed precisely, and it is best to practice until the technique is mastered. It is faster to retype a plate than to make an extensive correction, and once a paper plate has been damaged, it cannot be used and must be remade.

Corrections cannot be made on metal plates satisfactorily. However, the reproduction copy can be changed at will by cutting out, pasting over, or otherwise adding or removing copy. New negatives can then be made, followed by new plates. The process is quite flexible, and corrections of "repro copy" can be made up to the moment the final negative is shot.

Reduction or enlargement. Both can be accomplished with the photo-offset process. It is standard practice to prepare artwork within a 2-to-1 reduction, for such reduction refines drawings and eliminates many flaws that would show up on art prepared for 1-to-1 reproduction.

Speed. Machine speed is about 6,000 copies per hour. When excellence of reproduction is not essential, some machines will consistently produce as many as 9,000 copies per hour. On the other hand, if the operator is concerned with careful registration, it is better to plan on 3,000 to 4,000 copies per hour.

Cost of equipment. The cost of the so-called "office-type" offset presses starts at about $2,500. The larger presses cost from $4,000 to $30,000. In addition, for photo-offset work it is necessary to have such equipment as a copy camera ($1,400 to $10,000), plate-making equipment, light tables for stripping the negatives, and a dark room with the usual developing equipment. If you plan to set up a photo-offset production line, visit some plants that have been in operation for some time and get advice on the types and sizes of equipment that you would need.

Level of operators. Offset presses should be operated by professional pressmen for satisfactory results. Photolithography requires experienced and highly skilled technicians in all phases, including "repro copy" paste-up men, cameramen, filmstrippers, plate makers, and pressmen.

Comments. For an organization that has a steady output of reports, photolithography offers the most flexible and satisfactory method of reproduction. It is fast, versatile, and economical for short runs. If you do not have this equipment available, commercial lithographers can do your occasional jobs.

Figure 7-5. Typesetting machine. (Courtesy of the Intertype Company, a Division of the Harris-Intertype Corporation.)

Figure 7-6. Printing press. (Courtesy of Brandtjen & Kluge, Inc.)

7-1.6. Letterpress Process

Letterpress printing requires a complete printing plant, with type-setting machines (Fig. 7-5), presses (Fig. 7-6), collating machines, folders, and related equipment and a full staff of employees. In this process the image is prepared in reverse with the base material cut away in the areas that will not print, leaving the image areas raised above the base. An ink roller is passed over the raised image, which is then mechanically pressed against the paper, thereby transferring the image directly onto the paper.

To reproduce illustrations by the letterpress process, engravings are made in which the base material is etched away so that the image area stands above it. For photographs and other illustrations involving gradations of tone from light to dark, the image is broken up into dot patterns in which the dots get bigger as the tone varies from light to dark.

The letterpress process is seldom used for the reproduction of technical reports, because they usually are produced in small quantities. Because of the cost of setting the type and preparing engravings, this process is most economical for publications that have relatively few illustrations and large runs.

The quality of the product is excellent and normally surpasses that of any other reproduction process. If you expect to have your report reproduced by letterpress, visit your printer early and discuss with him any problems that you may have. Together you can work out the best methods of preparing your material to suit his equipment and methods.

7-2. COMPARISON OF REPRODUCTION PROCESSES

There are, of course, many factors that determine the method of reproduction that will be used on your report—not the least of which is the equipment that is available. Since this varies widely from one organization to another, no attempt will be made here to state precisely which method you should use. Instead, the different factors that should be considered are summarized in Table 7-1 for easy comparison. Reconcile what you would like with what you have available and try for the optimum selection.

7-3. POSSIBLE COMBINATIONS

Although it is usually most efficient to use one type of equipment for the production of all components of a report, there are circumstances that make it desirable to consider using combinations. Time, money, and available equipment all influence the decision, and it is quite impossible to select the one reproduction method that is the most efficient for all organizations at all times. In this section, some of the possible combinations will be discussed to indicate how you may be able to use the equipment that you have in order to get the best results in the time at your disposal.

7-3.1. Stencil and Photo-Offset

You can get good results by reproducing your text on a stencil duplicator and your illustrations by photo-offset. This will give you your entire report in black and white and still save the cost of photo-

TABLE 7–1

COMPARISON OF CHARACTERISTICS OF REPRODUCTION PROCESSES

Characteristics	Type-writer	Diazo	Spirit	Stencil	Offset		Letter-press
					Direct	Photo	
Number of copies:							
1–10	x	x	...	...	...	...	...
11–50	...	...	x	x	x	...	...
51–150	...	...	x	x	x	x	...
151–5,000	...	...	...	x	x	x	x
5,001–25,000	...	...	...	...	...	x	x
over 25,000	...	...	...	...	...	...	x
Kinds of copy:							
Text	x	x	x	x	x	x	x
Tables	x	x	x	x	x	x	x
Foldouts	...	x	...	...	:..	x	x
Line drawings:							
Simple	x	x	x	x	x	x	x
Complex	...	x	...	...	...	x	x
Halftones	...	x	...	...	...	x	x
Oversize or undersize	...	...	...	...	...	x	x
Quality of product:							
Image:							
Original	good	fair	fair	good	good	exc	exc
Copies	fair	fair	fair	good	good	exc	exc
Paper	poor	fair	good	fair	good	good	exc
Size limitations	8½ x 11	54 by any length	14 x 20	8½ x 14	10 x 15	48 x 54	48 x 54
Storage life of masters	...	indef	2 mo	indef	2 yr	indef	indef
Expected life of copies	indef	5 yr	5 yr	10 yr	indef	indef	indef

graphing the full report. If, for example, you have only one offset
machine, putting your text onto stencils will keep the offset press free
for reproduction of the illustrations. The stencil duplicator will produce an image that will last for 5 to 10 years, which is long enough
for most technical reports, and you have the flexibility of printing on
one or two sides of the sheet as you wish. Also, the masters can be
retained for a second printing. When planning a report for this
method of reproduction, the simplest arrangement is to place all the
text first, followed by the illustrations grouped at the rear. However,
it is easy to interleave the illustrations throughout the text as long as

you do not try to back up text with an offset illustration. The tables can be reproduced by either method, depending upon their complexity and whether or not they are of a size that requires reduction.

7-3.2. Direct-Image Offset and Photo-Offset

When more than one offset press is available, a bottleneck frequently develops at the lithographic camera. The load can be reduced by typing the text matter onto direct-image plates, which are ready for the press without going through the camera. Simple tables and line drawings can be placed on direct-image plates, but complex tables, complex line drawings, and tone illustrations should be automatically planned for photo-offset reproduction.

7-3.3. Typewriter and Photoprints

Reports can be reproduced by combining photoprints of the illustrations with text reproduced on typewriter (1 to 10 copies) or spirit hectograph (11 to 50 copies). The combination of typewritten text and photoprints of the illustrations gives maximum speed with complete control of the copies, but this combination is not efficient for more than a few copies. Any attempt to combine photoprints with text run on stencil duplicators or offset presses soon becomes prohibitively expensive. For example, 100 copies of a report with 10 tone illustrations would cost approximately $500 for the photographic work alone.

7-3.4. Spirit and Diazo Processes

Diazo prints of illustrations can be combined with text done on a typewriter, spirit duplicator, or stencil duplicator. When the illustrations are line drawings, this is an economical method of reproduction that can be used for as many as several hundred copies of a report if necessary. Unless you have a skilled photolithographer to prepare screened positives, however, do not plan to reproduce halftones on a diazo machine. It is also possible to prepare masters of the text matter on sheets of thin paper, which can then be used to reproduce a few preliminary copies on the diazo machine and later used as reproduction copy for the preparation of offset plates. Oversize drawings too big to be run on the offset press can be reproduced on a diazo machine and inserted in a report for which all of the other pages are run on the offset press.

7-3.5. Letterpress and Offset

The letterpress can be used economically to supply reproduction copy for eventual production on offset presses. This is useful when you need type faces that are not available to you with the composing machines at your disposal. For example, you may be preparing a report that contains complicated mathematical symbols that you do not have, or you may find that more elaborate headings in special faces are justified in a special publication. In these circumstances, you can have the material set by a commercial printer, who will supply you with proofs that can be pasted up into pages of reproduction copy. These can be combined with illustrations prepared for photo-offset reproduction. This combines maximum flexibility in type faces with the economy of photo-offset reproduction of complicated artwork. It is also economical if you must make last-minute changes because they can be cut into the "repro copy" by hand right up to the moment the copy goes before the photo-offset camera.

7-4. BINDING METHODS

Reports that are to be used extensively, or that are expected to be kept in filing cabinets or on bookshelves for several years, must be securely bound; there are a number of satisfactory methods available (see Fig. 7-7).

7-4.1. Side-Stitching

The simplest form of binding is to staple the pages together with two or three staples driven through the sheets near the left-hand edge. On informal reports of few pages, the stapling can be done with hand staplers. Formal reports, reports with many pages, and reports made with covers of a heavy stock must be bound with mechanical stapling machines. The binding can be given a finished appearance by adding an adhesive binding tape that covers the staples and the spine of the report. If possible, the top, bottom, and right side of the report should be trimmed after the binding has been completed.

Side-stitched bindings have one major drawback. The reports tend to snap shut unless they are held open in some manner, which makes them difficult to use when the reader wishes to leave them open on a desk or workbench. The thicker a report, the more inclined it is to close. This type of binding is satisfactory, then, for reports that are to be held in the hand while they are read, but it is not good for manuals, handbooks, or similar publications.

7-4.2. Metal Fasteners

A variation of the side-stitched binding is the metal fastener that is inserted through holes in the pages and folded over to bind them together. This type of binding is more expensive than stapling and takes more time. If you do not have a stapling machine, however, it is a satisfactory means of binding a few copies of a report. It is also useful when you are including bulky blueprints or oversize diazo prints folded to page size. Like stapled reports, reports bound with metal fasteners tend to snap shut.

7-4.3. Posts

Another variation of the side-stitched binding is accomplished by drilling or punching two or three holes near the left side of the pages and binding them together with screw posts. This type of binding is more expensive than staples or metal fasteners, but it is possible to bind much thicker reports with posts than with staples, and posts hold the pages more securely than metal fasteners. Inserting the screw posts is a hand job and time consuming.

7-4.4. Saddle-Stitching

Reports are said to be saddle-stitched when staples are inserted in the gutter between facing pages. Four pages are printed on each sheet of paper (two on the front and two on the back); the sheets are folded in the middle and collated so that the pages follow in proper sequence; and the sheets are then stapled with two or three staples in the fold.

For reports of comparatively few pages (8 to 60), this type of binding has definite advantages. It makes for maximum ease in reading, and the reports will lie open to any desired page. This is excellent for publications that must be left open on a desk or used in some similar manner.

This method of binding has some disadvantages, however. The number of pages in such a report is always a multiple of four, be-

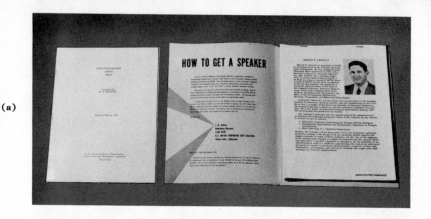

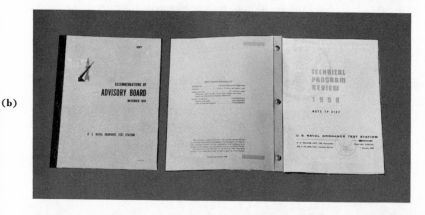

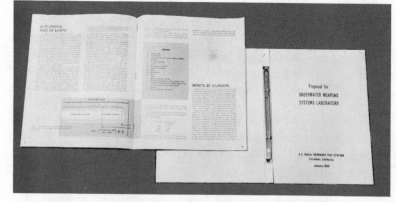

Figure 7-7. Available binding methods for report production. (a) Left, side-stitching (three staples along left margin); right, staples at the top. (b) Left, side-stitching covered with black

(d)

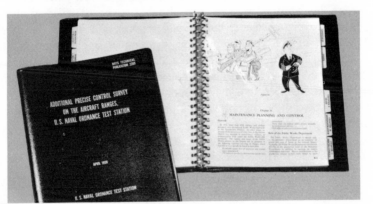

(e)

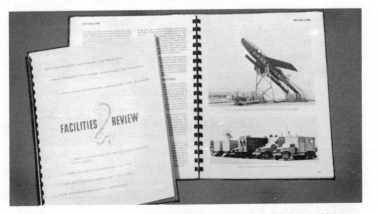

(f)

binding tape; right, post binding. (c) Left, saddle-stitching
(staples in the gutter); right, metal fasteners. (d) Book bound
by sewing and gluing. (e) Multi-ring binder. (f) Plastic binding.

cause any addition or deletion involves four pages. Of more concern are the problems of book design that are introduced in order to have the proper pages printed on the front and back of each sheet of paper. For example, in a 32-page report, pages 2 and 31 are printed side by side on a sheet backed up by pages 1 and 32. Also, a book planned for 8½- by 11-inch final size must be printed on a large press.

7-4.5. Sewing and Gluing

Reports bound by commercial binderies are usually sewn in signatures, and these are held together by sewing and gluing them to a backing. Normally, this package of signatures is then glued into hard covers, leatherette, or some other durable covers. They may also be glued into paper covers, but usually reports that justify the special treatment of hot-type composition, printing in signatures, and sewn and glued binding also justify the added protection of special covers. Most report writers need not be concerned with this type of binding. If you are involved in a major production that will be bound in hard covers, you will be supported by a production staff that will take care of these problems for you.

7-4.6. Multi-Ring Binders

There is a growing demand for reports inserted in multi-ring binders with either flexible or hard covers. There are many styles available, and quite a number of them are relatively inexpensive. They have the special advantage of complete freedom in regard to adding or removing pages as new information becomes available, or old information becomes obsolete. It is a comparatively easy matter to keep reports bound in this manner up to date by replacing obsolete pages with change pages. In addition, these bindings will lie open without any difficulty. The more rings in the binder, the more durable the report, because the pages are less apt to tear out; but, of course, the more rings, the more expensive the binding.

7-4.7. Plastic Bindings

Plastic bindings are popular for miscellaneous publications that justify the additional cost. Machines can be purchased with attachments that make it possible to insert or delete pages without too much trouble, although this is not so easy as it is with ring binders. Plastic binding comes in sizes from 1/8 to 2 inches, and, if you wish, you can have the title or other information stamped on the plastic binding, so that it can be read when the report is in a bookcase or file. Plastic binding is slow, however, and is not recommended for reports that are to be issued in large quantities. Also, the plastic has been known to break in use. Books with plastic bindings will lie open without trouble. The plastic bindings come in many different colors, and are effective for special jobs.

BIBLIOGRAPHY

The following list includes some of the publications available to report writers. Each of these offers much useful information and will be worth careful study by any of you who write more than an occasional report. There are, of course, many other excellent publications dealing with the various phases of report writing, and this bibliography is not intended in any way to be all-inclusive. Each book that you read will lead you to others.

Arkin, Herbert, and Raymond R. Colton. *Graphs: How to Make and Use Them,* Harper & Brothers, New York, 1940. 236 pp.

Collison, Robert L. *Indexes and Indexing,* John de.Graff, Inc., New York, 1953. 155 pp.

Howell, A. C. *A Handbook of English for Engineering Usage,* John Wiley and Sons, Inc., New York, 1940. 433 pp.

Hutchinson, Lois Irene. *Standard Handbook for Secretaries,* 6th Ed., McGraw-Hill Book Co., Inc., New York, 1952. 616 pp.

Kerekes, Frank, and Robley Winfrey. *Report Preparation,* The Iowa State College Press, Ames, Iowa, 1951. 448 pp.

Nelson, J. Raleigh. *Writing the Technical Report,* McGraw-Hill Book Co., Inc., New York, 1952. 356 pp.

Rhodes, Fred H., and H. F. Johnson. *Technical Report Writing,* McGraw-Hill Book Co., Inc., New York, 1941. 125 pp.

Sherman, Theodore A. *Modern Technical Writing,* Prentice-Hall, Inc., New York, 1955. 434 pp.

Skillin, Marjorie E., Robert M. Gay, and others. *Words Into Type,* Appleton-Century-Crofts, Inc., New York, 1948. 585 pp.

Smart, Walter K., and David R. Lang. *Smart's Handbook of Effective Writing,* Harper & Brothers, New York, 1943. 404 pp.

Spiker, Sina. *Indexing Your Book,* The University of Wisconsin Press, Madison, Wisconsin, 1955. 28 pp.

Sweet, Fred A. *Handbook for Writers, Editors, and Typists,* E. P. Dutton and Co., Inc., New York, 1939. 189 pp.

U. S. Geological Survey. *Suggestions to Authors of the Reports of the United States Geological Survey,* 5th Ed., GPO, Washington, 1958. 255 pp.

U. S. Government Printing Office. *Style Manual,* GPO, Washington, 1953. 492 pp.

University of Chicago Press. *A Manual of Style,* The University of Chicago Press, Chicago, 1956. 533 pp.

Walker, Helen M., and Walter M. Durost. *Statistical Tables, Their Structure and Use,* Teachers College, Columbia University, New York, 1937. 76 pp.

Weil, B. H. (Ed.). *The Technical Report,* Reinhold Publishing Corp., New York, 1954. 485 pp.

Wood, George McLane (Ed.). *Suggestions to Authors of Papers Submitted for Publication by the United States Geological Society,* 4th Ed., GPO, Washington, 1935. 126 pp.

GLOSSARY

backed up. Printed on the back. The term is applied to a sheet that has previously been printed on one side.

Bristol. A stiff, heavy paper made in various weights and colors and ranging from low to high grade.

callout. A word, phrase, number, or letter added to an illustration to identify, name, or explain an item shown in the illustration.

cap. Abbreviation for *capital letter*. The term *all caps* means that the specified word or words are to be set in capital letters.

change sheet. A sheet containing new information to. be inserted in a publication in place of a page containing original or earlier information that has become obsolete. The sheet that is replaced is then destroyed. (Also called *change page*.)

coated stock. A machine-finish paper coated with a mixture of clay, white fixer, and starch or casein. The surface finish varies from dull to glossy.

cold-type composition. The preparation of text and tabular matter by machines in which the type characters are precast and the image is obtained on paper by striking the character against the paper through an inked or carbon ribbon. This method of composition is similar to composition with a typewriter, except that the type fonts may be interchanged on a machine to get the desired variety of type. Many cold-type composing machines are equipped with attachments that make it possible to justify the right margins. This method of composition is used to prepare copy for reproduction by the offset process (although it is not restricted to the offset process).

collate. To gather or assemble the pages of a report in the proper sequence for binding.

cover stock. Heavy paper (for example, Bristol) used for covers of reports. There are different grades of stock and different kinds of finishes.

cut in. To insert an illustration, table, or other displayed matter on the same page with text.

descriptor. A word or phrase used to indicate the subject content of a report (a library term).

diazo. A group of light-sensitive compounds applied to paper (most commonly used), plastic, or acetate. In the *diazo process* of reproduction, the sensitized paper is exposed first to intense light and then to ammonia vapor, which results in an aniline-dye image.

dry process photoprint. A reproduction of a photograph made by the diazo process. A positive transparency made from a screened negative is used as the master.

flush. Aligned with the left or right margin—no indention.

fold out. An oversize page bound into a report and folded so as to fit within the dimensions of the standard pages. It is unfolded (folded out) when in use.

format. The physical make-up of a publication, including the shape, size, type style, margins, etc.

full measure. Length of a line of type used for running text in a publication; in typewriter typography, the average length of the lines of type in the text area.

gutter. The blank space resulting from the combined inside margins of facing printed pages.

halftone reproduction. Reproduction of a photograph or illustration in which the gradation of tone from light to dark is accomplished by breaking the tones of the original figure into dots of various sizes. With a fixed number of dots per square inch, smaller dots result in lighter tones and larger dots in darker tones. A *halftone negative* is obtained by photographing an original continuous-tone print or drawing with a camera in which a screen (contact or glass) is placed between the lens and a high-contrast film. The screen breaks up the image into a series of dots (from 65 to 300 per inch). In offset reproduction, the halftone negative is combined with the negative of the text and any other single-tone material (for example, ink drawings) on a page, and an offset plate is prepared from the combined negative. Copies are reproduced from this plate on the offset press. Proofs can be obtained of the combined negative by other photographic processes.

hot-type composition. The setting of text and tabular matter by machines in which new letters are cast individually or in lines from molten metal. The resulting type is then locked into blocks of desired dimensions and copies are produced by pressing sheets of paper against the inked type.

Proofs may be made from hot type for subsequent incorporation into reproduction copy used in the offset process, or the type may be used with a letterpress to produce an indefinite number of copies direct.

interleave. To insert a page or pages between other pages. Illustrations are said to be interleaved with the text of a publication when pages containing only illustrations and their legends are inserted between pages of text without changing the layout of the text to accommodate the interleaved items.

justify. To align printed matter along its left or right margin. Except in rare instances, left margins of text matter are justified. Right margins may or may not be justified depending upon the method of composing (that is, typewriter, cold type, or hot type).

leaders. A row of two or more periods (with or without spacing between them) used to lead the eye from one item to another on the same line.

master. An original from which additional copies may be reproduced. It may be matter typed or drawn on bond paper, a stencil, a direct-image offset plate, etc.

measure. Length of a line of type.

mounting board. A heavy paperboard upon which a photograph or other illustrative matter is cemented in order to give greater ease in handling and to protect the original item.

narrow measure. Length of a line of type that is shorter than the standard line used in a publication.

overlay. A sheet of transparent, translucent, or opaque material placed over a basic page of text, tabular matter, illustration, etc. during processing. The purpose may be to protect the basic matter, carry instructions, carry additional matter to be processed separately from the basic matter, etc.

register. To superimpose one image upon another in the precise position required to result in a single image with all parts in proper relationship to each other.

rule. A straight line. A rule may be drawn by a ruler or printed by the use of a strip of brass or type metal. Such lines may be of different thicknesses.

running head. A heading repeated at the top of each page of a publication. It is usually the title of a report, the report series number, or both. In large reports, the title may be repeated at the top of the left-hand pages, while the title of a chapter or major section is repeated at the top of the right-hand pages. Many other variations may be used.

running text. The continuing verbal matter of an author's work, as distinct from tabular matter, displayed matter, and illustrations.

show-through. The image of matter printed on one side of a sheet of paper that can be seen from the other side.

signature. A folded sheet upon which four or more pages of a book have been printed. The pages are printed (in multiples of four) and the sheet is folded in such a way that when the signature is sewn the pages fall in sequence forming a portion of the book. A signature usually consists of 16 pages but may vary from 4 to 64 pages depending upon the weight of the paper and the printing and folding equipment available.

subscript. A sign, letter, or symbol set below the line of type in relation to a word, letter, or number; for example: H_2O.

superscript. A sign, letter, or symbol set above the line of type in relation to a word, letter, or number; for example: x^2.

turnover line. A continuation of displayed matter or an entry in a table from the first line of such matter to a following line.

typography. The plan, arrangement, and appearance of certain details of printed matter.

vellum. A thin, fine-grained, translucent paper. It is available in various weights and grades. Sheets of vellum (called *vellums*) are used for the preparation of masters by typing or drawing on them with pencil or ink for subsequent reproduction.

INDEX

(Numbers in parentheses refer to sections.)

273

SOME DOVER SCIENCE BOOKS

SOME DOVER SCIENCE BOOKS

WHAT IS SCIENCE?,
Norman Campbell
This excellent introduction explains scientific method, role of mathematics, types of scientific laws. Contents: 2 aspects of science, science & nature, laws of science, discovery of laws, explanation of laws, measurement & numerical laws, applications of science. 192pp. 5⅜ x 8.   Paperbound $1.25

FADS AND FALLACIES IN THE NAME OF SCIENCE,
Martin Gardner
Examines various cults, quack systems, frauds, delusions which at various times have masqueraded as science. Accounts of hollow-earth fanatics like Symmes; Velikovsky and wandering planets; Hoerbiger; Bellamy and the theory of multiple moons; Charles Fort; dowsing, pseudoscientific methods for finding water, ores, oil. Sections on naturopathy, iridiagnosis, zone therapy, food fads, etc. Analytical accounts of Wilhelm Reich and orgone sex energy; L. Ron Hubbard and Dianetics; A. Korzybski and General Semantics; many others. Brought up to date to include Bridey Murphy, others. Not just a collection of anecdotes, but a fair, reasoned appraisal of eccentric theory. Formerly titled *In the Name of Science*. Preface. Index. x + 384pp. 5⅜ x 8.
                                                     Paperbound $1.85

PHYSICS, THE PIONEER SCIENCE,
L. W. Taylor
First thorough text to place all important physical phenomena in cultural-historical framework; remains best work of its kind. Exposition of physical laws, theories developed chronologically, with great historical, illustrative experiments diagrammed, described, worked out mathematically. Excellent physics text for self-study as well as class work. Vol. 1: Heat, Sound: motion, acceleration, gravitation, conservation of energy, heat engines, rotation, heat, mechanical energy, etc. 211 illus. 407pp. 5⅜ x 8. Vol. 2: Light, Electricity: images, lenses, prisms, magnetism, Ohm's law, dynamos, telegraph, quantum theory, decline of mechanical view of nature, etc. Bibliography. 13 table appendix. Index. 551 illus. 2 color plates. 508pp. 5⅜ x 8.
                         Vol. 1 Paperbound $2.25, Vol. 2 Paperbound $2.25,
                                                        The set $4.50

THE EVOLUTION OF SCIENTIFIC THOUGHT FROM NEWTON TO EINSTEIN,
A. d'Abro
Einstein's special and general theories of relativity, with their historical implications, are analyzed in non-technical terms. Excellent accounts of the contributions of Newton, Riemann, Weyl, Planck, Eddington, Maxwell, Lorentz and others are treated in terms of space and time, equations of electromagnetics, finiteness of the universe, methodology of science. 21 diagrams. 482pp. 5⅜ x 8.
                                                     Paperbound $2.50

CHANCE, LUCK AND STATISTICS: THE SCIENCE OF CHANCE,
Horace C. Levinson
Theory of probability and science of statistics in simple, non-technical language. Part I deals with theory of probability, covering odd superstitions in regard to "luck," the meaning of betting odds, the law of mathematical expectation, gambling, and applications in poker, roulette, lotteries, dice, bridge, and other games of chance. Part II discusses the misuse of statistics, the concept of statistical probabilities, normal and skew frequency distributions, and statistics applied to various fields—birth rates, stock speculation, insurance rates, advertising, etc. "Presented in an easy humorous style which I consider the best kind of expository writing," Prof. A. C. Cohen, Industry Quality Control. Enlarged revised edition. Formerly titled *The Science of Chance*. Preface and two new appendices by the author. Index. xiv + 365pp. 5⅜ x 8. Paperbound $2.00

BASIC ELECTRONICS,
prepared by the U.S. Navy Training Publications Center
A thorough and comprehensive manual on the fundamentals of electronics. Written clearly, it is equally useful for self-study or course work for those with a knowledge of the principles of basic electricity. Partial contents: Operating Principles of the Electron Tube; Introduction to Transistors; Power Supplies for Electronic Equipment; Tuned Circuits; Electron-Tube Amplifiers; Audio Power Amplifiers; Oscillators; Transmitters; Transmission Lines; Antennas and Propagation; Introduction to Computers; and related topics. Appendix. Index. Hundreds of illustrations and diagrams. vi + 471pp. 6½ x 9¼.
Paperbound $2.75

BASIC THEORY AND APPLICATION OF TRANSISTORS,
prepared by the U.S. Department of the Army
An introductory manual prepared for an army training program. One of the finest available surveys of theory and application of transistor design and operation. Minimal knowledge of physics and theory of electron tubes required. Suitable for textbook use, course supplement, or home study. Chapters: Introduction; fundamental theory of transistors; transistor amplifier fundamentals; parameters, equivalent circuits, and characteristic curves; bias stabilization; transistor analysis and comparison using characteristic curves and charts; audio amplifiers; tuned amplifiers; wide-band amplifiers; oscillators; pulse and switching circuits; modulation, mixing, and demodulation; and additional semiconductor devices. Unabridged, corrected edition. 240 schematic drawings, photographs, wiring diagrams, etc. 2 Appendices. Glossary. Index. 263pp. 6½ x 9¼. Paperbound $1.25

GUIDE TO THE LITERATURE OF MATHEMATICS AND PHYSICS,
N. G. Parke III
Over 5000 entries included under approximately 120 major subject headings of selected most important books, monographs, periodicals, articles in English, plus important works in German, French, Italian, Spanish, Russian (many recently available works). Covers every branch of physics, math, related engineering. Includes author, title, edition, publisher, place, date, number of volumes, number of pages. A 40-page introduction on the basic problems of research and study provides useful information on the organization and use of libraries, the psychology of learning, etc. This reference work will save you hours of time. 2nd revised edition. Indices of authors, subjects, 464pp. 5⅜ x 8.
Paperbound $2.75

THE RISE OF THE NEW PHYSICS (formerly THE DECLINE OF MECHANISM), *A. d'Abro*
This authoritative and comprehensive 2-volume exposition is unique in scientific publishing. Written for intelligent readers not familiar with higher mathematics, it is the only thorough explanation in non-technical language of modern mathematical-physical theory. Combining both history and exposition, it ranges from classical Newtonian concepts up through the electronic theories of Dirac and Heisenberg, the statistical mechanics of Fermi, and Einstein's relativity theories. "A must for anyone doing serious study in the physical sciences," *J. of Franklin Inst.* 97 illustrations. 991pp. 2 volumes.

Vol. 1 Paperbound $2.25, Vol. 2 Paperbound $2.25,
The set $4.50

THE STRANGE STORY OF THE QUANTUM, AN ACCOUNT FOR THE GENERAL READER OF THE GROWTH OF IDEAS UNDERLYING OUR PRESENT ATOMIC KNOWLEDGE, *B. Hoffmann*
Presents lucidly and expertly, with barest amount of mathematics, the problems and theories which led to modern quantum physics. Dr. Hoffmann begins with the closing years of the 19th century, when certain trifling discrepancies were noticed, and with illuminating analogies and examples takes you through the brilliant concepts of Planck, Einstein, Pauli, de Broglie, Bohr, Schroedinger, Heisenberg, Dirac, Sommerfeld, Feynman, etc. This edition includes a new, long postscript carrying the story through 1958. "Of the books attempting an account of the history and contents of our modern atomic physics which have come to my attention, this is the best," H. Margenau, Yale University, in *American Journal of Physics.* 32 tables and line illustrations. Index. 275pp. 5⅜ x 8.

Paperbound $1.75

GREAT IDEAS AND THEORIES OF MODERN COSMOLOGY, *Jagjit Singh*
The theories of Jeans, Eddington, Milne, Kant, Bondi, Gold, Newton, Einstein, Gamow, Hoyle, Dirac, Kuiper, Hubble, Weizsäcker and many others on such cosmological questions as the origin of the universe, space and time, planet formation, "continuous creation," the birth, life, and death of the stars, the origin of the galaxies, etc. By the author of the popular *Great Ideas of Modern Mathematics.* A gifted popularizer of science, he makes the most difficult abstractions crystal-clear even to the most non-mathematical reader. Index. xii + 276pp. 5⅜ x 8½.

Paperbound $2.00

GREAT IDEAS OF MODERN MATHEMATICS: THEIR NATURE AND USE, *Jagjit Singh*
Reader with only high school math will understand main mathematical ideas of modern physics, astronomy, genetics, psychology, evolution, etc., better than many who use them as tools, but comprehend little of their basic structure. Author uses his wide knowledge of non-mathematical fields in brilliant exposition of differential equations, matrices, group theory, logic, statistics, problems of mathematical foundations, imaginary numbers, vectors, etc. Original publications, 2 appendices. 2 indexes. 65 illustr. 322pp. 5⅜ x 8. Paperbound $2.00

THE MATHEMATICS OF GREAT AMATEURS, *Julian L. Coolidge*
Great discoveries made by poets, theologians, philosophers, artists and other non-mathematicians: Omar Khayyam, Leonardo da Vinci, Albrecht Dürer, John Napier, Pascal, Diderot, Bolzano, etc. Surprising accounts of what can result from a non-professional preoccupation with the oldest of sciences. 56 figures. viii + 211pp. 5⅜ x 8½.

Paperbound $1.50

COLLEGE ALGEBRA, *H. B. Fine*

Standard college text that gives a systematic and deductive structure to algebra; comprehensive, connected, with emphasis on theory. Discusses the commutative, associative, and distributive laws of number in unusual detail, and goes on with undetermined coefficients, quadratic equations, progressions, logarithms, permutations, probability, power series, and much more. Still most valuable elementary-intermediate text on the science and structure of algebra. Index. 1560 problems, all with answers. x + 631pp. 5⅜ x 8. Paperbound $2.75

HIGHER MATHEMATICS FOR STUDENTS OF CHEMISTRY AND PHYSICS, *J. W. Mellor*

Not abstract, but practical, building its problems out of familiar laboratory material, this covers differential calculus, coordinate, analytical geometry, functions, integral calculus, infinite series, numerical equations, differential equations, Fourier's theorem, probability, theory of errors, calculus of variations, determinants. "If the reader is not familiar with this book, it will repay him to examine it," *Chem. & Engineering News.* 800 problems. 189 figures. Bibliography. xxi + 641pp. 5⅜ x 8. Paperbound $2.50

TRIGONOMETRY REFRESHER FOR TECHNICAL MEN, *A. A. Klaf*

A modern question and answer text on plane and spherical trigonometry. Part I covers plane trigonometry: angles, quadrants, trigonometrical functions, graphical representation, interpolation, equations, logarithms, solution of triangles, slide rules, etc. Part II discusses applications to navigation, surveying, elasticity, architecture, and engineering. Small angles, periodic functions, vectors, polar coordinates, De Moivre's theorem, fully covered. Part III is devoted to spherical trigonometry and the solution of spherical triangles, with applications to terrestrial and astronomical problems. Special time-savers for numerical calculation. 913 questions answered for you! 1738 problems; answers to odd numbers. 494 figures. 14 pages of functions, formulae. Index. x + 629pp. 5⅜ x 8.
Paperbound $2.00

CALCULUS REFRESHER FOR TECHNICAL MEN, *A. A. Klaf*

Not an ordinary textbook but a unique refresher for engineers, technicians, and students. An examination of the most important aspects of differential and integral calculus by means of 756 key questions. Part I covers simple differential calculus: constants, variables, functions, increments, derivatives, logarithms, curvature, etc. Part II treats fundamental concepts of integration: inspection, substitution, transformation, reduction, areas and volumes, mean value, successive and partial integration, double and triple integration. Stresses practical aspects! A 50 page section gives applications to civil and nautical engineering, electricity, stress and strain, elasticity, industrial engineering, and similar fields. 756 questions answered. 556 problems; solutions to odd numbers. 36 pages of constants, formulae. Index. v + 431pp. 5⅜ x 8. Paperbound $2.00

INTRODUCTION TO THE THEORY OF GROUPS OF FINITE ORDER, *R. Carmichael*

Examines fundamental theorems and their application. Beginning with sets, systems, permutations, etc., it progresses in easy stages through important types of groups: Abelian, prime power, permutation, etc. Except 1 chapter where matrices are desirable, no higher math needed. 783 exercises, problems. Index. xvi + 447pp. 5⅜ x 8. Paperbound $3.00

FIVE VOLUME "THEORY OF FUNCTIONS" SET BY KONRAD KNOPP

This five-volume set, prepared by Konrad Knopp, provides a complete and readily followed account of theory of functions. Proofs are given concisely, yet without sacrifice of completeness or rigor. These volumes are used as texts by such universities as M.I.T., University of Chicago, N. Y. City College, and many others. "Excellent introduction . . . remarkably readable, concise, clear, rigorous," *Journal of the American Statistical Association.*

ELEMENTS OF THE THEORY OF FUNCTIONS,
Konrad Knopp
This book provides the student with background for further volumes in this set, or texts on a similar level. Partial contents: foundations, system of complex numbers and the Gaussian plane of numbers, Riemann sphere of numbers, mapping by linear functions, normal forms, the logarithm, the cyclometric functions and binomial series. "Not only for the young student, but also for the student who knows all about what is in it," *Mathematical Journal.* Bibliography. Index. 140pp. 5⅜ x 8.   Paperbound $1.50

THEORY OF FUNCTIONS, PART I,
Konrad Knopp
With volume II, this book provides coverage of basic concepts and theorems. Partial contents: numbers and points, functions of a complex variable, integral of a continuous function, Cauchy's integral theorem, Cauchy's integral formulae, series with variable terms, expansion of analytic functions in power series, analytic continuation and complete definition of analytic functions, entire transcendental functions, Laurent expansion, types of singularities. Bibliography. Index. vii + 146pp. 5⅜ x 8.   Paperbound $1.35

THEORY OF FUNCTIONS, PART II,
Konrad Knopp
Application and further development of general theory, special topics. Single valued functions. Entire, Weierstrass, Meromorphic functions. Riemann surfaces. Algebraic functions. Analytical configuration, Riemann surface. Bibliography. Index. x + 150pp. 5⅜ x 8.   Paperbound $1.35

PROBLEM BOOK IN THE THEORY OF FUNCTIONS, VOLUME 1.
Konrad Knopp
Problems in elementary theory, for use with Knopp's *Theory of Functions,* or any other text, arranged according to increasing difficulty. Fundamental concepts, sequences of numbers and infinite series, complex variable, integral theorems, development in series, conformal mapping. 182 problems. Answers. viii + 126pp. 5⅜ x 8.   Paperbound $1.35

PROBLEM BOOK IN THE THEORY OF FUNCTIONS, VOLUME 2,
Konrad Knopp
Advanced theory of functions, to be used either with Knopp's *Theory of Functions,* or any other comparable text. Singularities, entire & meromorphic functions, periodic, analytic, continuation, multiple-valued functions, Riemann surfaces, conformal mapping. Includes a section of additional elementary problems. "The difficult task of selecting from the immense material of the modern theory of functions the problems just within the reach of the beginner is here masterfully accomplished," *Am. Math. Soc.* Answers. 138pp. 5⅜ x 8.
Paperbound $1.50

NUMERICAL SOLUTIONS OF DIFFERENTIAL EQUATIONS,
H. Levy & E. A. Baggott

Comprehensive collection of methods for solving ordinary differential equations of first and higher order. All must pass 2 requirements: easy to grasp and practical, more rapid than school methods. Partial contents: graphical integration of differential equations, graphical methods for detailed solution. Numerical solution. Simultaneous equations and equations of 2nd and higher orders. "Should be in the hands of all in research in applied mathematics, teaching," *Nature.* 21 figures. viii + 238pp. 5⅜ x 8.   Paperbound $1.85

ELEMENTARY STATISTICS, WITH APPLICATIONS IN MEDICINE AND THE BIOLOGICAL SCIENCES, *F. E. Croxton*

A sound introduction to statistics for anyone in the physical sciences, assuming no prior acquaintance and requiring only a modest knowledge of math. All basic formulas carefully explained and illustrated; all necessary reference tables included. From basic terms and concepts, the study proceeds to frequency distribution, linear, non-linear, and multiple correlation, skewness, kurtosis, etc. A large section deals with reliability and significance of statistical methods. Containing concrete examples from medicine and biology, this book will prove unusually helpful to workers in those fields who increasingly must evaluate, check, and interpret statistics. Formerly titled "Elementary Statistics with Applications in Medicine." 101 charts. 57 tables. 14 appendices. Index. vi + 376pp. 5⅜ x 8.   Paperbound $2.00

INTRODUCTION TO SYMBOLIC LOGIC,
S. Langer

No special knowledge of math required — probably the clearest book ever written on symbolic logic, suitable for the layman, general scientist, and philosopher. You start with simple symbols and advance to a knowledge of the Boole-Schroeder and Russell-Whitehead systems. Forms, logical structure, classes, the calculus of propositions, logic of the syllogism, etc. are all covered. "One of the clearest and simplest introductions," *Mathematics Gazette.* Second enlarged, revised edition. 368pp. 5⅜ x 8.   Paperbound $2.00

A SHORT ACCOUNT OF THE HISTORY OF MATHEMATICS,
W. W. R. Ball

Most readable non-technical history of mathematics treats lives, discoveries of every important figure from Egyptian, Phoenician, mathematicians to late 19th century. Discusses schools of Ionia, Pythagoras, Athens, Cyzicus, Alexandria, Byzantium, systems of numeration; primitive arithmetic; Middle Ages, Renaissance, including Arabs, Bacon, Regiomontanus, Tartaglia, Cardan, Stevinus, Galileo, Kepler; modern mathematics of Descartes, Pascal, Wallis, Huygens, Newton, Leibnitz, d'Alembert, Euler, Lambert, Laplace, Legendre, Gauss, Hermite, Weierstrass, scores more. Index. 25 figures. 546pp. 5⅜ x 8.
                              Paperbound $2.25

INTRODUCTION TO NONLINEAR DIFFERENTIAL AND INTEGRAL EQUATIONS,
Harold T. Davis

Aspects of the problem of nonlinear equations, transformations that lead to equations solvable by classical means, results in special cases, and useful generalizations. Thorough, but easily followed by mathematically sophisticated reader who knows little about non-linear equations. 137 problems for student to solve. xv + 566pp. 5⅜ x 8½.   Paperbound $2.00

An Introduction to the Geometry of N Dimensions,
D. H. Y. Sommerville
An introduction presupposing no prior knowledge of the field, the only book in English devoted exclusively to higher dimensional geometry. Discusses fundamental ideas of incidence, parallelism, perpendicularity, angles between linear space; enumerative geometry; analytical geometry from projective and metric points of view; polytopes; elementary ideas in analysis situs; content of hyper-spacial figures. Bibliography. Index. 60 diagrams. 196pp. 5⅜ x 8.
Paperbound $1.50

Elementary Concepts of Topology, P. Alexandroff
First English translation of the famous brief introduction to topology for the beginner or for the mathematician not undertaking extensive study. This unusually useful intuitive approach deals primarily with the concepts of complex, cycle, and homology, and is wholly consistent with current investigations. Ranges from basic concepts of set-theoretic topology to the concept of Betti groups. "Glowing example of harmony between intuition and thought," David Hilbert. Translated by A. E. Farley. Introduction by D. Hilbert. Index. 25 figures. 73pp. 5⅜ x 8.
Paperbound $1.00

Elements of Non-Euclidean Geometry,
D. M. Y. Sommerville
Unique in proceeding step-by-step, in the manner of traditional geometry. Enables the student with only a good knowledge of high school algebra and geometry to grasp elementary hyperbolic, elliptic, analytic non-Euclidean geometries; space curvature and its philosophical implications; theory of radical axes; homothetic centres and systems of circles; parataxy and parallelism; absolute measure; Gauss' proof of the defect area theorem; geodesic representation; much more, all with exceptional clarity. 126 problems at chapter endings provide progressive practice and familiarity. 133 figures. Index. xvi + 274pp. 5⅜ x 8.
Paperbound $2.00

Introduction to the Theory of Numbers, L. E. Dickson
Thorough, comprehensive approach with adequate coverage of classical literature, an introductory volume beginners can follow. Chapters on divisibility, congruences, quadratic residues & reciprocity. Diophantine equations, etc. Full treatment of binary quadratic forms without usual restriction to integral coefficients. Covers infinitude of primes, least residues. Fermat's theorem. Euler's phi function, Legendre's symbol, Gauss's lemma, automorphs, reduced forms, recent theorems of Thue & Siegel, many more. Much material not readily available elsewhere. 239 problems. Index. I figure. viii + 183pp. 5⅜ x 8.
Paperbound $1.75

Mathematical Tables and Formulas,
compiled by Robert D. Carmichael and Edwin R. Smith
Valuable collection for students, etc. Contains all tables necessary in college algebra and trigonometry, such as five-place common logarithms, logarithmic sines and tangents of small angles, logarithmic trigonometric functions, natural trigonometric functions, four-place antilogarithms, tables for changing from sexagesimal to circular and from circular to sexagesimal measure of angles, etc. Also many tables and formulas not ordinarily accessible, including powers, roots, and reciprocals, exponential and hyperbolic functions, ten-place logarithms of prime numbers, and formulas and theorems from analytical and elementary geometry and from calculus. Explanatory introduction. viii + 269pp. 5⅜ x 8½.
Paperbound $1.25

A SOURCE BOOK IN MATHEMATICS,
D. E. Smith
Great discoveries in math, from Renaissance to end of 19th century, in English translation. Read announcements by Dedekind, Gauss, Delamain, Pascal, Fermat, Newton, Abel, Lobachevsky, Bolyai, Riemann, De Moivre, Legendre, Laplace, others of discoveries about imaginary numbers, number congruence, slide rule, equations, symbolism, cubic algebraic equations, non-Euclidean forms of geometry, calculus, function theory, quaternions, etc. Succinct selections from 125 different treatises, articles, most unavailable elsewhere in English. Each article preceded by biographical introduction. Vol. I: Fields of Number, Algebra. Index. 32 illus. 338pp. 5⅜ x 8. Vol. II: Fields of Geometry, Probability, Calculus, Functions, Quaternions. 83 illus. 432pp. 5⅜ x 8.
Vol. 1 Paperbound $2.00, Vol. 2 Paperbound $2.00,
The set $4.00

FOUNDATIONS OF PHYSICS,
R. B. Lindsay & H. Margenau
Excellent bridge between semi-popular works & technical treatises. A discussion of methods of physical description, construction of theory; valuable for physicist with elementary calculus who is interested in ideas that give meaning to data, tools of modern physics. Contents include symbolism; mathematical equations; space & time foundations of mechanics; probability; physics & continua; electron theory; special & general relativity; quantum mechanics; causality. "Thorough and yet not overdetailed. Unreservedly recommended," *Nature* (London). Unabridged, corrected edition. List of recommended readings. 35 illustrations. xi + 537pp. 5⅜ x 8.   Paperbound $3.00

FUNDAMENTAL FORMULAS OF PHYSICS,
ed. by D. H. Menzel
High useful, full, inexpensive reference and study text, ranging from simple to highly sophisticated operations. Mathematics integrated into text—each chapter stands as short textbook of field represented. Vol. 1: Statistics, Physical Constants, Special Theory of Relativity, Hydrodynamics, Aerodynamics, Boundary Value Problems in Math, Physics, Viscosity, Electromagnetic Theory, etc. Vol. 2: Sound, Acoustics, Geometrical Optics, Electron Optics, High-Energy Phenomena, Magnetism, Biophysics, much more. Index. Total of 800pp. 5⅜ x 8.
Vol. 1 Paperbound $2.25, Vol. 2 Paperbound $2.25,
The set $4.50

THEORETICAL PHYSICS,
A. S. Kompaneyets
One of the very few thorough studies of the subject in this price range. Provides advanced students with a comprehensive theoretical background. Especially strong on recent experimentation and developments in quantum theory. Contents: Mechanics (Generalized Coordinates, Lagrange's Equation, Collision of Particles, etc.), Electrodynamics (Vector Analysis, Maxwell's equations, Transmission of Signals, Theory of Relativity, etc.), Quantum Mechanics (the Inadequacy of Classical Mechanics, the Wave Equation, Motion in a Central Field, Quantum Theory of Radiation, Quantum Theories of Dispersion and Scattering, etc.), and Statistical Physics (Equilibrium Distribution of Molecules in an Ideal Gas, Boltzmann Statistics, Bose and Fermi Distribution. Thermodynamic Quantities, etc.). Revised to 1961. Translated by George Yankovsky, authorized by Kompaneyets. 137 exercises. 56 figures. 529pp. 5⅜ x 8½.
Paperbound $2.50

MATHEMATICAL PHYSICS, *D. H. Menzel*
Thorough one-volume treatment of the mathematical techniques vital for classical mechanics, electromagnetic theory, quantum theory, and relativity. Written by the Harvard Professor of Astrophysics for junior, senior, and graduate courses, it gives clear explanations of all those aspects of function theory, vectors, matrices, dyadics, tensors, partial differential equations, etc., necessary for the understanding of the various physical theories. Electron theory, relativity, and other topics seldom presented appear here in considerable detail. Scores of definition, conversion factors, dimensional constants, etc. "More detailed than normal for an advanced text . . . excellent set of sections on Dyadics, Matrices, and Tensors," *Journal of the Franklin Institute*. Index. 193 problems, with answers. x + 412pp. 5⅜ x 8. Paperbound $2.50

THE THEORY OF SOUND, *Lord Rayleigh*
Most vibrating systems likely to be encountered in practice can be tackled successfully by the methods set forth by the great Nobel laureate, Lord Rayleigh. Complete coverage of experimental, mathematical aspects of sound theory. Partial contents: Harmonic motions, vibrating systems in general, lateral vibrations of bars, curved plates or shells, applications of Laplace's functions to acoustical problems, fluid friction, plane vortex-sheet, vibrations of solid bodies, etc. This is the first inexpensive edition of this great reference and study work. Bibliography, Historical introduction by R. B. Lindsay. Total of 1040pp. 97 figures. 5⅜ x 8. Vol. 1 Paperbound $2.50, Vol. 2 Paperbound $2.50, The set $5.00

HYDRODYNAMICS, *Horace Lamb*
Internationally famous complete coverage of standard reference work on dynamics of liquids & gases. Fundamental theorems, equations, methods, solutions, background, for classical hydrodynamics. Chapters include Equations of Motion, Integration of Equations in Special Gases, Irrotational Motion, Motion of Liquid in 2 Dimensions, Motion of Solids through Liquid-Dynamical Theory, Vortex Motion, Tidal Waves, Surface Waves, Waves of Expansion, Viscosity, Rotating Masses of Liquids. Excellently planned, arranged; clear, lucid presentation. 6th enlarged, revised edition. Index. Over 900 footnotes, mostly bibliographical. 119 figures. xv + 738pp. 6⅛ x 9¼. Paperbound $4.00

DYNAMICAL THEORY OF GASES, *James Jeans*
Divided into mathematical and physical chapters for the convenience of those not expert in mathematics, this volume discusses the mathematical theory of gas in a steady state, thermodynamics, Boltzmann and Maxwell, kinetic theory, quantum theory, exponentials, etc. 4th enlarged edition, with new material on quantum theory, quantum dynamics, etc. Indexes. 28 figures. 444pp. 6⅛ x 9¼. Paperbound $2.75

THERMODYNAMICS, *Enrico Fermi*
Unabridged reproduction of 1937 edition. Elementary in treatment; remarkable for clarity, organization. Requires no knowledge of advanced math beyond calculus, only familiarity with fundamentals of thermometry, calorimetry. Partial Contents: Thermodynamic systems; First & Second laws of thermodynamics; Entropy; Thermodynamic potentials: phase rule, reversible electric cell; Gaseous reactions: van't Hoff reaction box, principle of LeChatelier; Thermodynamics of dilute solutions: osmotic & vapor pressures, boiling & freezing points; Entropy constant. Index. 25 problems. 24 illustrations. x + 160pp. 5⅜ x 8. Paperbound $1.75

CELESTIAL OBJECTS FOR COMMON TELESCOPES,
Rev. T. W. Webb
Classic handbook for the use and pleasure of the amateur astronomer. Of
inestimable aid in locating and identifying thousands of celestial objects. Vol I,
The Solar System: discussions of the principle and operation of the telescope,
procedures of observations and telescope-photography, spectroscopy, etc., precise
location information of sun, moon, planets, meteors. Vol. II, The Stars:
alphabetical listing of constellations, information on double stars, clusters, stars
with unusual spectra, variables, and nebulae, etc. Nearly 4,000 objects noted.
Edited and extensively revised by Margaret W. Mayall, director of the American
Assn. of Variable Star Observers. New Index by Mrs. Mayall giving the location
of all objects mentioned in the text for Epoch 2000. New Precession Table
added. New appendices on the planetary satellites, constellation names and
abbreviations, and solar system data. Total of 46 illustrations. Total of xxxix
+ 606pp. 5⅜ x 8.   Vol. 1 Paperbound $2.25, Vol. 2 Paperbound $2.25
The set $4.50

PLANETARY THEORY,
E. W. Brown and C. A. Shook
Provides a clear presentation of basic methods for calculating planetary orbits
for today's astronomer. Begins with a careful exposition of specialized mathematical topics essential for handling perturbation theory and then goes on to
indicate how most of the previous methods reduce ultimately to two general
calculation methods: obtaining expressions either for the coordinates of planetary positions or for the elements which determine the perturbed paths. An
example of each is given and worked in detail. Corrected edition. Preface.
Appendix. Index. xii + 302pp. 5⅜ x 8½.   Paperbound $2.25

STAR NAMES AND THEIR MEANINGS,
Richard Hinckley Allen
An unusual book documenting the various attributions of names to the
individual stars over the centuries. Here is a treasure-house of information on
a topic not normally delved into even by professional astronomers; provides a
fascinating background to the stars in folk-lore, literary references, ancient
writings, star catalogs and maps over the centuries. Constellation-by-constella-
tion analysis covers hundreds of stars and other asterisms, including the
Pleiades, Hyades, Andromedan Nebula, etc. Introduction. Indices. List of
authors and authorities. xx + 563pp. 5⅜ x 8½.   Paperbound $2.50

A SHORT HISTORY OF ASTRONOMY, *A. Berry*
Popular standard work for over 50 years, this thorough and accurate volume
covers the science from primitive times to the end of the 19th century. After
the Greeks and the Middle Ages, individual chapters analyze Copernicus, Brahe,
Galileo, Kepler, and Newton, and the mixed reception of their discoveries.
Post-Newtonian achievements are then discussed in unusual detail: Halley,
Bradley, Lagrange, Laplace, Herschel, Bessel, etc. 2 Indexes. 104 illustrations,
9 portraits. xxxi + 440pp. 5⅜ x 8.   Paperbound $2.75

SOME THEORY OF SAMPLING, *W. E. Deming*
The purpose of this book is to make sampling techniques understandable to
and useable by social scientists, industrial managers, and natural scientists
who are finding statistics increasingly part of their work. Over 200 exercises,
plus dozens of actual applications. 61 tables. 90 figs. xix + 602pp. 5⅜ x 8½.
Paperbound $3.50

PRINCIPLES OF STRATIGRAPHY,
A. W. Grabau

Classic of 20th century geology, unmatched in scope and comprehensiveness. Nearly 600 pages cover the structure and origins of every kind of sedimentary, hydrogenic, oceanic, pyroclastic, atmoclastic, hydroclastic, marine hydroclastic, and bioclastic rock; metamorphism; erosion; etc. Includes also the constitution of the atmosphere; morphology of oceans, rivers, glaciers; volcanic activities; faults and earthquakes; and fundamental principles of paleontology (nearly 200 pages). New introduction by Prof. M. Kay, Columbia U. 1277 bibliographical entries. 264 diagrams. Tables, maps, etc. Two volume set. Total of xxxii + 1185pp. 5⅜ x 8.   Vol. 1 Paperbound $2.50, Vol. 2 Paperbound $2.50,
                                                                                        The set $5.00

SNOW CRYSTALS, W. A. Bentley and W. J. Humphreys

Over 200 pages of Bentley's famous microphotographs of snow flakes—the product of painstaking, methodical work at his Jericho, Vermont studio. The pictures, which also include plates of frost, glaze and dew on vegetation, spider webs, windowpanes; sleet; graupel or soft hail, were chosen both for their scientific interest and their aesthetic qualities. The wonder of nature's diversity is exhibited in the intricate, beautiful patterns of the snow flakes. Introductory text by W. J. Humphreys. Selected bibliography. 2,453 illustrations. 224pp. 8 x 10¼.   Paperbound $3.25

THE BIRTH AND DEVELOPMENT OF THE GEOLOGICAL SCIENCES,
F. D. Adams

Most thorough history of the earth sciences ever written. Geological thought from earliest times to the end of the 19th century, covering over 300 early thinkers & systems: fossils & their explanation, vulcanists vs. neptunists, figured stones & paleontology, generation of stones, dozens of similar topics. 91 illustrations, including medieval, renaissance woodcuts, etc. Index. 632 footnotes, mostly bibliographical. 511pp. 5⅜ x 8.   Paperbound $2.75

ORGANIC CHEMISTRY, F. C. Whitmore

The entire subject of organic chemistry for the practicing chemist and the advanced student. Storehouse of facts, theories, processes found elsewhere only in specialized journals. Covers aliphatic compounds (500 pages on the properties and synthetic preparation of hydrocarbons, halides, proteins, ketones, etc.), alicyclic compounds, aromatic compounds, heterocyclic compounds, organophosphorus and organometallic compounds. Methods of synthetic preparation analyzed critically throughout. Includes much of biochemical interest. "The scope of this volume is astonishing," *Industrial and Engineering Chemistry*. 12,000-reference index. 2387-item bibliography. Total of x + 1005pp. 5⅜ x 8.   Two volume set, paperbound $4.50

THE PHASE RULE AND ITS APPLICATION,
Alexander Findlay

Covering chemical phenomena of 1, 2, 3, 4, and multiple component systems, this "standard work on the subject" (*Nature*, London), has been completely revised and brought up to date by A. N. Campbell and N. O. Smith. Brand new material has been added on such matters as binary, tertiary liquid equilibria, solid solutions in ternary systems, quinary systems of salts and water. Completely revised to triangular coordinates in ternary systems, clarified graphic representation, solid models, etc. 9th revised edition. Author, subject indexes. 236 figures. 505 footnotes, mostly bibliographic. xii + 494pp. 5⅜ x 8.
                                                                                        Paperbound $2.75

A COURSE IN MATHEMATICAL ANALYSIS,
Edouard Goursat

Trans. by E. R. Hedrick, O. Dunkel, H. G. Bergmann. Classic study of fundamental material thoroughly treated. Extremely lucid exposition of wide range of subject matter for student with one year of calculus. Vol. 1: Derivatives and differentials, definite integrals, expansions in series, applications to geometry. 52 figures, 556pp. Paperbound $2.50. Vol. 2, Part 1: Functions of a complex variable, conformal representations, doubly periodic functions, natural boundaries, etc. 38 figures, 269pp. Paperbound $1.85. Vol. 2, Part 2: Differential equations, Cauchy-Lipschitz method, nonlinear differential equations, simultaneous equations, etc. 308pp. Paperbound $1.85. Vol. 3, Part 1: Variation of solutions, partial differential equations of the second order. 15 figures, 339pp. Paperbound $3.00. Vol. 3, Part 2: Integral equations, calculus of variations. 13 figures, 389pp.   Paperbound $3.00

PLANETS, STARS AND GALAXIES,
A. E. Fanning

Descriptive astronomy for beginners: the solar system; neighboring galaxies; seasons; quasars; fly-by results from Mars, Venus, Moon; radio astronomy; etc. all simply explained. Revised up to 1966 by author and Prof. D. H. Menzel, former Director, Harvard College Observatory. 29 photos, 16 figures. 189pp. 5⅜ x 8½.   Paperbound $1.50

GREAT IDEAS IN INFORMATION THEORY, LANGUAGE AND CYBERNETICS,
Jagjit Singh

Winner of Unesco's Kalinga Prize covers language, metalanguages, analog and digital computers, neural systems, work of McCulloch, Pitts, von Neumann, Turing, other important topics. No advanced mathematics needed, yet a full discussion without compromise or distortion. 118 figures. ix + 338pp. 5⅜ x 8½.
                                          Paperbound $2.00

GEOMETRIC EXERCISES IN PAPER FOLDING,
T. Sundara Row

Regular polygons, circles and other curves can be folded or pricked on paper, then used to demonstrate geometric propositions, work out proofs, set up well-known problems. 89 illustrations, photographs of actually folded sheets. xii + 148pp. 5⅜ x 8½.   Paperbound $1.00

VISUAL ILLUSIONS, THEIR CAUSES, CHARACTERISTICS AND APPLICATIONS,
M. Luckiesh

The visual process, the structure of the eye, geometric, perspective illusions, influence of angles, illusions of depth and distance, color illusions, lighting effects, illusions in nature, special uses in painting, decoration, architecture, magic, camouflage. New introduction by W. H. Ittleson covers modern developments in this area. 100 illustrations. xxi + 252pp. 5⅜ x 8.
                                          Paperbound $1.50

ATOMS AND MOLECULES SIMPLY EXPLAINED,
B. C. Saunders and R. E. D. Clark

Introduction to chemical phenomena and their applications: cohesion, particles, crystals, tailoring big molecules, chemist as architect, with applications in radioactivity, color photography, synthetics, biochemistry, polymers, and many other important areas. Non technical. 95 figures. x + 299pp. 5⅜ x 8½.
                                          Paperbound $1.50

THE PRINCIPLES OF ELECTROCHEMISTRY,
D. A. MacInnes

Basic equations for almost every subfield of electrochemistry from first principles, referring at all times to the soundest and most recent theories and results; unusually useful as text or as reference. Covers coulometers and Faraday's Law, electrolytic conductance, the Debye-Hueckel method for the theoretical calculation of activity coefficients, concentration cells, standard electrode potentials, thermodynamic ionization constants, pH, potentiometric titrations, irreversible phenomena. Planck's equation, and much more. 2 indices. Appendix. 585-item bibliography. 137 figures. 94 tables. ii + 478pp. 5⅝ x 8⅜.
Paperbound $2.75

MATHEMATICS OF MODERN ENGINEERING,
E. G. Keller and R. E. Doherty

Written for the Advanced Course in Engineering of the General Electric Corporation, deals with the engineering use of determinants, tensors, the Heaviside operational calculus, dyadics, the calculus of variations, etc. Presents underlying principles fully, but emphasis is on the perennial engineering attack of set-up and solve. Indexes. Over 185 figures and tables. Hundreds of exercises, problems, and worked-out examples. References. Two volume set. Total of xxxiii + 623pp. 5⅝ x 8.
Two volume set, paperbound $3.70

AERODYNAMIC THEORY: A GENERAL REVIEW OF PROGRESS,
William F. Durand, editor-in-chief

A monumental joint effort by the world's leading authorities prepared under a grant of the Guggenheim Fund for the Promotion of Aeronautics. Never equalled for breadth, depth, reliability. Contains discussions of special mathematical topics not usually taught in the engineering or technical courses. Also: an extended two-part treatise on Fluid Mechanics, discussions of aerodynamics of perfect fluids, analyses of experiments with wind tunnels, applied airfoil theory, the nonlifting system of the airplane, the air propeller, hydrodynamics of boats and floats, the aerodynamics of cooling, etc. Contributing experts include Munk, Giacomelli, Prandtl, Toussaint, Von Karman, Klemperer, among others. Unabridged republication. 6 volumes. Total of 1,012 figures, 12 plates, 2,186pp. Bibliographies. Notes. Indices. 5⅜ x 8½.
Six volume set, paperbound $13.50

FUNDAMENTALS OF HYDRO- AND AEROMECHANICS,
L. Prandtl and O. G. Tietjens

The well-known standard work based upon Prandtl's lectures at Goettingen. Wherever possible hydrodynamics theory is referred to practical considerations in hydraulics, with the view of unifying theory and experience. Presentation is extremely clear and though primarily physical, mathematical proofs are rigorous and use vector analysis to a considerable extent. An Engineering Society Monograph, 1934. 186 figures. Index. xvi + 270pp. 5⅜ x 8.
Paperbound $2.00

APPLIED HYDRO- AND AEROMECHANICS,
L. Prandtl and O. G. Tietjens

Presents for the most part methods which will be valuable to engineers. Covers flow in pipes, boundary layers, airfoil theory, entry conditions, turbulent flow in pipes, and the boundary layer, determining drag from measurements of pressure and velocity, etc. Unabridged, unaltered. An Engineering Society Monograph. 1934. Index. 226 figures, 28 photographic plates illustrating flow patterns. xvi + 311pp. 5⅜ x 8.
Paperbound $2.00

APPLIED OPTICS AND OPTICAL DESIGN,
A. E. Conrady
With publication of vol. 2, standard work for designers in optics is now complete for first time. Only work of its kind in English; only detailed work for practical designer and self-taught. Requires, for bulk of work, no math above trig. Step-by-step exposition, from fundamental concepts of geometrical, physical optics, to systematic study, design, of almost all types of optical systems. Vol. 1: all ordinary ray-tracing methods; primary aberrations; necessary higher aberration for design of telescopes, low-power microscopes, photographic equipment. Vol. 2: (Completed from author's notes by R. Kingslake, Dir. Optical Design, Eastman Kodak.) Special attention to high-power microscope, anastigmatic photographic objectives. "An indispensable work," *J., Optical Soc. of Amer.* Index. Bibliography. 193 diagrams. 852pp. 6⅛ x 9¼.

Two volume set, paperbound $7.00

MECHANICS OF THE GYROSCOPE, THE DYNAMICS OF ROTATION,
R. F. Deimel, Professor of Mechanical Engineering at Stevens Institute of Technology
Elementary general treatment of dynamics of rotation, with special application of gyroscopic phenomena. No knowledge of vectors needed. Velocity of a moving curve, acceleration to a point, general equations of motion, gyroscopic horizon, free gyro, motion of discs, the damped gyro, 103 similar topics. Exercises. 75 figures. 208pp. 5⅜ x 8.

Paperbound $1.75

STRENGTH OF MATERIALS,
J. P. Den Hartog
Full, clear treatment of elementary material (tension, torsion, bending, compound stresses, deflection of beams, etc.), plus much advanced material on engineering methods of great practical value: full treatment of the Mohr circle, lucid elementary discussions of the theory of the center of shear and the "Myosotis" method of calculating beam deflections, reinforced concrete, plastic deformations, photoelasticity, etc. In all sections, both general principles and concrete applications are given. Index. 186 figures (160 others in problem section). 350 problems, all with answers. List of formulas. viii + 323pp. 5⅜ x 8.

Paperbound $2.00

HYDRAULIC TRANSIENTS,
G. R. Rich
The best text in hydraulics ever printed in English . . . by former Chief Design Engineer for T.V.A. Provides a transition from the basic differential equations of hydraulic transient theory to the arithmetic integration computation required by practicing engineers. Sections cover Water Hammer, Turbine Speed Regulation, Stability of Governing, Water-Hammer Pressures in Pump Discharge Lines, The Differential and Restricted Orifice Surge Tanks, The Normalized Surge Tank Charts of Calame and Gaden, Navigation Locks, Surges in Power Canals—Tidal Harmonics, etc. Revised and enlarged. Author's prefaces. Index. xiv + 409pp. 5⅜ x 8½.

Paperbound $2.50

Prices subject to change without notice.

Available at your book dealer or write for free catalogue to Dept. Adsci, Dover Publications, Inc., 180 Varick St., N.Y., N.Y. 10014. Dover publishes more than 150 books each year on science, elementary and advanced mathematics, biology, music, art, literary history, social sciences and other areas.